TRAVELS *with* MYSELF *and* ANOTHER

Idaho, 1940

TRAVELS *with* MYSELF *and* ANOTHER

MARTHA GELLHORN

JEREMY P. TARCHER • PUTNAM

a member of Penguin Putnam Inc.

New York

Most Tarcher/Putnam books are available at special quantity discounts for bulk purchase for sales promotions, premiums, fund-raising, and educational needs. Special books or book excerpts also can be created to fit specific needs. For details, write Putnam Special Markets, 375 Hudson Street, New York, NY 10014.

Jeremy P. Tarcher/Putnam
a member of
Penguin Putnam Inc.
375 Hudson Street
New York, NY 10014
www.penguinputnam.com

First published in 1978 by Eland

First Jeremy P. Tarcher/Putnam Edition 2001
Copyright © 1978 by Martha Gellhorn
Introduction copyright © 2001 by Bill Buford

photo on page iv © Lloyd Arnold/Archive Photos, print courtesy of The John F. Kennedy Library; photo on page xxii by Ruth Rabb; photo on page 8 courtesy of The John F. Kennedy Library; photo on page 58 © U.S. Navy, courtesy of The John F. Kennedy Library; photo on page 106 by Ruth Rabb; photo on page 240 courtesy of The John F. Kennedy Library; photo on page 284 courtesy of The John F. Kennedy Library; photo on page 292 © Lloyd Arnold/Archive Photos, print courtesy of The John F. Kennedy Library

Library of Congress Cataloging-in-Publication Data

Gellhorn, Martha, 1908–1998
Travels with myself and another / Martha Gellhorn.
p. cm.
Originally published: London: Allen Lane, 1978.
ISBN 1-58542-090-5
1. Gellhorn, Martha, 1908–1998—Journeys. 2. Voyages and travels.
I. Title.
G465.G44   2001   00-049749
910'.92—dc21

Printed in the United States of America

1 3 5 7 9 10 8 6 4 2

This book is printed on acid-free paper. ∞

BOOK DESIGN BY JENNIFER ANN DADDIO

For Diana Cooper with long-lasting love

CONTENTS

The good traveller doesn't know where he's going.
The great traveller doesn't know where he's been.
CHUANG TZǓ

Leap before you look.
OLD SLAVONIC MAXIM

"Oh S. the sights are worse than the journeys."
SYBILLE BEDFORD, *A VISIT TO DON OTAVIO*

INTRODUCTION

M y dear William. Note: that's William. Not Bill. You must change your name. No one will ever take you seriously as Bill. Bill Buford? No, it just won't do. And your hair. You've got to do something with your hair. And that beard? Shave it. You look like Allen Ginsberg." I'm quoting Martha Gellhorn, a characteristic letter, imperious, forthright, even bullying. Martha was a novelist, a war correspondent and, with the publication of *Travels with Myself and Another* in 1978 (when she was just turning sixty), a travel writer of a wildly original voice. She died in 1998. I had the privilege of publishing some of her work during her last decade, her ninth.

"I forgot to add, William. You must buy new trousers that don't look like what the well-dressed young elephants are wearing this year. How else can you win the Iranian's love?" The Iranian in question was a particularly elusive girlfriend. Martha tutored me on matters of the heart, and on drinking (you could never drink enough), on my appearance (a disaster), and on my manners—especially my manners: my manners, in Martha's eyes, were catastrophic.

"I'll be in London for a few days later this month," she wrote me after we had a row arising out of another one of my behavioral misdemeanors, and the exchange must have lead to Martha's being so rude—and I infer this from the correspondence that I'm rereading for the first time—that I sank into a sulk.

"If you don't return my call, I'll sadly take it that you wish to sever relations forever. A pity. But think about it, William. I may be the only old person you know, and elders and betters are necessary as I know with despair, now that all of mine are dead."

The elementary facts of her life: born in 1908, in St. Louis, the place, according to Martha, that everyone flees from (and thus the ideal nurturing ground for a travel writer); bossy, straight-talking, cigarette-smoking; the boozy reporter of wars and of the plight of the down-and-out; also a writer of short stories, novellas, and novels. She was married to Ernest Hemingway, and she hated the fact that, whenever her work was written about, his name was invariably mentioned as well, just as I'm mentioning it now. But it's hard to avoid. The two of them met when the world was at its most dramatic. They fell in love at the outbreak of the Spanish Civil War and divorced once World War II had ended— and in between was Cuba and big-game hunting and trips to China and battlefields in Finland and Barcelona and the beaches of Normandy. She rarely admits his existence, which makes his depiction here, in "Mr. Ma's Tigers," a great rarity. He's the U.C. referred to, the Unwilling Companion (she wouldn't, of course, use his name), and he comes across as a rascal of pranks and charm, held affectionately dear. It's Martha, for instance, who insists that, despite Hemingway's enthusiasm for Chinese fireworks, he simply has got to stop lighting them in the bedroom. Could there be any two people more romantic? By then he was Papa Hemingway, and she was, what, blonde and thin and sassy, a starlet of the highest order, a young Lauren Bacall, except that she was a whole lot brainier than a young Lauren Bacall, but just as sexy. There was a glamour about Martha Gellhorn, the glamour of black-and-white movies. It was in her manner and her way with the ways of the world. She was a dame.

In 1983, I hadn't read Martha Gellhorn, but I was living in England

and editing a literary magazine and putting together an issue of travel writing, and someone said I should ask her to contribute. I had missed the publication of *Travels with Myself and Another*, which appeared only five years before. I now believe I missed it because the book was written before its time (and therefore hadn't fully caught on), even though most of the episodes described in it occurred many years before. Curiously, the book tells us as much about Gellhorn as the places she visits (curiously, because she was deeply private), and, in this, writing stories about journeys that are, finally, about many more things than the journeys themselves, she prefigures the works of people like Bruce Chatwin and Paul Theroux and Jonathan Raban and the renaissance of first-person adventure writing. I contacted Gellhorn—I got her address from someone—and a piece about a trip to Haiti was the result (something I only now recall had been originally intended for this volume but wasn't finished in time). The piece was dramatic and eventful (a white woman on an island of angry blacks who nearly gets stoned) and full of what I would come to recognize as Gellhorn rage—the irrepressible, passionate rage against injustice. Gellhorn alludes to this rage in her account of visiting Mrs. Mandelstam (Mrs. M.), the widow of the great poet, one of the last and most moving essays in this volume. At some point, the famous widow describes living in constant fear, and she asks Martha if she, too, feels fear all the time. "No," Martha says in reply (sharply, I imagine, definitively, without hesitation). "I feel angry. Every minute about everything." No one was so capable of rage or of being so poetic expressing it.

"The Big Picture always exists," she wrote, and by Big Picture she means the drama of power brokers and politicians and corporations. "And I seem to have spent my life observing how desperately the Big Picture affects the little people who did not devise it and have no control over it." She was engaged by politics but hated politicians, and the ones who figure in this volume, like those who appeared throughout her life, are insufferably boring (and, in the Gellhorn vocabulary, there is no more damning thing to be). "I expected powerful political people to be boring," she writes here, on meeting Chiang Kai-shek and his wife. "It comes from no one interrupting or arguing or telling them to shut up. The more powerful the more boring." Politics, she declares during her trip across the equator of Africa (she had never been; it seemed like a journey worth taking; why not?), is the bungling management of the affairs of men. "It is a game played among themselves by a breed of professionals. What has politics to do with real daily life, as real people live it?"

I was astonished by Gellhorn when I finally met her. I felt I had discovered her and didn't know why it had taken me so long. This American in Britain, this throwback to a time when truth was truth, and right was right, and wrong was an identifiable thing that must be fought at all costs—she was all these things, and I fell for her. I wanted to do everything for her. I wanted to publish her in my magazine. I wanted to publish her books. I wanted to be her agent. I wanted to see her work translated, brought back into print, made into movies. And, for a brief period (both of us fools), she let me be all these things—editor, publisher, agent, the works. But I was still in my twenties and briefly believed that there was nothing I couldn't do, and she, nearly fifty years older, probably should have known better. I know now that I had put myself in a role that she was already familiar with: the incompetent male charmer whom she had to tell what to do and how to do it. I had chills of recognition rereading Martha's account of travelling across East Africa, with a driver, Joshua, who knew neither East Africa nor how to drive. (And only Martha would end up with a driver who can't drive and then go on to spend more time with him than any other travelling companion in her life.) On meeting Joshua ("black imitation Italian silk pipestream trousers, white shirt, black pointed shoes, black sunglasses in ornate red frames, holding a cardboard suitcase"), Martha knew he was probably not right. "Instinct, which I regularly ignore, told me that Joshua was not the man for the job." Instinct told her, I'm sure, that I was not the man for the job as well, but we carried on until it became too obvious to ignore.

Her letters to me are postmarked Belize and Kenya and Tanzania and the south of Spain. Martha was fundamentally a loner (in this volume, you'll note that people are rude, incompetent, unreliable, drunk, and they smell very bad; Martha never travelled for people; it was natural beauty she sought, the view of the Rift Valley, a beach on the Indian Ocean, a giraffe in the wild). Her social life, true to character, was conducted mainly through letters, written late at night, in solitude, and these stories were often first told in letters home—letters that Martha recovered in order to write this book.

She was happiest in places hot enough that she could wear little—she lived for swimming—but her home was a cottage in north Wales, Catscradle, atop a blustery, exposed hill (again, every travel writer needs a place from which to flee), where she lived alone, drank booze, read mystery novels, and wrote, until she got tired of her company and came into London. Her days there were tightly organized—drinks and dinners and maybe a nightcap. She didn't have parties—she rarely saw people in groups—but met with her friends, one by one. John Pilger, Paul Theroux, James Fox, Nicholas Shakespeare, John Hatt, Jeremy Harding—journalists, adventurers. Those were some of her regular men friends. We'd see each other—one of us on the way out, while another was arriving. She had some women friends, but Martha liked men, was easy around them, and could be flirty and coquettish even at the age of eighty-five. One evening, she recounted her being thrown off a press boat during the Normandy invasion (Hemingway, with whom she was by then in a relationship of unmitigated acrimony, had taken her credentials), and her being summarily returned to Britain. By her own account, she flirted her way back onto another boat (a hospital ship), stowed away in a broom closet, and saw the invasion firsthand. It was a telling incident: unintimidated by one of the most dangerous military operations of the war (and so fearless in a male way) and yet utterly capable of making men melt (devastating in her distinctly female way). And of course Hemingway.

I brought him up the first time I went to her London flat for dinner. It was the forbidden subject. "William," she said, "I have only one response to people when they bring up his name. And that's to show them the door." She didn't show me the door. In fact, the taboo having been broken, she went on to talk about him at length—both that evening and on many occasions thereafter. Yes, she resented him for all kinds of reasons, but he was the only man she talked about. She mentioned her next husband only once—that was Thomas Matthews, the editor of *Time* magazine—and that was to express her regret at having been married to the man. "I don't know what happened," she said. "It's as if, for ten years, I just stopped thinking. I did no work. I did no writing. Just endless entertaining—grand dinners with crystal and china and men in dinner jackets serving us."

But Hemingway was present on a first-name basis. Sometimes it was Ernest the monster (how he terrified his children) and sometimes Ernest the myth (he was, in her words, "shy in bed," and had, she was convinced, slept with no more than five women). She was fed up with him by the end of World War II—he was bloated and self-centered and indifferent to history—but she had respect for the writing. She talked about the philosophy of his sentences and that business of paring them back until they were as direct and true as they could possibly be—something she did herself in her own, tough, often staccato prose, one that often hangs on one perfectly chosen word, usually a simile: the flamingoes, in East Africa, lifting off and spreading in a coral pink streamer against the sky, and "the sound of flight was like silk tearing." Mr. Slicker, another one of Martha's wholly inappropriate guides, tells Martha how the locals value the texture of skin in a woman—this is the quality they find beautiful—and Martha understands why, "since the ladies were mainly huge bottoms, like carrying your own pillow."

These are very Gellhorn sentences—careful, witty, spare. On our many, always boozy nights together, she talked like this and said many more things, vivid and indiscreet at the time, but usually uttered under the influence of her liquor cabinet or the bottles of wine that we had at dinner ("tight as a tick" was one of her phrases), and few details now remain. Once I recall writing something down on a napkin—Martha had gone to the loo, having just revealed some wonderfully salacious anecdote—but I was myself so drunk that I later blew my nose into it and then threw it away.

There was a growing suspicion among Martha's friends that she would never die. She had too much energy, too much determination to be curtailed by something as ordinary as mortality. She had a ninetieth birthday coming up. Surely she'd make that. And there was the prospect of another war, in Iraq, in the Balkans—Martha wouldn't allow herself to miss those. But she will. And she did.

I feel lucky to have known her, this proof of the human spirit, the naysayer to naysayers. I know her friends do, too. Now we just have her books. And, among my favorites is this one, *Travels with Myself and Another,* in part because it's her most revealing book, the closest thing we'll get to an autobiography. It's also one of her most forthright—energetic, vicious, self-deprecating, bigoted, witty, and outrageous. It's very Gellhorn.

— Bill ("William") Buford

PREFACE

We can't all be Marco Polo or Freya Stark but millions of us are travellers nevertheless. The great travellers, living and dead, are in a class by themselves, unequalled professionals. We are amateurs and though we too have our moments of glory we also tire, our spirits sag, we have our moments of rancour. Who has not heard, felt, thought, or said, in the course of a journey, words like: "They've lost the luggage again, for God's sake?" "You mean we came all this way just to see this?" "Why do they have to make so damn much noise?" "Call that a room with a view?" "I'd rather kick his teeth in than give him a tip."

But we persevere and do our best to see the world and we get around; we go everywhere. Upon our return, no one willingly listens to our travellers' tales. "How was the trip?" they say. "Marvellous," we say. "In Tbilisi, I saw . . ." Eyes glaze. As soon as politeness permits or before, conversation is switched back to local news such as gossip, the current political outrage, who's read what, last night's telly; people will talk about the weather rather than hear our glowing reports on Copenhagen, the Grand Canyon, Katmandu.

The only aspect of our travels that is guaranteed to hold an audience is disaster. "The camel threw you at the *Great Pyramid* and you broke your leg?" "Chased the pickpocket through the Galeria and across Naples and lost *all* your travellers' cheques and your passport?" "Locked and forgotten in a *sauna* in Viipuri?" "Ptomaine from eating *sheep's eyes* at a Druze feast?" That's what they like. They can hardly wait for us to finish before they launch into stories of their own suffering in foreign lands. The fact is, we cherish our disasters and here we are one up on the great travellers who have every impressive qualification for the job but lack jokes.

I rarely read travel books myself, I prefer to travel. This is not a proper travel book. After presenting my credentials so you will believe that I know whereof I speak, it is an account of my best horror journeys, chosen from a wide range, recollected with tenderness now that they are past. All amateur travellers have experienced horror journeys, long or short, sooner or later, one way or another. As a student of disaster, I note that we react alike to our tribulations: frayed and bitter at the time, proud afterwards. Nothing is better for self-esteem than survival.

It takes real stamina to travel and it's getting worse. Remember the old days when we had porters not hijackers; remember when hotels were built and finished before you got there; remember when key unions weren't on strike at your point of departure or arrival; remember when we were given generous helpings of butter and jam for breakfast, not those little cellophane and cardboard containers; remember when the weather was reliable; remember when you didn't have to plan your trip like a military operation and book in advance with deposit enclosed; remember when the Mediterranean was clean; remember when you were a person not a sheep, herded in airports, railway stations, ski-lifts, movies, museums, restaurants, among your fellow sheep; remember when you knew what your money would bring in other currencies; remember when you confidently expected everything to go well instead of thinking it a miracle if everything doesn't go wrong?

We're not heroic like the great travellers but all the same we amateurs are a pretty tough breed. No matter how horrendous the last journey we never give up hope for the next one, God knows why.

TRAVELS *with* MYSELF *and* ANOTHER

Grumetti Serengeti Tanzania, early 1970s

One

CREDENTIALS

I was seized by the idea of this book while sitting on a rotten little beach at the western tip of Crete, flanked by a waterlogged shoe and a rusted potty. Around me, the litter of our species. I had the depressed feeling that I spent my life doing this sort of thing and might well end my days here. This is the traveller's deep dark night of the soul and can happen anywhere at any hour.

No one suggested or recommended this sewer. I found it unaided, studying a map on the cheap night flight to Heraklion. Very pleased with myself too because I'd become so practical; before leaping into the unknown I actually telephoned the Greek Tourist Office in London and received a map of Crete, a list of hotels and the usual travel bumpf written in the usual purple prose. Reading matter for the plane.

Way off there, alone on a bay, was a place named Kastelli with one C Class hotel. Just the ticket; far from the beaten track, the C Class hotel was sure to be a sweet little taverna, clean, no running water, grape arbour. I pictured Kastelli as an unspoiled fishing village, sugar cube houses clustered behind a golden beach. All day I would swim in lovely water, the purpose of the journey; at night I would drink ouzo in the grape arbour and watch the fishermen lollop about like Zorba under the moon.

It took as long to get from Heraklion to Kastelli, by three buses, as from London to New York by Jumbo Jet. All buses sang Arab-type Musak. Kastelli had two streets of squat cement dwellings and shops; the Aegean was not in sight. The C Class hotel was a three-storey cement box; my room was a cubby-hole with a full complement of dead flies, mashed mosquitoes on the walls and hairy dust balls drifting around the floor. The population of Kastelli, not surprisingly, appeared sunk in speechless gloom, none more so than the proprietor of the C Class hotel where I was, also not surprisingly, the only guest. On the side of the Post Office, across from my room, a political enthusiast had painted a large black slogan. Amepikanoi was the first word, and I needed no Greek to know that it meant Yank Go Home. You bet your boots, gladly, cannot wait to oblige; but there was no way out until the afternoon bus the next day.

I had made prodigious efforts to reach this death trap for the purpose of swimming and swim I would. In the morning, a twenty-minute walk past a disused factory and some hideous small unoccupied villas brought me to a café by the sea, which provided unspeakable food and a closet half filled with mouldy potatoes for undressing. And so to the beach, like a minor garbage pit, the sea having cast up rubbish to join the crushed cigarette packs, tin cans, dirty papers, bottles left by previous swimmers. Anyhow nobody else was here and the water looked fine, transparent and calm over sand but too shallow for swimming. Beyond the little promontory, the waves were choppy with whitecaps, no obstacle to a dedicated swimmer. Once out into the deep water the current grabbed me and began to move me at speed westwards. Next stop Malta.

We are supposed to learn by experience; fat lot of good that does if you only remember experience too late. Flailing for shore, I remembered the circular current of Mauritius where I was caught and borne for a time on a fast scary round trip of that island. Such currents might be a disagreeable feature of large isolated islands; the kind of information it would be helpful to know. A few minutes earlier I had been warning myself not to get dashed against the promontory on the return trip; a few minutes later I did my best to get dashed and clung with fingers and fingernails, washed away, clinging again, until I could pull back into the still protected water. And now sat on the sand, bleeding gently from scratches, somewhat winded, and in despair.

Où sont les plages d'antan? I remember when beaches had no debris on them except seaweed and were safe and often so deserted that I was the sole naked tenant. The coves around the small Caribbean islands, the water turquoise and Nile green; bays in Cuba surrounded by jungle; Mexico on the Gulf and on the Pacific; beaches backed by umbrella pines along the Var coast, the Mediterranean side of Italy all the way down to Calabria, the Costa Brava and the great beach at Zarauz; marvellous beaches in the state of Washington; miles of white sand by the Indian Ocean in Kenya. The natural world is my true love; therein my particular love, the beautiful junction of sea and land, was lost forever, defiled and overrun. I was reduced to a contemptible muck heap outside Kastelli. The future loomed coal black; nowhere to go that was worth going to. I might as well stop travelling.

Stop travelling? Come, come. That was carrying despair to preposterous lengths. I'd been in much worse places than Kastelli. Furthermore millions of other travellers set forth with high hopes and land symbolically between a waterlogged shoe and a rusted potty. I was not unique, singled out for special misfortune. Besides, I was in the same position towards travel as a leopard is towards his spots. I had been a traveller all my life, beginning in childhood on the streetcars of my native city which transported me to Samarkand, Peking, Tahiti, Constantinople. Place names were the most powerful magic I knew. Still are. And I had been hard at the real thing since my twenty-first year, when I decided that it would be a good plan to see everywhere and everything and everyone and write about it.

A pep talk was called for and delivered. If you can't learn from experience at least you can use it. What have you done with your long rich experience of horror journeys and fetching up in dumps like this? Moaning is unseemly; get to work. Work is the best remedy for despair. Okay. All right. Agreed. But first, let's get out of Kastelli.

The trouble is that experience is useless without memory. Serious travel writers not only see and understand everything around them but command erudite cross references to history, literature and related travels. I couldn't even remember where I'd been. I think I was born with a weak memory as one can be born with a weak heart or weak ankles. I forget places, people, events, and books as fast as I read them. All the magnificent scenery, the greatest joy of travel, blurs. As to dates—what year? What month?—the situation is hopeless. I am still waiting for the promised time, said to arrive with advancing age, when you forget what you ate for breakfast but the past becomes brilliantly clear, like a personal *son et lumière*. I know exactly what I ate for breakfast, can reconstruct the main events of the last month if I try, otherwise the past is veiled in cloud with gleams of light.

The lowest points of some horror journeys were unforgettable but I needed details. For the first time ever, I began to search through old papers, archaeology in the sitting room. Like the moss-free rolling stone, a roving writer gathers few papers. There were letters to my mother who wisely saved perhaps ten percent of the avalanche total, and nine diaries scribbled only to remind me where I'd been that year and not looked at since, and some confused notes and published and unpublished bits and pieces. Rummaging in that stuff made me unhappy. Even when glimpses of the past were funny they were sad because the years were gone and the people with them. And my memory was growing more—not less—muddled. A different approach seemed indicated.

Before selecting the best of the worst journeys, I ought to remember the countries I'd been in. By been in, I mean stayed long enough to learn something of the local life and customs. Not like India (India then) where I landed at Karachi and took a quick look at the cows and the poor scabrous children and made a beeline back to the airport to get away. Or

French Guiana where I spent a mere three repelled hours. Or Venezuela or the Philippines, absolute amnesia. It was slow work. I kept remembering a country in the middle of the night. Finally my list was complete: fifty-three countries, which includes every state in the Union except Alaska.

When I tried to think of islands, memory fainted and failed. The Caribbean is pock-marked by islands; it was easier to remember the names of the four where I had not been, Barbuda, Barbados, Isla de Margharita, Jamaica. And the Greek islands from Corfu to Rhodes with plenty of little ones between, and Capri and Ischia and Sicily and Mallorca and Elba and Corsica and Gozo and Comino and Bermuda and Bali and Honolulu and Hawaii and Guam and Midway and Wake and Macao and Gran Canaria and Sao Miguel and probably others.

This is the countries list, willy-nilly as I remembered them. France, Great Britain (four parts), Germany, Austria, Switzerland, Liechtenstein, Italy, Spain, Andorra, Canada, Mexico, Cuba, Greece, Surinam, Haiti, Dominican Republic, China, Hongkong, Burma, Malaya, Netherlands, East Indies, Portugal, Finland, Holland, Denmark, Sweden, Poland, Russia, Cameroun, Chad, Sudan, Kenya, Uganda, Tanzania, Egypt (including the Gaza Strip when Egyptian, and later when Israeli), Israel, Lebanon, Jordan, Yugoslavia, Luxemburg, Mauritius, Tunisia, Morocco, Algeria, Thailand, South Vietnam, Turkey, San Marino, Republic of Ireland, Czechoslovakia, Costa Rica, Malta, the United States of America up, down, and across.

Once launched on this memory exercise, statistics went to my head. I calculate that I made repeated trips to twenty-four of those countries, ranging from two sojourns in the Netherlands East Indies to countless travels in Europe, the Caribbean, and East Africa. As a base, from which to move, I lived in seven countries where I established eleven permanent residences. A residence is a flat or house that you rent or buy or, if insane, build. I built one and a half houses in two countries and in my opinion house-building is far worse than any horror journey. The point is that you start from scratch with the notion that you are going to live there quite a while, maybe for the rest of your life. You then use the residence for several years and abandon it, usually with all its contents.

Residences are different from temporary furnished quarters of which I remembered seventeen before I stopped trying to remember. Some temporary furnished quarters preceded permanent residences, some were linked to jobs, but mostly they were and continue to be bolt-holes for writing. At home, wherever home is, there are interruptions. I settle in temporary furnished quarters in foreign places where I know nobody and enter into a symbiotic relationship with a typewriter. This is stationary travel in contrast to travelling travel and I love it. No matter how unsatisfactory the work or how drab the furn. bdstr., I have the scenery, chosen with care, sea or mountains, and the joys thereof.

How very odd that one bends one's own twig and it stays bent. Who could have foreseen the permanent effect of childhood journeys on streetcars? No other manner of living would have interested me so much and so long and I will surely go on until I drop trying to see more of the world and what's happening in it.

Despite the amount of ground covered, I never thought of writing about travel. Here goes.

*With Hemingway and Madame Chiang Kai Shek
in China, 1941*

Two

MR MA'S TIGERS

By the beginning of 1941, the Sino-Japanese war had been going on so long and was so far away that it ranked more as an historic fact than a war. Compared to the survival of Britain, the Far East was stale and trifling. But something new had been added to the old China story; Japan was now joined to the Axis as the third partner in what they named "the New Order". My boss, the editor of *Collier's* and one of the nicest men I ever knew, concluded that the Japanese, having already invaded Indochina, did not intend to sit upon their hands and would soon start destroying the East as their partners were destroying the West. He agreed that I should report on the Chinese army in action, and defences against future Japanese attack around the South China Sea.

The Germans had done fearsomely well, Europe was lost and silenced but, like countless millions of others, I didn't believe at any time that Britain would be defeated, that America would stay neutral and that Hitlerian Germany would conquer and rule and poison life on this planet. After long years we were going to win but it would be the end of the world. End of the world? I felt a driving sense of haste: hurry, hurry, before it's too late; but don't remember what I meant. I was determined to see the Orient before I died or the world ended or whatever came next.

The Orient: pictures in my mind since childhood, not reality. Reality was in the other direction, across the Atlantic.

All I had to do was get to China. On this super horror journey I wheedled an Unwilling Companion, hereinafter referred to as U.C., into going where he had no wish to go. He had not spent his formative years mooning on streetcar travels and stuffing his imagination with Fu Manchu and Somerset Maugham. He claimed to have had an uncle who was a medical missionary in China and took out his own appendix on horseback. He was also forced to contribute dimes from his allowance to convert the heathen Chinese. These facts seemed to have turned him against the Orient. I went on wheedling until he sighed gloomily and gave in. That was scandalous selfishness on my part, never repeated. Future horror journeys were made on my own. It was all right to plunge oneself neck deep in the soup but not to drag anyone else in too.

Early in February 1941, we set out from San Francisco for Honolulu by boat. We imagined this trip would be like the already distant good old days when one crossed from New York to France, on a French ship, wallowing in delicious food and drink and luxury. U.C. always had the right idea about pleasure, which is grab it while you can. Instead of the hoped-for delights, we were batted about the decks like ping-pong balls, hurled into nailed-down furniture unless unnailed-down furniture hurled itself into us until finally, incapable of standing upright, we retired to our berths where we lay eating and drinking and trying not to be flung from berth to floor.

Trays crashed off our laps, bottles spilled; the ship proceeded with the motion of a dolphin, lovely in a dolphin and vile in a ship. U.C. muttered a lot: why had nobody warned us, if he had known the Pacific was this kind of ocean he would never have set foot on it, a man should stick with the waters he knew, as a matter of fact he knew and respected many lakes and rivers too, and look at it any way you want, M., this is a bad sign. The sea voyage lasted roughly forever. Somewhere, over those detestable grey waves, Honolulu would be a haven of sun, swimming, peace and stationary land. Nobody warned us about the traditional aloha-welcome either.

I made a full airmail report to my mother:

"There were finally eighteen leis on each of our necks. U.C. had a face of black hate. He said to me, 'I never had no filthy Christed flowers around my neck before and the next son of a bitch who touches me I am going to cool him and what a dung heap we came to and by Christ if anybody else says aloha to me I am going to spit back in his mouth.' You get the feeling?

"Leis were not the end of it. Among the hordes of greeters who swarm aboard, ready to sling leis on their friends, were photographers. A fat man we never saw before came up to us. He was Irish and drunk. He said to U.C., 'I'm as big a man as you are and I can drink as much.' Then he staggered and U.C. caught him. 'Here,' he said to a nearby photographer. 'Take a picture of me too. I'm a fine man where I come from.' So I said quickly, to forestall worse, 'You bet you are,' and this is the picture. Us three. He stumbled away and we never saw him again."

That photograph is one of the few, the sadly few, which has survived my multiple changes of residence. U.C. is grinning like a wolf with bared fangs above necklaces of flowers; in profile, flower-draped too, I seem to be falling over backwards and look dazed; between us the fat man, flowerless but glass in hand, managed to lean affectionately against us both. Seeing the way people carry cameras, everyone else has always known the value of recording one's travels on film. I have only now understood what I've missed: instead of massive albums I have a single thin folder of photos to make me laugh in my declining years.

The report continues: "Also arrived on board an aunt of U.C.'s, an actual full-blooded aunt, U.C. said; she was the leechiest of all with a fine disregard of anyone's feelings or fatigue (U.C.'s face was now white and wet with sweat and horror, the ground was coming up to hit me and I couldn't see from headache, it was like a lecture tour with all the gushing cannot-be-shaken-off people). We got rid of her at the dock and there was Bill looking very nice, clean, solid, reasonable, unexcited and dull; he took us to this hotel where we fell upon liquor to carry us through and had a good talk with him, about the defence stuff, shop talk which interests us and which I at least must know. Then he left but not before he had extracted a promise (Louise sent him to get it) that we would dine with the local American King and Queen of the island that night. This is a place where hospitality is a curse and no one can be alone. We lunched with the aunt and a dreary gathering of people who should have been missionaries but were not even kind, just stupid people with nothing to drink and I was afraid I was going to faint from boredom and you can imagine U.C. At last we got an hour to ourselves on the beach and then people began to call at our hotel; then we went to dinner. Some life, what?

"The dinner was for about fifty people in a vast torch-lit patio with a fountain playing, the most spectacular house outside a movie set I have ever seen, and to me not beautiful, but rich, rich, rich. There is a strike of streetcar workers going on and they all said with vicious hard voices: let them strike till they starve but don't give in, it will spoil these beautiful islands . . . The stockholders are now getting 80 percent on their investment; they cannot possibly compromise and only get 6 percent. Let them starve, the guests kept saying, over the creamy food and the champagne; let them starve. So that was very delightful and instructive."

Finding this letter was a lucky surprise, authentic hot news of the day, especially as I remembered nothing about Honolulu except being there, disliking it and touring Pearl Harbor with Bill. The planes stood wing tip to wing tip, the warships nudged each other ("like the Sargasso Sea", from notes), the Japanese fishing boats were anchored alongside, ideal for Japanese Intelligence. Bill, a soldier, was appalled by the set-up but not a five-star general, thus unable to scare sense into anyone. U.C. said it was the system so popular in the First World War: get everything and everyone packed in one place and get the whole lot wiped out. When Pearl Harbor was indeed wiped out ten months later, with 3,300 American officers and men killed, my countrymen were whipped into fury against "the stab in the back", but my fury was directed against the U.S. General Staff who provided the world's richest target for the Japanese.

We retreated to Hawaii, undiscovered by tourists, peaceful and simple. My notes are bright with descriptions of beauty, cane fields and cattle range country, tea gardens, fishing villages, enchanting Japanese children, but all I remember is climbing and scrabbling over volcanic lava in a vain search for the Hawaiian chamois or some such animal. U.C. enjoyed Hawaii more than I did; he was by no means on fire with impatience for the Orient. Then I hear the unchanging voice of my soul (in another letter to my mother): "In half an hour we go to the Clipper. I am very, very excited and pleased and glad to be off. To think that all the names of all the places are real; and I will be there . . . I don't care where we go; it is all new, I want to see it all."

Air travel was not always disgusting. Those big PanAm flying boats were marvellous. We flew all day in roomy comfort, eating and drinking like pigs, visiting the Captain, listening to our fellow travellers, dozing, reading, and in the late afternoon the plane landed on the water at an island. The passengers had time for a swim, a shower, dinner, and slept in beds. Since that was air travel at its best, it has naturally disappeared.

On the way to Hongkong, at Guam, we were introduced to spearfishing by a passenger whom I described to my mother as "a character like Lawrence of Arabia, a marine aviator en route to Egypt", and that's all I now know about him, sinful bad memory. I never speared any fish nor tried to. I thought it unwise and improper to dive into depths where I didn't belong and interfere with activity I didn't understand. Keeping a respectful distance on the surface, I have watched underwater scenery and fish with joy all these years. Fish must perceive me as a rowboat. It is not that easy in life to find an unfailing source of joy.

U.C. took to Hongkong at once. Hongkong bore no resemblance to the present city as seen on TV, a forest of skyscrapers, a mini New York set against the great triangular mountain. Travellers of the next century, always supposing there are any, will scarcely know whether they are in

Buenos Aires or Chicago, skyscrapers all the way, skyscrapers to break the heart. When we saw it, the working city of Hongkong at the base of the Peak looked as if nailed together hurriedly from odd lots of old wood and sounded like a chronic Chinese New Year. It was brilliant with colour in signs and pennants; the narrow streets were jammed by rickshaws, bicycles, people, but not cars; the highest building was an imposing square bank and it wasn't very high. The gentry lived in gracious homes up the sides of the Peak, social position established by height.

We stayed in an old hotel downtown, perhaps the only hotel there was: big rooms with paddle fans on the ceilings, antique bathrooms, a large public lounge with large beat-up leather chairs; very Maugham to me. U.C., in the twinkling of an eye, collected a mixed jovial entourage, ranging from local cops with whom he went pheasant-shooting to fat wealthy crook-type Chinese businessmen who invited him to Chinese feasts. A bald middle-aged Caucasian of obscure nationality and occupation, self-styled "General," was a special favourite, and a huge polite thug from Chicago named Cohen whom U.C. believed to be a hit man for some Chinese warlord.

U.C. could not bear party chatter, or discussions of politics or the arts, but never tired of true life stories, the more unlikely the better. He was able to sit with a bunch of men for most of a day or most of a night, or most of both day and night though perhaps with different men, wherever he happened to have started sitting, all of them fortified by a continuous supply of drink, the while he roared with laughter at reminiscences and anecdotes. It was a valid system for him. Aside from being his form of amusement, he learned about a place and people through the eyes and experiences of those who lived there.

Though a hearty talker in my own right and given to laughing loudly at my own jokes, I was a novice drinker and had a separate approach to learning. I wanted to see for myself, not hear. U.C. did not mind what I did as long as he didn't have to do it too. Much as I like conversation, I like it only in bursts for a few hours, not marathons, and seldom in group formation. I slipped away from the large leather chairs. U.C. used to say, kindly, "M. is going off to take the pulse of the nation."

Four days after arrival, I left Hongkong alone to fly via Chungking and Kunming to Lashio, the Burma end of the Burma Road, and returned immediately the same way, material for a *Collier's* article. The airline, called China National Aviation Company (CNAC), consisted of two DC3s and three DC2s, elderly machines and no nonsense about comfort. Compared to passenger planes now, these were flying beetles. The floor sloped steeply, the chairs were canvas on metal frames, the toilet, behind a green curtain, gave a small circular view of the ground below.

DC3s could carry twenty-one passengers, DC2s fourteen passengers, but seats were removed to make space for the freight load. Five thousand kilos of mail and fifty-five million dollars in banknotes (very heavy) were average monthly freight; the same planes also hauled wolfram and tin out of China. Except for the Burma Road, CNAC was the only contact between the outside world and "Free" China, in effect the one third of China not occupied by the Japanese and ruled by the Generalissimo, Chiang Kai-shek. Trucks took fourteen days to reach Chungking from Rangoon on the spectacular corkscrew of the Burma Road, and broke down and rolled off precipices in alarming numbers. The five small tatty planes of CNAC kept "Free" China in business.

There were seven surviving American CNAC pilots, ten Chinese and Chinese-American copilots, same for twelve radio operators, and two stewardesses. The pilot on my round trip jaunt was Roy Leonard who looked and sounded like a nice ordinary Midwesterner. He became my hero within an hour of being airborne. He was thirty-three or four, medium height, brown hair, thin, matter-of-fact, invariably good tempered, and as much at home and at ease in China as if China were Indiana. I never learned why he came to China but he had been flying here for years, for a time as Chiang's private pilot. I felt I was watching a genius at work, and I watched closely, settling at once into the pilot's cabin.

The Japanese encircled Hongkong and had shown themselves hostile by fatally attacking two CNAC planes. CNAC simply changed its methods. Now CNAC planes climbed high above Hongkong, at night, in bad weather, before crossing the Japanese lines. Flights were postponed or cancelled if the weather was too good. Passengers were informed of the departure time a few hours in advance. By daylight, the Hongkong airfield looked discouragingly short, with the sea at one end and the cliffside of the Peak at the other. It was less worrying at night when you couldn't see what was happening.

We left Hongkong at 4.30 a.m. in a high wind in a DC2; freight, seven Chinese passengers, me and Roy Leonard. I cannot remember a radio operator nor find mention of him in my muddled old pencil notes; there was certainly no copilot or stewardess. In principle every plane did carry a radio operator whose job was to pick up weather reports and, before landing, make sure the landing field was not being bombed or under water. The passengers were given a rough brown blanket and a brown paper bag for throwing up. The plane was not heated or pressurized.

We climbed, as if climbing a spiral staircase, in tight jolting circles over Hongkong until we reached fourteen thousand feet. All lights went off except the dim light in the pilot's cabin and we crossed the Japanese lines, brightly lit far below. In half an hour, the storm hit us. I had been watching the flickering exhaust flame on a wing, but the wing vanished into cloud that looked grainy and hard as granite. Hail sounded like a threshing machine. Everything froze including the air speed indicator. Roy explained that if the speed dropped below sixty-three miles per hour the plane stalled and went into a spin, but there was no cause for anxiety; he opened his window a crack and judged air speed that way; he'd done it often. The wind-screen was a sheet of frost. Inside this cloud mass, elevator draughts lifted and dropped the plane, one's stomach making the same vertical movements. I had untroubled confidence in Roy so the behaviour of the plane didn't disturb me but I was perishing of cold. Behind in the cabin, the passengers vomited or hid beneath their blankets from the sound and the fury. This lasted for an hour and a half, after which Roy remarked that the rest of the trip would be easy. We were still flying blind in cloud but I thought it would be bad manners to mention that.

We landed at 10 a.m. at Chungking. The airstrip was a narrow island in the Yangtze, beneath the cliffs. For two months a year, this island lay under sixty feet of water and was subject to weird nightly rises in the river level. When we circled to land, I saw Chungking on the cliff top, looking like a greyish brown expanse of rubble. The passengers departed gratefully. While the plane was refuelled, Roy and I sat on the damp ground and ate a sumptuous breakfast of one bowl of dry rice and tea. That was the only nourishment until we got the same repast in the late afternoon at Kunming. I said there was no nonsense about comfort.

More passengers arrived and we took off for Kunming. The country was visible all afternoon, mountains, changing in colour and marked with a jigsaw pattern of small cultivated fields. A few grey villages, a few isolated farmhouses appeared in this vastness, and paths like animal tracks. Roy flew the plane as if riding a horse, meandering along valleys, "I go where I'm looking," he said. He was trying out a new route, the idea being to baffle the Japanese.

At one point I observed that this was a remarkable plane as it seemed able to stand still in the air. We were low in a valley between massive mountains. Roy said we weren't exactly standing still but headwinds were sixty miles per hour so it kind of slowed us. Then he started to play an odd game of peek-a-boo, flying up to peer over mountains, dropping back; he was trying to see how things were at Kunming. "Yep," he said, and we flew straight in to land. The sky above Kunming was smoky and yellow with dust but clear of Japanese planes; the day's bombing had finished. Every day, ground crews scurried around shifting the runway markers, white-painted oil drums, and filling in new bomb craters to get ready for the arrival of the CNAC plane.

Again passengers left with relief and another lot arrived and we were off, flying at thirteen thousand feet above the gorges of the Burma Road. The high altitude was necessary because here the appalling down-draughts plunged the plane thousands of feet in seconds towards the valley floor. We were always cold to frozen but I began to feel ashamed (soft, nothing worse than being soft) because I was also flushed and my legs and arms twitched and my mind seemed peevishly dislocated and I thought with horror that I might burst into tears for no reason. Confessing some of these symptoms to Roy, with a forced laugh, he said it was only lack of oxygen and I'd be all right when we got to Lashio after ten that night. Flare pots lit the runway at Lashio; it was much easier on the nerves to land in the dark when you couldn't see what a mess you were landing on. Sixteen hours and 1,494 miles, if flying like a crow, seemed to me a fairly mammoth trip, but this was a regular weekly run for Roy and the other pilots.

The CNAC rest house, near the Lashio field, was a wooden shack with iron cots and a shower, heaven itself, a chance to wash and sleep in spite of suffocating heat. Roy went off in the early morning with a .22 rifle to bag game; I wandered in the village bazaar, Burma rubies and eggs in banana-leaf baskets and pretty little Burmese women bathing under a tap. The Japanese usually bombed Kunming between 10 and 11 a.m. but it was unsafe to count on their schedule. Today they were late. We hung about sweating, which made a nice change, until the radio reported that twenty-seven Jap planes had bombed Kunming at 1 p.m. for half an hour but were now gone, so we could take off. Back as we'd come, over the Burma Road by daylight, beautiful, hopeless country, jagged mountain after mountain and a brown ribbon of road. Those hot green mountains were breeding grounds for the malarial mosquito; malignant malaria, which is fatal, was another hazard of the road journey. We landed at Kunming at five-thirty in the afternoon dark, a city shrouded in smoke and lit by fires.

I had been in Finnish cities during bombing attacks, and Madrid was swept almost daily by artillery fire; but Kunming was in a class by itself. It was a big walled city, entered by a great carved painted gate. The houses were made of timber or mud brick, with curving eaves. The Japanese claimed to have destroyed it but, as they destroyed, the Chinese residents repaired. Endurance was the Chinese secret weapon. The Japanese should have understood that, and everybody else had better remember it.

First, we smelled smoke and the stink of burst drains. Electric light lines were down like snakes over heaps of rubble. On the sides of a fresh crater, twenty-five feet wide, a little house half tottered, half held, and the family was eating inside by candle light. There was no sound except hammering. Enormous crowds of silent people were putting their houses together as best they could, by the light of candles and kerosene lamps. Something had gone wrong with the fire hose, water could not be pumped from the river. Two tall fires blazed while a mile-long chain of Chinese passed buckets of water from hand to hand. No one was wailing or crying; everyone, even small children, worked in silence.

Part of the city was still lit by electric light. Noisy eaters were bowed over rice bowls in an eating house. A long queue stood outside a movie theatre waiting to see a film called "Kentucky." We took rickshaws to the hotel since we couldn't find our way on foot over the rubble and around the new craters. The hotel was a small dirty café downstairs and a few dirty little rooms upstairs. The Greek owner welcomed Roy as a friend, and was in splendid form. Every day that his hotel escaped intact was like a special favour from God. He said, *"L'alerte est très correcte ici."* The people had two to three hours warning so they could run from the city. Pre-alarm was one balloon, floating over the town; then two balloons were floated and the siren wailed, really time to get moving. For the final urgent alert the balloons were hauled down and the siren wailed steadily. The only casualties were people who got sick and tired of running off into the fields every day, and stayed and took their chances.

The penalty for looting was death. "They shot about 400 and since then there has been no problem." Today had been unusual, only forty minutes' warning and the Japanese, whom the Greek called *"ces bandits,"* were late. Kunming was defenceless and the Burma Road traffic did not pile up there. Roy thought the Japanese used Kunming as safe practice in bombing and cross-country navigation for their trainee pilots.

We dined on fried eggs and warm beer, very jolly, and went early to bed as we had to be off before dawn and well lost, flying low between the mountains, before the Japanese came back on their usual morning raid.

Landing at Hongkong the third night was as impressive as the rest of the trip. We had been flying in what looked like bechamel sauce for hours; Hongkong was invisible but the Peak is always there as a threat for straying planes. Roy wheeled and turned, wheeled and turned, saw the field for an instant through a rift in the clouds, dropped lower, still on that circular flight pattern, saw more, and finally we skimmed the house-tops, ceiling two hundred metres, and landed neatly. The Chinese passengers had a tendency to clap, with tears in their eyes, at every safe arrival.

There can have been nothing else like CNAC in the history of civil aviation. I doubt if there were ever any other pilots like those. They flew by compass, eyesight and experience; help from the ground was limited to contact when nearing cities, the all-clear signal for take-off, and whatever weather reports they could pick from the air. I remember one weather report: "The moon is beaming," not really much help. The pilots earned one thousand dollars a month for eighty-five flying hours and ten dollars for each extra hour. Men do not risk their lives every week for such money. They were immensely proud of their fantastic little airline. And I think they were in love with their kind of flying, the man and the machine off on their own against the Japanese and the weather and the mountains and the landing fields.

That was not a horror journey, never a dull moment. Glowing with adrenalin and high spirits, I would gladly have started again on the next flight.

U.C. had finished a long piece of work before we left the U.S. and if I hadn't coaxed him to China, he would have been loafing somewhere probably with a fishing rod. Since he was done out of that, he loafed around Hongkong with an ever-growing band of buddies. He had learned to speak coolie English, a language related to West African pidgin and Caribbean English, and was seen laughing with waiters and rickshaw coolies and street vendors, all parties evidently enjoying each other. He loved Chinese food and would return from feasts with his Chinese crook-type friends swearing they'd been served by geisha girls, and describe the menu until I begged him to stop, due to queasiness. He was ready to try anything, including snake wine, the snakes presumably coiled and pickled in the bottom of the jug.

Local customs charmed him, for instance ear-cleaning. Salesmen with trays of thin sticks, topped by tiny coloured pom-poms, roamed the streets; these sticks were ear cleaners. Customers would pause, in the middle of those bustling crowds, to prod away at their ears with the detached expression, U.C. said, of people peeing in a swimming pool. The Chinese passion for firecrackers also delighted him. U.C. bought them every day and was very disappointed when I insisted that he stop lighting them in our rooms, where they raced like exploding worms over the floor. He found someone to box with and went to the races, saying that dye sweated off the horses and cunning Oriental fraud prevailed. From the first he was much better at the glamorous East than I was, flexible and undismayed.

U.C. wrote to my mother of the Hongkong pleasures so far, adding that "M. is very happy, treating the men like brothers and the women like dogs." U.C. was not the most accurate fellow on earth (neither am I) and I cannot think of any women whom I could have treated like dogs. I remember only Emily Hahn with cigar and highly savvy on the Orient and I was never foolish enough to be disdainful of her, and Madame Sun Yat Sen, tiny and adorable and admirable unlike her sisters Madame Chiang and Madame Kung who were the limit. The CNAC men and their wives were my chosen companions.

I wasn't entirely happy either as I was taking the pulse of the nation and growing more despondent by the day. Opium dens, brothels, dance halls, mah-jong parlours, markets, factories, the Criminal Courts; it was my usual way of looking at a society from the bottom rather than from the top. An opium den, to an old student of Fu Manchu, should have been velvet and gilt and voluptuous sin; these sad little rooms—more like a corridor than a room—with three tiers of bare board shelf-size bunks, were where the coolies smoked opium at ten cents for three tiny pills, because opium was cheaper than food, took away the appetite, and rested the strained and tired muscles. In one such room, behind a basket factory, a girl of fourteen fixed the pipes and when not so occupied played gently with a pet tortoise. Another such den (what a word) was an airless hole behind a carpenter's shop; the carpenters worked from 8 a.m. to 5 p.m., then ate their one daily meal and worked again from 7 p.m. to 10 p.m. A girl of fifteen earned seventy cents a day there; the poor skinny smokers could fondle her as part of the services. Next door, two families lived in a space about the size of a double Pullman berth.

The Chinese, great gamblers, paid one cent an hour to play in a mahjong parlour and bet ten cents a game; they played in concentrated silence. The streets were full of pavement sleepers at night. The brothels were small square wood cubicles, lining a narrow passage; two dollars a night per man per girl. The crimes were street vending without a licence, and a fine no one could pay. These people were the real Hongkong and this was the most cruel poverty, worse than any I had seen before. Worse still because of an air of eternity; life had always been like this, always would be. The sheer numbers, the density of bodies, horrified me. There was no space to breathe, these crushed millions were stifling each other.

When finally I visited a dank ill-lit basement factory where small children carved ivory balls within balls, a favourite tourist trinket, I could not bear to see any more. I had a mild fit of hysterics.

"They look about ten years old," I shouted at U.C. "It takes three months to make one of those damned things, I think it's eight balls within balls. They'll be blind before they're twenty. And that little girl with her tortoise. We're all living on slave labour! The people are half-starved! I want to get out, I can't stand this place!"

U.C. considered me thoughtfully. "The trouble with you, M., is that you think everybody is exactly like you. What you can't stand, they can't stand. What's hell for you has to be hell for them. How do you know what they feel about their lives? If it was as bad as you think, they'd kill themselves instead of having more kids and setting off firecrackers."

From agonizing over the lot of my Chinese fellow men, I fell into a state of hysterical disgust with hardly a pause. "*Why* do they all have to spit so much?" I cried. "You can't put your foot down without stepping on a big slimy glob! And everything stinks of sweat and good old night-soil!" The answer of course could be that spitting was due to endemic tuberculosis, and as for the stink, I had seen where and how the people lived. I knew I was being contemptible. To avoid more hysterics, U.C. moved us to a country hotel at Repulse Bay. We couldn't go farther because we hadn't yet received our papers and permissions for the journey to the interior. The hotel at Repulse Bay was as near English as possible, set in lovely gardens and done up in chintz. Soft-footed servitors bore pink gins around the place. No spitting and no smells, no visible poverty. U.C. teased me about my contentment in this clean non-Oriental enclave but was quite happy himself; he'd had enough company and was satisfied to read and walk over the hills.

We decided to walk to a sampan city for lunch, balmy weather, nice walk, and the prospect of rare fish dishes. The sampan city entranced me, from a distance, because it looked like picturesque China in the movies. A Chinese woman staggered along the dirt road towards us, pleasing U.C. who was partial to Chinese drunks. I think he felt that the Hongkong Chinese, given to gambling, rice wine and firecrackers, had great *savoir vivre*. The woman then began to vomit blood and collapsed. U.C. said, "She's had it, poor old lady," and hurried me off.

We had just seen the cholera epidemic in close-up. The cholera epidemic was due to practice air-raid alerts, lately discontinued. The night-soil coolies, terrified by the sound of the siren, dumped their baskets of excrement and fled; and cholera followed. I believe U.C. was more impressed by the sight of that woman dying than he ever said; he became the Medical Officer on our China travels. In China, water is like justice in that it has to be boiled and seen to be boiled; U.C. supervised this.

U.C. also checked the quinine intake, which I'd have forgotten or muddled. He arranged extra shots against all the available diseases. By myself, I'd have wrung my hands and groaned and caught every germ and ended up dead.

Reporting on the Chinese army in action seemed a rational project in New York but absurd in China due to distances, lack of roads and transport, and any form of communication and the quiescence of the war. The Japanese held the best three quarters of China and had no need to push farther; they bombed without opposition when they felt like it. No front was anywhere near remote Chungking so U.C. decided we would do a short aerial jump over the neighbouring mountains and the Japanese, and make our way back towards the Canton front which was next door to Hongkong. I now think it astounding that this trip ever got arranged; at the time, not knowing the practical obstacles, I fumed and fretted and complained of the delay. What more natural, I asked, than for war correspondents to look at war?

My glimpse of conditions inland had given me ideas: I stocked up on Keating's Flea and Lice Powder, Flit, thermos bottles for boiled water, disinfectant for unboiled water, towels, mosquito nets and bedrolls and fancied we were comfortably equipped. U.C. did the tedious staff work and bought not enough whisky but how could he guess that Chinese generals would down this new tasty drink like water. As it worked out, we flew for an hour and a half from Hongkong to Namyung, where the true horror journey began, and took seven days on the ground to travel half of that distance.

On 24 March 1941, we presented ourselves with our gear in the middle of the night at the Hongkong airfield and stood around in a gale-force wind until the flight was scrubbed. Visibility at Namyung: zero. The next day we left at 11 a.m. for Namyung in blanketing cloud. From notes: "lovely landing (blind)." Showing off to myself, as an old China aviation hand. It was raining at Namyung. Here we met the first batch of our Chinese escorts. I described them to my mother as "two Chinese officers, both officers by courtesy, since one was in the Political and one in the Transport Department. Mr Ma, the politico, our interpreter, early showed himself to be a dope . . . Mr Ho, the transport king, was as efficient as humanly possible in this repellent country and we liked him very much. He spoke a language that resembled French and had a vocabulary of some thirty words." Yet Mr Ho, whom we approved, is sunk without trace while Mr Ma lives on tenderly preserved in my memory.

Mr Ma was all round; round specs, round nose, round cheeks, round, permanently smiling or open (waiting to smile) mouth. He said he had been educated at the University of Michigan which we didn't believe for a minute and as time went on we doubted that he understood either English or Chinese. The smile was infuriating; poor Mr Ma, so hard-working and good-natured, he couldn't help being a fool.

In China, vehicles were manned by the driver and the mechanic, who leaped out to start the car, tinker with the engine, change tyres, and put rocks behind wheels to keep the vehicle from rolling away. We set out in a small old Chevrolet, seven of us and both U.C. and I bigger than any Chinese. Wedged in, we got our first taste of the infrequent roads. Not roads; rivers of mud, rutted, gouged, strewn with boulders. You caught your breath after each back-breaking crash. The tyres, not unnaturally, exploded like firecrackers. This drive lasted until dark when we arrived at our hotel, the Light of Shaokwan, in the city of that name.

Mr Ma had assured us of the elegance of the hotel so we were a bit daunted to begin with. We had a room with two sets of planks for beds, a trembling bamboo table, a brass washbowl full of dubious water and a spittoon to empty it into, a hard bamboo chair and a bamboo stool, two toy kerosene lamps, malarial mosquitoes and a stand-up hole-in-the-floor toilet down the corridor. The toilet must have been unique, in that I do not mention it with hatred, possibly a jar of water was provided for flushing. It was still raining—it was always raining—and cold, but cold did not discourage the mosquitoes.

I wondered aloud about the washing arrangements: how exactly were two people to manage with one bowl of water? Did we both wash our teeth in the same water, then our faces? U.C. told me earnestly not to wash at all and if I dreamed of brushing my teeth I was a nutcase. I had better control my mania for keeping clean. "Cheer up," U.C. said, battling with a mosquito net. "Who wanted to come to China?"

We spent only three days in Shaokwan, a record of speed, making the necessary politeness visits. They drove me to frenzy, all the politeness visits, then and later, and U.C. was heroic. The burden fell squarely on him; he alone had to swap compliments and reply to flowery toasts. As a woman, I was expected only to smile. I was free to be a mere presence, mute and suffering, though sometimes so beside myself that I went off into insane giggles, which were ignored. Mr Ma translated, a slow and wearisome affair. Thinking it over, after these many years, I put a proper value on U.C.'s patience and courtesy, neither his most familiar qualities, and believe he must have been upholding the honour of the United States. He was also obliged to deliver rousing speeches. How did he survive it? Enjoying Chinese food helped him a little, and tolerance of rice wine, yellow kerosene to me. At Shaokwan I noted: "Lunch with General Yu. Looks like Buddha. Staff of generals, Chu, Chiang, Wong, Chen etc. Bottoms up on Chinese fire-water. Vast food. Many compliments exchanged before lunch. U.C. terrific. Drink tea at separate table before and after meal. Home to mosquitoes."

Waiting for who knows what further permissions, we drove with a General Chu, and certainly without enthusiasm, on the ruinous road to a monastery. U.C. was no sightseer. I remember it enough to remember that I thought here was a religion, whatever it might be, even more unappealing than most. From notes: "2 gates each with huge wood statues of angry painted devils 25 feet high. Inside temple, 396 clay Buddhas, 3 enormous gold Buddhas. Great bell. Priests in blue, all filthy, look like cretins. 6 shaved spots on head show full priest. Fine trees. No one knows names."

We drove for three quarters of an hour each way, shaken and bruised, to breakfast with the Provincial Governor, to save his face; he could not be upstaged in hospitality by the General. He gave us jasmine tea, tasting like cologne, and sweet biscuits. I would have blessed Shaokwan had

I known what lay ahead. Instead I was panting to leave, thinking to escape compliments and Generals and spraying the Light of Shaokwan with Flit and eating quinine and reading on a bamboo stool. "Whatever else you can say about war," I informed U.C., "when you get to the front, it's not boring." U.C. raised his eyebrows but refrained from comment.

We left Shaokwan in a very old truck; in the cab, driver, mechanic and us; behind, our troops, three officers—"a nice General Staff Officer named Tong, who only spoke Chinese, had joined us," also sunk without trace—and four soldiers in faded cotton uniforms, all looking about twelve years old. The road outdid itself. We braced one hand on the roof of the truck, one foot on the dashboard, and despite being joined together like Siamese quadruplets on the front seat, we were badly battered. The trip lasted three hours and covered thirty-five miles, which was all the road there was. Being new and unbroken in spirit, we were still able to laugh whenever we had breath in our bodies. My notes say: "Kind of truck you can hurt yourself in." So we came to the banks of the North River, marked on the map as a wandering rivulet, but as wide as the Mississippi and crowded like everywhere in China. Our water-borne transport was an antique rusty Chriscraft towing a large covered sampan by a rope that looked like a raffia clothesline. It was the sole motorboat on the river.

The pilot or captain of the Chriscraft was a skinny little ancient, with a few grey wisps of beard and a bamboo pipe. He sat crosslegged and silent on a high stool, up forward in the cabin. A tiny boy, his grandson, apparently lived in the toilet, a closet of unutterable stench and filth, and served the Captain as a steward, bringing him bowls of rice and tea, filling his pipe. Every other hour, he pumped out the Chriscraft to prevent it from sinking. On the sampan, the military contingent settled in with the sampan family, descendants of the Chriscraft ancient. There were two women, one new baby (who cried all the way), two boys and two men. The women cooked for everyone on charcoal braziers. The teenage soldiers made up beds for the officers and boiled water for our thermoses.

Everything was fine except no room for U.C. and me. We moved to the small sloping roof of the Chriscraft where we disposed ourselves on coiled ropes and boathooks, not the best mattresses, and were glad to be out in the air, away from the pervasive odours, if not the pervasive sounds. U.C. said, "You'll have to get used to it, M. You wanted to come to China." Everybody has idiosyncrasies. One of mine, involuntary and unfortunate, is a reaction to the sound of hawking up phlegm, collecting it in the mouth and spitting it out. My reaction is to retch. Nothing violent, no carry-through, but an instant sudden spasm. This hawking was background music from the sampan.

I didn't mind belches, no matter how long, rumbling and gaseous. I was inured to non-stop Chinese talk which is not melodious but a nasal, harsh sing-song. The hawking got me. "Put cotton in your ears," U.C. said. "You won't miss anything." We had no cotton. In time, I managed to retch so that it looked like swallowing. No one noticed except U.C. who would leer at me, mockingly. The punishment didn't begin to fit the crime. Who brought us to China?

We had a nice view from the cabin roof. Small temples sprouted out of rock cliffs. Sailing junks were pulled up river with chanting like the Volga Boatmen. Bamboo and pine grew by the shore. Sandbanks showed like whales' backs in the stream. We saw an egret and then a single black duck. "That's the best sign so far," U.C. said. It was quite beautiful and calm. In forty-five minutes the tow-rope snapped. Mr Ma was looking at pictures in *Time*. Mr Ho slept. The baby cried.

At 4 p.m. the sampan drew close to the Chriscraft for the dinner hour. If all went well, we got two meals a day, at approximately nine in the morning and four in the afternoon. A bowl of rice and tea, unless being entertained with compliments and gastronomy by Generals. We had whisky with boiling hot water from our thermoses for dessert. The river shone silver in the evening light; blue-black mountains stood out against a greenish sky. As we passed the poor river villages, huts on stilts, massed sampans, U.C. said, "They think happy days are here again. Tourists are coming back to the North River." Then he slept, a talent I envied. In the starless night we began to run aground on sandbars. A man from our sampan took soundings with a boathook. Other unseen boat people shouted at us; I suppose we were a traffic block. After the fifth being stuck and grinding off, the tow-rope wrapped around the propeller, the Chriscraft went in circles and the sampan was bumping our stern. The military lay snugly tucked in, on the floor of the sampan, asleep in their long underwear.

"Mr Ma! Mr Ma! Do these boats usually go down the river at night?" Mr Ma, wakened, put on his glasses.

"Oh yes, all the time. Very often, maybe."

"Do they *want* to go now? Or have you ordered it?" I could too easily imagine being stuck forever with the propeller broken.

"They say they can't see a thing."

"Well then, let's anchor."

"We go back to that town now. Is more safe."

Somehow we untangled and chugged inshore to a sampan village, the shape of the moored boats showing in the flicker of kerosene lamps. Their smells and noise and mosquitoes blew in a cloud around us. U.C. woke, sat bolt upright, and announced, "This town is called Tintack, the disease centre of South China." He stumbled to his feet among the coiled ropes and called benignly, "You boys got any cholera we haven't got?" Women shrieked, babies howled, people leapt away from us, retreating to distant sampans. I scolded U.C. for frightening the populace out of its wits. He said he was only trying to be friendly, the boys must feel lonely stuck off by themselves with their cholera. Hadn't I seen the black flag? I remarked testily that he was making it up, even Mr Ma wouldn't be so idiotic as to anchor us in a cholera epidemic. U.C. went back to sleep while I listened to a man, on our sampan or an adjacent one, slowly and noisily suck in three bowlfuls of food, then counted his belches. Talk resumed in the village. Men chanted on the shore, more Volga Boatmen stuff. For three hours of darkness, China was almost quiet. By the dawn's early light I saw the black flag.

We landed at nine-thirty in the morning rain, twenty-four hours after leaving the luxurious Light of Shaokwan. We didn't land anywhere special. We slithered up a mud bank like all the mud banks along the river. A platoon of soldiers in soaked cotton uniforms and eight stable coolies with eight diminutive horses stood at attention to receive us. Men and beasts shook with cold. U.C. took the platoon's salute in fine style and remarked that his horse was lucky as he could ride and walk at the same time so the horse would really have six legs. I went to get on my horse which kicked ferociously; Mr Ma, beating a retreat, slipped and fell flat in the thick mud. We set off in a downpour, all members of the party past speech.

The gait of the awful little horses was unlike any known horse movement; there was no way you could ride them painlessly. When two got close to each other, they kicked and bit; the stable coolies screamed at them and beat them on the nose with long sticks. We proceeded through waterlogged country in the unremitting downpour along a creek rushing with dirty grey water, as from a gigantic sudsy washtub. After plenty of this, we arrived at a Cadet Training School where we were to inspect two new buildings. The sentries screeched *Attention!*, the horses kicked, bit and trumpeted and we dripped into the premises. We were treated to tea, grapefruit, and compliments.

No memory of those buildings remains except for the photographs that decorated the walls of the officers' mess: Hitler, Mussolini, Daladier, Chamberlain, Roosevelt, Stalin, Goering, Chiang. "Great statesmen of the world, more or less," Mr Ma said. We made farewell compliments and rode five miles farther in the downpour to Division Headquarters. The triumphal arches started to appear now. I have never since seen or heard of triumphal arches for the Press. Our rarity value probably explained them and the Political Department, whose work they were, had little else to occupy it. The arches were of paper, hand-printed, smearing in the rain, and rigged up on poles across the track. "Welcome to the Representatives of Righteousness and Peace." "Welcome to our International Friends." "Consolidate all Democracy Nations." "We will resist Untill Finall Victory [*sic*]." Similar messages greeted us everywhere

on that long trek. Once a man ran alongside our cavalcade to ask where
we were going next so the Political Department could put up an arch. My
favourite was mysterious: "Democracy only Survives Civilization." U.C.
and I brooded on that one but could reach no conclusion.

"Mr Ma, what trees are those?"

"Ordinary trees."

U.C. laughed and disguised it as a belch. I already knew that Mr Ma
was useless as a fount of knowledge but couldn't stop myself. Mr Ma,
with his frail grasp of language, was our only link to people and places.
On the river, I had pointed to one of the barges being hauled upstream
by chanting men and asked, "What do those boats carry, Mr Ma?"

"Cargo, more or less." "Watchumacallit" served as Mr Ma's all-
purpose word.

Gay chatter did not enliven any day but that first sodden day was
also blind. If there was anything to see we couldn't see it through the
lashing rain. We tried to wring water from our trouser legs before meeting the General (Lin, Liu, Chen, Chang, what does it matter?) who had
an unhoped-for coal brazier to sit by while we imbibed technical information about his Division. Chiang's armies were divided into nine war
zones; we were visiting a sector of the Seventh War Zone. The area was
about the size of Belgium with a population of 30 million civilians and
150,000 soldiers. There were no roads and obviously no motorized transport. I never saw so much as a two-wheeled cart. The population of Belgium is 10 million and it seems a tightly packed little country.

Only narrow footpaths crossed this vast stretch of land, leading to
and from countless villages, each village more pathetic and graceless than
the next, rural slums of mud brick. Headquarters were sometimes a new
wood house, sometimes a house made of lashed mats on stilts above the
duck pond. The pond water was rotting garbage and mud rather than
water, pigs rooted in the muck, flies swarmed, and over all villages hung
the smell of China: night-soil, the deadly national manure.

I noted much now meaningless detail about the formation, training,
weaponry, and actions of the Twelfth Army Group which held this sector

of the front. The revealing note is: "Soldiers always look like sad orphanage children." They were to weep over, those unfortunate boys, usually barefooted with puttees on their bare legs, dressed in cotton uniforms. They were paid a token wage, something like $2.80 U.S. a month, and an even smaller rice allowance. With this money they had to buy their own food. Rice was plentiful but they could not afford to buy what they needed; the soldiers, not the generals, were very thin. Punishment and discipline were Prussian. Though we inspected everything in sight, we never saw a military hospital, not even a medical aid station. I alternated between pitying the soldiers most and pitying the peasants most.

Our first night in the peaceful combat zone was like the others; we shivered in our wet clothes on our board beds, dozed, waked to shiver some more and at six in the morning we were called. U.C. mounted his miniature horse at seven and rode five miles back to the Training Camp to deliver a rousing speech to graduating cadets. I am more and more amazed that he didn't strangle me. When he returned, I asked what he had said to the boys. He glared at me. "Just don't be funny about it, M. I may have had to do worse things but I doubt it."

We set off at ten and rode and walked in clear cold weather until late afternoon, twenty-five miles with occasional refreshing draughts of boiled hot water from our thermoses but no food. It was hill country, like an endless rollercoaster. In the valleys, peasants ploughed the fields behind water buffaloes, peasants and buffaloes struggling along up to their middles in grey mud. We passed through slatternly villages, each adorned with a triumphal arch for us and a duck pond with malaria for them. No one had ever seen any white foreign devils before. The children either screamed in excitement or sobbed in fear. The adults were stony-faced, exhausted by life, and also marred and scarred by unimaginable diseases. "If only our noses don't drop off," U.C. murmured, after seeing one more peasant with a little red hole in a ravaged face.

"It looked so beautiful from the air," I told U.C. wistfully. "The mountains and the fields. And now it looks like nothing."

"It looks big," U.C. said.

We rested beside the track under a spreading nameless tree. Trees were rare, being a luxury. The land was used to produce food. The steep hills grew bushes and tall grass; perhaps all serviceable trees had been cut down for building timber. Even here, in the middle of nowhere, there was passing traffic. A merchant with a string of sandals around his neck, a merchant carrying a carton of toothpicks, a man bearing a coffin on his back. "That one's got good steady work, plenty of customers," U.C. said.

I noticed that some of the unending hills were black stubble and asked Mr Ma, probably testing whether I could still speak, "Why do they burn off the hills, Mr Ma?"

"To get rid of the tigers."

"*Tigers*, Mr Ma?"

"Yes, many, more or less. You see, tigers eat some kind of tender little roots and sweet grasses, and when it is all burned, they get hungry and go away."

U.C. lay back on the stony ground and raised his face to heaven with the radiant smile of one who has heard angels singing. Mr Ma's vegetarian tigers have taken on a complex and changing symbolism over the years, and always rejoin me in the blackest hours of other horror journeys.

Before the day was over, my notes state: "U.C.'s horse fell on him." U.C. stretched his arm over the saddle and under the horse's belly and picked it up, muttering about cruelty to animals, and started to walk with it. I said sharply, "Put that horse down."

He said, "I will not, poor bloody horse."

I said, "You're insulting the Chinese. Put it down!"

He said, "My first loyalty is to this horse."

I said, "*You must drop that horse! Please!*"

"Okay, poor old horse, walk by yourself if you can." All afternoon the stable coolie behind me held his stomach and groaned.

That night we were spared generals. U.C. could not have coped with compliments. We shivered and slept in some sort of shed with a mat as partial wall between us and our military men. Or U.C. slept. I listened, discovering that when they began the hawking with a long phlegmy cough it was even worse.

The morning ride was a mere four miles in rain before our breakfast of tea and rice. The General, named Wong, looked like a Chinese Kewpie doll, very sweet. We did solemn map work with him. He showed us how the Japanese had driven up from Canton in a three-pronged attack, almost reaching Shaokwan in 1939 and again in May 1940. General Wong explained the order of battle in case of future Japanese attack: the forward machine-gun posts on the hills would delay the enemy, the reserves would come up, and the Japanese would be pulverized by artillery and mortar fire.

This sounded improbable due to the Japanese having planes and the Chinese not. Anyway I believed that the only reason the Japanese didn't take Shaokwan or anywhere else they chose was because China was roadless and immense and the Japanese, as insanely cruel as the Nazis, had taught the Chinese peasants to hate in the same way that their Nazi allies taught the Russian peasantry. Scorched earth is the peasants' weapon. Twice the peasants hereabouts burned their crops and their stored rice, killed what animals they couldn't lead away, and left emptiness for the Japanese. Chinese soldiers were sons of peasants. Though they were offered $1,000 U.S. for any Japanese prisoner taken alive, there were no living prisoners. Like Russia, China is not a sensible country to invade.

In the afternoon we attended a meeting on the parade ground, the regiment in serried ranks, soldiers trembling with cold and a hundred village elders huddled and shivering. It wasn't so bad because U.C. didn't have to make a speech; we listened to Mr Ma's translation of speeches rendered impenetrable now by "whatchumacallit." Mr Ma was falling apart from so much translating. "They say if the U.S. whatchumacallit, we will do the rest . . . They say greetings to the American whatchumacallit, hope very happy with whatchumacallit army." Speeches were redundant since the area was festooned with signs, giving us the word for the day. "Down with the Nipponese. The World will be Lighter." "Support to President Roosevelt Speech." "Help to Democracy Nation." "International Help and Sympathy Always Appreciated."

Mr Ma said this large village was a thousand years old, and it might well have been. They built their villages like rabbit warrens, house stuck to house, on aimless, narrow mud lanes. No gardens, no open ground except around the duck pond. Perhaps the need for rice paddies forced them to live in a tight huddle, always too many people in too little space; or perhaps they liked it that way because the enormity of their land chilled them.

We were quartered in a stone house in a stone room on a stone floor. It was very cold. The door opened on to the street and the smell thereof. The mosquitoes were competing with the flies and losing. The whisky, our only source of warmth, had run out owing to Generals' enthusiasm for it. I lay on my boards, a foot off the floor, and said in the darkness, "I wish to die."

"Too late," answered U.C. from across the room. "Who wanted to come to China?"

Why this village presented a particular problem I no longer know. In the cold grey morning I was faced with the unfair fact that a female cannot modestly relieve herself, and no place to retire in a landscape of bare rice paddies, a sea of mud. The village latrine was a public monument, a bamboo tower, reached by a fragile bamboo ladder, the top screened in mats. Beneath, a five-foot-tall Ali Baba jar stood on the ground to collect valuable human manure.

"I can't do it," I said, staring at the tower.

"Nobody asks you to," said U.C. "You haven't seen any Chinese women fooling around with modesty, have you? I recommend the duck pond, it's the popular spot here."

"No."

"Put up or shut up, M., we have to start for the next speeches."

Cautiously, I climbed the ladder, nervous about the bamboo structure but comforted by the mat screens. At this moment, someone hammered on the nose cap from a Japanese bomb, which served in these villages as air raid siren. I looked down to see the peasants evaporating; the village was empty, even the pigs had departed. Far below, in the street, U.C. grinned up at me.

"What now, M.? What now?"

"Nothing!" I shouted, enraged by my ridiculous situation. "Here I am and here I stay!"

"The best of Chinese luck to you," U.C. called and withdrew to a doorway. A squadron of Japanese planes passed, very high and very fast. It must have been the regular run to Kunming. I had an excellent view. I picked my way carefully down the ladder where U.C. met me, laughing heartily.

"Oh poor M., what an inglorious death it would have been. M., the intrepid war correspondent, knocked off in the line of duty. But where? But how? the press of the world inquires."

I had no time to nurse my self-pity because we were jolting off again, under a lowering sky, on the interminable track. Mr Ma promised great excitements for the day. The army was going to put on manoeuvres for us. "Ground strafing," U.C. said to himself. "What sort of Japanese planes have you seen, Mr Ma?"

Mr Ma became Clausewitz. "They throw a bomb," he explained carefully, "when they want to knock down a house. If they see many people on a road more or less they come down and machine-gunning them."

We reached a barracks and one more General. We rode another hour to the area where the Chinese Army was to show us how it operated in combat. This was the real front, to the extent that the Chinese had their machine-guns on these hills and, three kilometres away, the Japanese had the same. We stationed ourselves with binoculars to watch our boys simulate an attack on Japanese fortified mountain positions. They did well too, it looked a most competent and intelligent manoeuvre. Under the grey sky, among the humping mountains, the mortars made a loud jolly noise, like all the firecrackers in China united. Echoes of explosions racketed between the hills. We enjoyed the bangs, the sprightliest event so far. U.C., much invigorated, said, "The Japs think it's mutiny in the

Chinese army! They're signalling Tokyo for orders to advance! They expect to take Shaokwan day after tomorrow! In two weeks they'll be at the gates of Chungking! Excitement has spread to Canton! The city is a veritable hotbed of rumours!"

The General looked puzzled, Mr Ma agape. He had never heard U.C. speak like that. He was used to U.C. droning, "Tell the General we greatly appreciate . . . Tell the General we deeply admire . . . Tell the General his Division is unrivalled in the world."

"Speak slower again, sir," Mr Ma said.

"No, no, don't bother, Mr Ma. It was only technical stuff to help M. with her piece on the Canton Front."

At night, a further entertainment had been arranged: plays presented by the Political Department. Wind blew over the parade ground; six bonfires were lighted around the edges. The troops, eighteen hundred of them, squatted on the damp ground while we sat in the place of honour on chairs beside the General. After three quarters of an hour, they got an acetylene lamp to work and light the stage. First there were speeches. Mr Ma pretended to translate but mumbled gibberish. Three piercing blasts on a whistle heralded the producer who stepped before the blue denim curtains on the small stage and announced the name of the play, "Group of Devils."

The curtains jerked open, like all school plays, revealing the cast of characters, a Chinese workman, a painted Chinese lady (a girl political worker), and three Japanese officers. The workman was the lady's husband, masquerading as the janitor. The plot was uncomplicated. The lady, a loyal Chinese spy, lured the Japanese officers to give away secrets. The Japanese officers wore paper hats like Japanese military headgear and moustaches of lamp black. The Japanese officers desired the painted lady with lewd explicit energy. The husband–janitor slyly ridiculed and insulted the Japanese officers. This went on for some time and at last all three Japanese officers were shot on stage. The audience adored it, roaring with laughter and applauding like thunder.

The second play, "Cross Section of Canton," performed by the same actors, was not such a smash hit. Evidently I missed its finer points. The audience responded with gloom until the old father bit the Japanese soldier and was hauled off to be buried alive. After which his son collared the bitten Japanese soldier and kicked him round the stage, preparatory to slicing him in two. The audience then laughed happily. The curtain fell on the son with upraised sword, the Japanese soldier on his knees fearfully begging for his life. This was greeted with warm applause and laughter and cheerful cries, no doubt Chinese for *"Bravo."*

We laughed too, partly from pleasure to hear others laughing, partly from relief, after three hours in the wind. Mr Ma said, "All these plays are true. It cuts the General deeply in his feelings to see these plays."

U.C. said, "Remember, M., when you come to China next time, bring your long underwear."

"I'd rather jump off the Empire State building in long underwear than come to China again."

"I put nothing past you," U.C. said sombrely. "Nothing."

The Japanese had been shown as loud, rude, ridiculous, tactless, and bullying: they were grotesque joke figures. Yet this audience was not green troops; they had been here the year before during the successful Japanese advance; they knew the Japanese. I couldn't imagine any audience of European or American soldiers laughing its head off at a play about the antics of Germans, those clumsy, noisy, nasty, comical cowards. What did it mean? A profound difference between the Oriental and the Occidental mind?

On his best day, in a country he liked, with plenty to drink, U.C. wasn't the man to sit still for such waffling speculation. I must have emerged from behind my fixed smile to ask the General about this odd attitude to the Japanese; otherwise I cannot account for my notes: "the General told atrocity stories." If the General told us atrocity stories, he at least didn't think the Japanese a big laugh. Mr Ma chipped in with a tale of eight village girls. "Since village girls are very particular about their virginity, they resisted furiously. But they were nuded and very seriously raped." Dear Mr Ma, he could make anything shine with foolishness.

And so the Representatives of Righteousness and Peace turned back for the return trip to the river. Mr Ho broke his silence on a cold three-hour ride in mist and rain. I wonder if my notes are translated literally from his alleged French or whether Mr Ma intervened. "Bad territory" (the field of politics). "The civils are taking up all the money from the poor people . . . I did not want to be military either. Look. I kill you. You kill me. At once. Necessary. That is very bad also . . . The world is stupid . . . Perhaps our God is angry." Mr Ho was a Catholic. He earned 120 Chinese dollars a month, fake money anyhow, but a pair of shoes cost $200. He had a wife and eight children in Macao.

I have no memory of what U.C. was doing. I rode with my head down like the horse, nodding wearily like the horse. We passed again the rice paddies and the awful straining work of the peasants. "Mr Ma," I am sure I sounded half crazed. "What fun do people have in China?"

"Chinese people are very serious. Just work. For pleasure only talk and eat."

War isn't funny after all, not a time to dance in the streets. But there wasn't any war here, there was an undeclared truce. I was sure this China had always been drowning in hopeless poverty and disease, war only made the normal state somewhat worse.

We slumped in to Wongshek and the 189th Division, where solemn blue-clad soldiers stood in the rain and U.C. had to make a speech, gagging over the words. School children greeted us with pennants, cheers and a song. Then there was another speech to villagers. We inspected a training camp, a barracks, classrooms. The signs said: "Warm Welcome to American News Reporters." U.C. was outraged: he didn't care what they called me but he was *not* a News Reporter. "Welcome American Friends Directing our Defective Points." "It is good for closer relations of China and America, honoured visitors coming to see our country." No other news reporters or foreigners had ever been here, nor had any of the military brass from Chungking. U.C. and I agreed that this was due to their good sense. Unlike us, they must have known about travel conditions in China and also how this war worked. Chiang's armies served as a defensive rearguard but were nowhere engaged in driving the Japanese out of China. Without air support, there wasn't much they could do even if the Japanese had been Chiang's major concern.

U.C. said, "Cheer up, M. You saw the Chinese army, you can't be blamed if there's no action."

The Chinese army settled down to live permanently wherever stationed. The soldiers got no home leave; how could they get home to begin with? They built their barracks and schools, they trained, they stayed. They would stay as long as the Japanese stayed. Two years now in the same place for the men we'd seen. Illiterate peasant families could not write to their illiterate soldier sons, and we saw no system for transporting mail and couldn't imagine one. Nobody bothered with this lost corner of the land. Perhaps U.C. pitied that neglect, and from kindness, in the daily grind of his speeches and toasts, tried to give these forgotten people a sense of importance. I just kept moaning "God help them all" but was hardly able to maintain a polite smile.

The farewell luncheon was sensational. Generals and colonels clustered around a long table. Dish followed dish; when you lost count, the grandeur was out of sight. Chopsticks had a life of their own in my hands so I had to use a tin fork and spoon which I carried in my pocket. I was stuffing in the welcome food and failed to observe that the party had turned into a booze battle. U.C. alone against fourteen Chinese officers. One of them rose and made a toast to which U.C. replied; then he and U.C. drank bottoms up. The grisly yellow rice wine, Chinese vodka. While one toaster rested another rose, obliging U.C. to spout fancy words and again drink bottoms up. When all fourteen had finished the first round, they returned to the fray. U.C., breathing rather hard, looked like a man who is winning in a brawl against overwhelming odds.

Slowly officers grew scarlet in the face and slid beneath the table; others went green-white and fell as if shot. U.C. was planted on his feet like Atlas. I mumbled that he would have a seizure, was it worth it, patriotism is not enough, remember Nurse Cavell. But he was gleaming with the pride of combat. No question now about the honour of the United States, his personal honour was at stake, he was ready to drink them down if he died in the process. General Wong became purple and his eyes watered and he had trouble focusing so that when he tottered upright he directed his toast to the wall rather than to U.C. Mr Ma was so drunk that he was unable to translate U.C.'s most beautiful toast to the Generalissimo's glorious and heroic armies. Half the company lay under the table, most of the remainder rested their heads upon it. U.C. towered above us, swaying but triumphant. General Wong, in whose power lay reprieve, apologized for the disgrace of having no more rice wine to offer his honoured guests.

U.C. walked with care. "I guess that showed 'em, eh M.?"

"How do you feel?"

"Like a man who is never going to make a speech or a toast again."

This orgy began at the peculiar lunch hour of ten-thirty in the morning. We were aboard the Chriscraft by one o'clock. We made a ceremonial departure, chugging a hundred yards upriver to anchor and wait for a soldier who had vanished in the village. It was raining. I don't know why I harp on the rain; there was only one day without rain. The cabin of the Chriscraft seven days before (days like years) had seemed to me unfit for human habitation. It reeked from the toilet, the two short bunks were covered in cloth that was dark and greasy with age-old dirt. I sprinkled Keatings Powder on the bunks and we roosted there like homing pigeons. U.C. had a nap. By three o'clock the missing soldier was found and we moved out into the river. U.C. read.

I shouted above the clanging of the Chriscraft motor, "The worst is over!"

U.C. glanced at me and returned to his book.

"Mr Ma says we'll be at Shaokwan by noon tomorrow. More or less. Then we'll catch the train to Kweilin. He says we can get anything we want to eat on the train and we'll have a first class compartment to ourselves. It ought to be interesting, really, it's the only train in the whole Republic of China. Don't you think so?"

U.C., reading, had begun to wag his head like a pendulum.

"And the CNAC boys will pick us up in Kweilin and it's nothing from there to Chungking. I figure we'll be in Chungking by late afternoon, day after tomorrow."

U.C. went on reading and head-wagging.

"And in Chungking it *has* to be all right. After all, Whatchumacallit is rich and he's lived in the U.S. and Europe, he must have a good house. He gave me the impression of a man who liked his comforts." I was talking about a Chinese potentate, perhaps Chiang's ambassador in Washington, I've forgotten his exact position, who offered me his Chungking house because I had Connections. I accepted with thanks, knowing he thought my Connections would be useful to him, knowing myself that they wouldn't. My Connections were the Roosevelts. I loved Mrs Roosevelt and since the President could charm the birds off the trees he could easily charm me. In those days, the White House had not become an imperial palace and was also definitely not a Nixon bazaar for buying and selling favours. Loaning his house to me was the Chinese potentate's miscalculation.

"Baths and sheets and real beds and dry clean clothes and no more mosquito nets. Dear God, I can hardly wait."

U.C. looked at me. "You go on hoping, M. They say hope is a natural human emotion. I'll read."

The night was routine, no way to lie on the short bunks, cramps in the legs, cold: nothing special. By noon we were ready to disembark. By three o'clock we had reached the original embarkation point on the river bank but the road back to Shaokwan was impassable due to rain. It was impassable enough before, now it was flooded out. We got off the boat and strolled through the mud to a village where we bought firecrackers and wine in a stone jug. A runner was sent four kilometres to fetch more gasoline for the Chriscraft, because we had to proceed afloat to Shaokwan.

We sat on the Chriscraft roof in a light drizzle and set off the anaemic firecrackers, not up to U.C.'s standards, and drank the wine. In the thermos cup, the wine was a menacing pink colour, thickish, slimy; it looked like hair oil and perhaps tasted like hair oil though I cannot say having never tried hair oil not even in China. All I hoped for was alcoholic warmth and numbing. We were still drinking at six o'clock when the runner returned. Holding the stone jug to pour, I heard something scrape inside.

"What's in here?" I said, shaking the jug.

"It's called spring wine," U.C. said evasively. "It was all Mr Ma could get. Considered very high class, the Chinese drink it as an aphrodisiac."

"What's in this jug?"

"M., are you sure you want to know?"

"Yes."

"Well, snakes. But *dead*. M., if you throw up, I swear I'll hold it against you."

While we were in the depths of Kwantung Province, the Chriscraft pilot had improved his property; instead of the thin tow-rope, he now possessed a stout steel cable. At eight o'clock, in midstream in the black night, this cable wrapped around the propeller, all thirty feet of it. The Chinese talked between themselves very loudly and at length. The tiny boy looked miserable. No one wanted to dive into the river and try to file off the cable. U.C. had never uttered a word of complaint, like a Resistance hero who refuses to speak under torture. He simply sank into deeper silences. I complain more than I eat usually, but on this journey did not dare to, being the guilty party, and limited myself to groaning and sighing and calling upon God. The situation was so hopeless now that I too sank into silence, indifferent, numb from despair rather than from snake wine.

We ate dinner on the sampan, rice and tea. We went back to the Chriscraft. As there were no lights we couldn't read. We waited. At nine-thirty, we piled on to the sampan which was hitched to a paddle-wheel river steamer. The river steamer was a modern version of nineteenth-century steerage travel, the Chinese packed in like cattle. Mr Ma, Mr Ho, the mute Mr Tong, U.C., and I slept in the small rear section of the sampan on the floor. Forward, the rest of our unlucky world: the baby crying, the adults coughing, hawking, spitting, farting, belching through the long night.

We must have become almost Chinese by then, capable of brute endurance. Except for one stationary hour when the steamer broke down, we were towed up the North River more slowly than walking while the steamer stopped everywhere to disgorge and engorge passengers. At ten o'clock on the second morning we climbed out of the sampan at Shaokwan. We had been on the river for forty-three hours.

We thanked the boy soldiers and tipped them which created some happiness for a change. Our officers escorted us to the station where we asked them not to wait; we might be there for hours and were drained dry of compliments. I wanted to kiss Mr Ma, having come to see him as a fool of God, but knew he would be shocked so contented myself with shaking hands and smiling until my face hurt. At last we were alone in our first class compartment, leaning on the window ledge to observe the crowd. Farther up the platform a band of laughing, chatty, light-hearted lepers was waving goodbye to a travelling leper friend.

I said, "I can't bear it. I can't bear another minute or another sight."

"So far," U.C. said, quietly studying the genial group, "we've still got our noses."

The first class compartment was coated with cinders, the floor a mat of fruit peels and cigarette butts. In a rage I roamed the train until I found the porter, a blank embittered youth in khaki shorts and sandals. Writing to my mother: "I forced the train boy to make some pretence of cleaning our compartment. All cleaning in China is done with a damp rag. The rag is dark grey from dirt and smells so putrid that you have to leave wherever it's being used. If anything was not already filthy and germ-laden, it would be after the passage of the rag. There was nothing to eat. We bought oranges and hardboiled eggs (both safe) at a station. The country suddenly became beautiful as did the weather. It was very hot in the train. The blue and brown mountains were good to see. Without enough food, no drink except boiled water, with dirty lumpy itchy plush seats, and cinders in our eyes, it was still the most comfortable day we have had. That trip lasted 25 hours and covered not quite 400 miles."

I had seen another Caucasian board the train at Shaokwan and made a bet with U.C.

"Bet you twenty dollars Chinese he comes from St Louis."

"Why?"

"I think it's a law. When you get to the worst farthest places, the stranger has come from St Louis."

"Done."

I moved along the unsteady train until I saw the man, reading alone in his cindery compartment. I asked if he was American. Yes. Did he come from St Louis? He looked only slightly surprised and said Yes. I said thank you and left and collected twenty Chinese dollars.

U.C. thought about that. Hours later he said, "Maybe it's something you catch from the water. Maybe it's not your fault." Since I too come from St Louis.

In Kweilin, U.C.'s superhuman resignation wore out, he lost his temper. He stamped around the room, kicking what little there was to kick, shouting, "The sons of bitches, the worthless shits, the motherfuckers, the *bastards.*" Twelfth Army HQ had some means of communication with Kweilin which in turn could signal Hongkong. U.C. had sent a message days before to Kweilin asking them to relay it to Hongkong: a request for CNAC to pick us up in Kweilin. The Kweilin people had not bothered to do anything.

Kweilin was not on the scheduled CNAC route; it was only a stop to load or unload freight. In Hongkong we had arranged to be called for on a freight flight. The weather changed back to normal, solid rain blowing in a gale. Kweilin nestled among extraordinary mountains, sharp, pointed, pyramidal mountains, furred by trees, unlike any I have seen anywhere else, beautiful and romantic, when you could see them rising through cloud. They were no consolation and hazardous terrain for landing aircraft. We were well and truly stuck in the Palace Hotel, Kweilin.

And stuck in the most severe squalor to date. Mashed bedbugs on the walls, bedbugs creeping over the board beds, peering from the wood floor. Bedbugs smell apart from their bite. Two bamboo chairs, a small table, a kerosene lamp, a bowl of dirty water without spittoon for emptying it. Down the corridor, a fine modern porcelain toilet in a cement cubicle but not geared to modern plumbing; the bowl overflowed across the floor. The sight was more appalling than the stench though the stench was superlative. I flung Keatings Powder everywhere until our room looked as if it had been hit by a powdered-mustard cyclone. We argued as to whether sleeping on the floor was safer than on the board beds.

I cannot imagine how we passed those days, clinging to the remnants of sanity. U.C. did say once that if only he had a target pistol he could shoot the bedbugs; they were slow but small and therefore a sporting shot. I think he tried to make a slingshot but must have failed. He beat them down with a shoe. I wrote a long yowling letter to my mother. "China has cured me. I never want to travel again. The hardships (truly beyond belief) would be bearable but the boredom is not . . . Perhaps, before this war, when foreigners lived in luxury on little money in restricted European areas, they had a nice time. But that life as I saw it in Hongkong is as dull as any country club. The real life of the East is agony to watch and horror to share." My mother knew me well; she had received my cries from the pit over the years; I daresay she read this letter with amusement and sympathy for U.C. who had to endure me as well as the glamorous Orient.

At last the CNAC plane arrived, packed with cargo. The cargo was bales of handsome paper money, millions and millions of dollars, manufactured for the Republic of China in Britain and Hongkong. This money was worth the paper it was printed on. We sat on the bales, yelling with laughter at the pilot's jokes. The joy to be back among our own kind. I am certain that the barrier between the races—white, black, brown, yellow—is not only due to colour prejudice and the dissimilarity of customs and values. It is largely due to boredom, the real killer in human relations. We do not laugh at the same jokes. We bore each other sick. Later, whenever I saw the Chinese laughing together I said, translate please, quick, quick, to get the joke. On hearing the translation, I hid behind a bewildered smile. What on earth were the chumps laughing at?

From the riverbed airstrip to the city of Chungking on the high bluff above, you toiled up a precipice of steps. I don't know how we reached the dreamed-of loaned house. The front door opened into the sitting room. U.C. took one look at that room and one whiff of the air and walked into the bedroom where he laughed so hard he had to lie down. I sat on a chair, turned to stone. The sitting room was furnished with fidgety little varnished tables and Grand Rapids grey plush armchairs and sofas, tricked out in crocheted doilies for head-rests. The doilies were black from greasy dirt, but some were hidden by the lustrous hair of three young Chinese thugs. The thugs lolled on chairs and sofas and did not trouble to rise or speak as we entered. They stared at us through lizard eyes. They wore sharp striped suiting and pointed shoes. They had evidently been using our quarters: beneath the cheap pink satin bedspread, the sheets and pillow cases bore the dark stains of their hair oil. In the bathroom, another fine imported porcelain toilet overflowed on the tile floor.

U.C. had laughed himself to a standstill. He rose and straightened his clothes. "Well, I guess I'll go out and see what the boys in the corner saloon are drinking. What'll you do?"

I planned to go mad. "Stare at the wall."

Someone, not me, I was past any effort at self-preservation, must have cleaned the bathroom and changed the bed linen. Two pails of water provided *le confort moderne.* You lifted off the cistern top and poured in water which then thrillingly flushed the toilet; the other pail was for washing in the bowl. I stood in the bathtub and gave myself a daily shower with a teacup.

The thugs remained in the sitting room.

"Who *are* they?" I asked U.C.

"Probably Whatchumacallit's bodyguard, seconded to spy on us. Nobody passed them the word that we're the Representatives of Righteousness and Peace."

We stayed in Chungking for several weeks but the place returns to me only in flashes. It was never meant to be a capital city, its sole advantage being that the Japanese couldn't reach it. I see it as grey, shapeless, muddy, a collection of drab cement buildings and poverty shacks, the best feature a lively market. The Japanese bombed when they wished though not while we were there. The citizens fled to caves as air raid shelters; 396 had lately been killed by suffocation and stampeding feet when a bomb closed the mouth of such a cave. Crowds of thin cotton-clad expressionless people swarmed in the streets. Lepers abounded. They were beggars and forgivably spiteful; you hurried to find money in your purse; if not quick enough, they touched your shrinking skin.

U.C. was in fine spirits; I was not. He found entertaining company, all vanished from my memory, and doubtless Embassy whisky. I think he had got the hang of China by then and was, as they say, adjusted. He went off by air to Chengtu, a top secret area in the north where tens of thousands of Chinese peasants were chopping away mountains with hand shovels and spreading the earth in basketloads to make a tremendous landing field for Flying Fortresses. U.C. said it must have looked like that when the slaves built the Pyramids. The good humour of the peasants touched him; they sang at their work; they competed by villages, their pennants flying; the day's best team set off firecrackers at night in a victory celebration. Given more time and without me around, groaning and sighing steadily, U.C. might have developed into a happy Old China Hand. He did not value cleanliness far above godliness like me, and wasn't reduced to despair by all the manifestations of disease. He saw the Chinese as people, while I saw them as a mass of downtrodden valiant doomed humanity. Long ago, annoyed by the way I left convivial gatherings before anyone else, U.C. declared as dogma, "M. loves humanity but can't stand people." The truth was that in China I could hardly stand anything.

Dr Kung, the Finance Minister, took an avuncular shine to me and presented me with a big box of chocolates from which he had eaten his favourites and a red satin Chinese dress, embroidered in yellow and purple flowers. U.C. said that was no uncle's dress, it looked like the latest model they were wearing in the Chungking whorehouses. Dr Kung also organized a feast, placing me at his right. With his chopsticks, he selected choice morsels to put in my bowl: sea slugs, bits of black rubber with creepers, thousand-year eggs, oily black outside with blood-red yolks. U.C., unimportant in the middle of the table, had a wonderful time at that luncheon party. He watched me as I grew pale and babbled that everything was too delicious but I couldn't eat another mouthful, no really I can't, Dr Kung (desperately coy), you wouldn't want me to get so fat I couldn't wear my lovely red dress.

At a party somewhere, I met Madame Kung. She reminded me of stout rich vulgar matrons in Miami Beach hotels. The CNAC pilots were down on her for demanding that they offload passengers to make room for her trunks, whenever she flew to Hongkong. She was good at clothes; I remember her dress as one of the most beautiful I have ever seen. It was the classical Chinese model, never bettered anywhere, of black velvet. The little buttons that close these gowns from collar to knee are usually made of silk braid; hers were button-size diamonds. She said she had ruby and emerald buttons too. Sapphires were out because they didn't really show. I can't have been suffering too much or I would remember more.

Two visits stand out with rare clarity though I didn't know at the time how exceptional they were. The Generalissimo and Madame Chiang invited us to lunch, an intimate foursome. The Generalissimo wanted to hear news of the Canton front. Their house was modest, also furnished by Grand Rapids including doilies but clean and thug-free. Display in Chungking was useless. Madame Chiang did not stint herself when abroad, once taking a whole floor at the Waldorf. Madame Chiang, still a beauty and a famous vamp, was charming to U.C. and civil to me. Madame Chiang translated. U.C. and I agreed that the Generalissimo understood English as well as we did. He was thin, straight-backed, impeccable in a plain grey uniform and looked embalmed. I didn't take to him but felt rather sorry for him; he had no teeth. Reporting this later to an American Embassy wallah, he exclaimed over the honour showered on us; it was the highest compliment to be received by the Generalissimo with his teeth out.

I have been fascinated to find careless, casual notes on that luncheon conversation. As I reconstruct it, the Generalissimo asked U.C. what he thought of some articles that had appeared in the western press about the Chinese Communists; neither of us had read them and anyway had no opinions. The Generalissimo then went on to state that the Communists were "skilful propagandists without much fighting ability. The C.P. doesn't possess military strength and the government has no need to resort to force against them. If the C.P. tries to create trouble, injurious to the war, the government would use little measures to deal with them as disciplinary questions arose. The Fourth Route Army incident in China was very insignificant. Intensive C.P. propaganda in the U.S. made America believe the C.P. was necessary to the war of resistance. On the contrary, the C.P. was hampering the Chinese army."

He repeated this, according to my notes, in various ways, four separate times. Madame Chiang then said she got letters from the U.S. saying the Kuomintang (Chiang's) armies fired at the backs of the Fourth Route Army (Mao's men) while it was withdrawing according to orders; the Generalissimo said this was not true, his soldiers never fired on the Fourth Route Army and the Communists disarmed Kuomintang forces whenever possible, to get more weapons and territory. Madame Chiang said, "We are not trying to crush them."

If U.C. understood this talk, he didn't mention it to me. I would have been bored but I expected powerful political people to be boring; it comes from no one interrupting or arguing or telling them to shut up.

The more powerful the more boring. With thirty-five years' hindsight, I see that the Chiangs were pumping propaganda into us, as effective as pouring water in sand. We had no idea of what was really going on in China, nor that the Generalissimo and Madame Chiang, to whom power was all, feared the Chinese Communists not the Japanese. They were not fools. The Japanese would disappear some day; historically the Japanese were like an attack of boils. The true threat to the Chiangs' power lay in the people of China and therefore in the Communists who lived among and led the people. I didn't need political expertise to decide, in a few hours, that these two stony rulers could care nothing for the miserable hordes of their people and in turn their people had no reason to love them. An overlord class and tens of millions of expendable slaves was how China looked to me. War wasn't excuse enough for the terrible wretchedness of the people.

Madame Chiang and U.C. were hitting it off all right until I thrust my oar in. I asked Madame Chiang why they didn't take care of the lepers, why force the poor creatures to roam the streets begging. She blew up. The Chinese were humane and civilized unlike Westerners; they would never lock lepers away out of contact with other mortals. "China had a great culture when your ancestors were living in trees and painting themselves blue." Which ancestors? Apes or ancient Britons? I was furious and sulked. To appease me, Madame Chiang gave me a peasant's straw hat which I thought pretty and a brooch of jade set in silver filigree which I thought tacky. I didn't know how to refuse these gifts and was not appeased. U.C. behaved with decorum until we had done our bowing and scraping and departed. Then he said, laughing like a hyena, "I guess that'll teach you to take on the Empress of China."

"Why don't they do something for their people, instead of bragging about their past? All the big shots we've met don't give a damn about anything except their perks and their power. I wouldn't trust any of them. This is a rotten place. What's the matter with them?"

"Whatchumacallit. Maybe. More or less."

In the market, a tall blonde Dutch woman, wearing a man's felt hat and a flowered cotton dress over trousers, approached me furtively and asked if we wanted to see Chou En-lai. The name Chou En-lai meant nothing to me; I said I would ask U.C. I told U.C. that some sort of loon had sidled up to me in the market with this proposition and he said, "Oh yes, he's a friend of Joris." Joris Ivens, a darling man, is a Dutch documentary filmmaker who worked in China in 1938 or 1939. The Dutch woman had instructed me to return to the market with my answer. There followed a scene straight from James Bond but long preceding James Bond.

Our orders were to wander around the next day, until sure we were not tracked by our own thugs or any others, and meet in the market. The Dutch lady then led us through a maze of alleys, further throwing off pursuit. Finally we were bundled into rickshaws and blindfolded for the last lap. Blindfolds removed, we found ourselves in a small whitewashed cell, furnished with a table and three chairs, Chou En-lai behind the table. I was semi-stuffy, as I thought we were playing cops and robbers, and was always quick to disapprove silliness in others. I have no idea what Chou was doing or how he handled his life in Chungking where he was in constant danger.

Chou wore an open-neck short-sleeved white shirt, black trousers and sandals, the dress of an underpaid clerk. He too had a translator. We spoke French but knew by his brilliant amused eyes that he understood without translation. Unneeded interpreters may have been an inscrutable Oriental custom or maybe they served as living tape recorders. In any case, none of the stickiness of translation hampered us. For the first and only time we were at home with a Chinese. We laughed at the same jokes. I suppose U.C. told him about the Canton front. Neither of us could have asked intelligent questions about the Long March, the Communists, where they were and how they were operating, because we didn't know anything about these subjects, nor know who Chou was. He was a Communist living underground which made sense, thinking back belatedly and dimly to Malraux's *La Condition Humaine,* wherein Chiang was depicted ordering Communists to be thrown live into the boilers of locomotives. (I blush to remember my ignorance.)

U.C. was knowledgeable in exact detail about anything that interested him but China had not been on his list. Chou must have thought us brainless boobs of the first water, though that didn't affect our shared merriment. I wish I had Chou quotations to pass on to posterity but don't remember a word. Anyway, we had listened to words until we were punch-drunk. It wasn't what Chou said, but what he was. He sat in his bare little room, in his nondescript clothes, and he *was* Somebody. We thought Chou a winner, the one really good man we'd met in China; and if he was a sample of Chinese Communists, then the future was theirs. As for me, I was so captivated by this entrancing man that if he had said, take my hand and I will lead you to the pleasure dome of Xanadu, I would have made sure that Xanadu wasn't in China, asked for a minute to pick up my toothbrush, and been ready to leave.

Months later, we were convoked to Washington to answer questions about China. We went surlily and told those desk Intelligence Officers that the Communists would take over China, after this war. Why? Because the Chiang lot were hell and it was hypocritical bilge to talk about Chinese democracy, there was less than none, and the people would welcome any change, even two-headed men from Mars, but as it happened the best man in the country was a Communist and it was safe to assume he had some comrades like him. We were called Cassandras as usual and branded fellow travellers as usual. I was astonished when Chou surfaced as Foreign Minister of the new China, that lovely man from the whitewashed cellar in Chungking. All documentary films and travel books about Chou's China show that it is an immeasurable, almost inconceivable, improvement over Chiang's China. Never mind that it would be deadly for people like us; people like us were a drop in that remembered ocean of human misery.

At some point during this Chungking interval, I got China Rot on my hands. It was a very common and distasteful disease, a violent form

of athlete's foot (I think). Suddenly I observed that the skin between my
fingers was rotting away in a yellowish ooze laced with blood. U.C. took
one look at this mess and said for God's sake find a doctor, call the U.S.
Embassy, do something; this might be the first step to losing your nose.
The details are now hidden in the usual mists of time but the result was
that I wore large white motorman-type gloves over a malodorous
unguent; the unguent stained the gloves and I was about as alluring as a
leper. The doctor had assured me that I would not lose my fingers but the
disease was highly contagious. U.C. lacked sympathy.

"Honest to God, M.," he said, "you brought this on yourself. I told
you not to wash."

Even an unsurpassed and unsurpassable horror journey must one
day end, though I often thought it would not. We planned to fly to Rangoon with CNAC, where U.C. would catch the Clipper for home. My assignment was not finished, I had to look at the defences of neighbouring
countries and meant to whisk round Singapore and Java and return to the
newly glamorous Occident a month later. I skipped down the long steps
from Chungking to the river and the plane. Farewell forever to awful
China. U.C. was prepared for the flight with half a bottle of gin and his
Lily Cup. Where and how U.C. acquired his Lily Cup, I never knew. He
carried it, folded in the breast pocket of his jacket; he was inseparable
from it; he guarded it jealously; he shared it with no one, it was his dear-
est private property.

The plane was almost full of Chinese passengers, very jolly to be
leaving. For a brief spell they remained sprightly, but the plane was soon
behaving like a butterfly in a hurricane, tipping from wing to wing and
floating in large zig-zags over the scenery. That quieted the passengers.
Then we hit the up and down draughts over the Burma Road. Instead of
moving ahead we seemed to be in an express elevator. The passengers
began to wail loudly. U.C. and I, not subject to airsickness, admired the
pilot. We were well strapped in and U.C. had just carefully filled his Lily
Cup when the plane was seized by a colossal current and hurled upwards
like a rocket. Despite strapping we rose in our seats. Screams of fear rent

the air, mixed with sobs and the sound of violent vomiting. Having soared into outer space, the plane now dropped, like a descending rocket.

Folk wisdom claims (by what proof I'd like to know) that a drowning person sees his whole life in a flash before the final fatal swallow. I can testify that in however many seconds of that descent, I did a lot of thinking. I knew the wings had to fall off. Possibly we would crash before the wings ripped away but, in any case, survival was impossible. I wanted to tell U.C. that I regretted bitterly having nagged him into this horror journey and would never forgive myself for causing his death, cut off in his prime, his work unfinished, his children fatherless; my heart was breaking with sorrow for U.C. and racked by guilt. U.C., in a strange rigid position, held his Lily Cup with both hands, his eyes fixed on the cabin ceiling. Except for the Lily Cup, he might have been praying. In the tumult of passenger shrieks, I laid my oozing gloved hand on his sleeve and said, "I'm sorry, I'm sorry," as I had no time to make a speech. U.C. did not hear or notice. I closed my eyes, because I thought I'd rather not actually see a wing take leave of the fuselage.

The plane, close to ground level, slowly rose complete with wings. We regained whatever normal flying height was, though nothing was normal on a CNAC flight, and the plane advanced in butterfly style. U.C. smiled happily.

"I didn't lose a drop," he said. "The gin shot out of my Lily Cup and I watched it and caught it after it hit the roof. Not a single drop."

"Thank God," I said, breathless at still having breath.

"You know, M.," U.C. said, "for someone who doesn't believe in Him, you've sure as hell been in close contact with the Lord since you came to China."

Rangoon may be the pearl of the Orient for all I know. The heat was indescribable. This must have been the dog days before the monsoon rains. You felt you could cut the heat and hold it like chunks of wet blotting paper. It finished U.C.; he was a beached whale; he couldn't breathe and I, who love heat, was far from blooming. The only way to sleep or in fact live was to lie naked on the marble floor under the paddle fan in the hotel bedroom. I was never entirely naked since I couldn't remove my motorman's gloves even to shower. The catch in China Rot is that you spread it merely by touching your skin; scratch your head and you had another crop of China Rot. I was pretty tired of those gloves and their smell; U.C. tended to stay upwind of me.

I was obliged to visit the airline office but saw none of the famous pagodas, nothing except other heat-crushed people. U.C. had to sign for his ticket so walked beside me once, blinded by sweat, not so blinded that he couldn't see Burmese priests, languid young men dressed in orange cotton sarongs or orange cloths fastened on one shoulder, brass begging bowls in hand. "Religious bums," U.C. snarled.

Time resumed its frightful habit of standing still but finally we were gasping through the last night. I wanted to praise U.C. for his generosity, above and beyond the call of duty, in coming to China, his forbearance in not murdering me, his jokes, and let him know that I grieved for his time wasted on a season in hell. My brain was boiled; I couldn't form sentences. With tears in my eyes, I touched his shoulder and said, "Thank you."

He wrenched away, shouting, "Take your filthy dirty hands off me!"

We looked at each other in shocked silence. Were these to be the parting words between us after all the shared horrors of a super horror journey? Then we rolled on the marble floor, laughing in our separate pools of sweat.

U.C. missed the best of the Orient. Singapore and Batavia were a whirl of gaiety, specially Singapore with all the charming chaps in uniform fresh from Britain to defend that bastion of Empire. The gaiety might have been on the feverish side. I think the Dutch consciously and the British unconsciously sensed that they were living in the last act before the fateful curtain. There was much to criticize but, compared to the Chinese Imperial Boss Class as just seen, the European Imperial Boss Class was Florence Nightingale. British colonialists were warped by a colour complex, the meanest stupidity of the British Empire, shaming to newcomers from Britain. The Dutch were not. The Dutch were enlightened and honourable rulers though their good deeds didn't help them later. I wasn't hired to study the problems of Empire. Those were not horror journeys and have no place in this book. I lived in luxury, clean as a whistle, cured of China Rot, dashed about on military business and rounds of pleasure with marvellous companions of the road, and concealed my foreboding for those who had to stay.

I was right about one thing: in the Orient, a world ended.

With Captain V. C. Griffin at the Naval Air Station
in San Juan, Puerto Rico, 1942

Three

MESSING ABOUT
IN BOATS

During that terrible year, 1942, I lived in the sun, safe and comfortable and hating it. News reached us at regular hours on the radio and none of it was good. But we didn't understand how bad it was; piecemeal and (I now see) wisely censored, the news gave us no whole view. The only war I understood or could imagine was war on land and that was enough to shake the heart with the Germans moving like a tidal wave into Russia and Rommel rampaging in the desert. I think my ignorance was typical; the general public, which is most of us, did not realize that the fatal danger was on the sea. We would have lost the war if we went on losing ships at the appalling rate of 1942. Cargo ships, ungratefully neglected in the annals of glory, without which Britain would have starved and our war everywhere from Russia to North Africa halted like an engine out of fuel. 1,508 Allied merchant ships, 8,336,258 gross tons, sank to the bottom of the sea in one year. I can't make a picture of that for myself let alone for anyone else. The nearest I can come is that it was like bleeding to death.

Then American news broadcasts began to tell, with great excitement, of German submarines sinking ships along the eastern seaboard of the U.S., and in the Gulf of Mexico and the Caribbean and as far south as Brazil. I was leery of the tone; it sounded boastful as if suggesting that we too, in our impregnable safety, were endangered. Which we weren't. There has been no war on American soil since 1865. The suffering in Europe and the Orient was and is beyond American conception; no one can know what modern war means until it happens at home. But I was going into a decline from hearing about the war on the radio instead of being where I wanted to be, with the people whose lives were paying for it. I could get a short leave of absence from private obligations and domestic duties and at least escape the radio by roaming around the Caribbean to report on this sideshow, this minor if any submarine warfare in nearby waters.

Thirty-four years late, I bestirred myself to look up the facts and found with amazement that 251 merchant ships were sunk in 1942 in the Caribbean alone. In August and September, the months when I was dawdling through the area, the losses were heaviest, seventy-one ships in sixty-one days. As I had no idea of this at the time, nor could have had since it was highly classified information, I intended to do my best with the mild material at hand. I love journalism, it is always a chance to see and learn something new and I was interested by everything I saw, though hardly overcome by the importance of the assignment.

In Haiti, interned Nazis, German residents, well treated and swelling with pride, expected Germany to win next year and expected to be powerful Gauleiters. Puerto Rico had become a huge naval and air base; I begged a ride in a Flying Fortress on anti-submarine patrol. The crew was fun but the trip was like bus travel, flying with CNAC had spoiled me. The small brown gentle Puerto Ricans, who lived and died too young in shameful slums, were the people I liked best. Their sons volunteered eagerly for the U.S. Army, fifty dollars a month and as much as they wanted to eat was the first chance they'd ever had for a decent life.

All survivors, sailors from the torpedoed merchant ships, were brought to Puerto Rico before being sent off on other ships. You could recognize them at once in the waterfront bars, gaunt men in new cheap civilian clothes, suffering a different kind of shell-shock. I hung about listening with pity and admiration but knew that I wasn't understanding. Lifeboats were outside my experience.

"I guess the tenth day was about the worst. I just about gave up hope that day." "One of the chaps went a little wacky about the fourteenth day, remember, Bert?" "You didn't look too good yourself, John." "You can see it around their eyes, see, they get sort of a cuckoo look in their eyes. Had one chap wanted to kill hisself." A boy alone at the Condado bar kept telling me that kapok was much better than the old lifebelts, they ought to have it in all ships. He came from Brooklyn. He'd been adrift for eighteen days in a lifeboat. He spoke of a man who got caught in the ropes of a lifeboat just after the torpedo struck. "The guy must of jumped or something but not far enough and he was hung there, see what I mean, you know, dead." What was it like in the lifeboat? "I don't remember, I guess it was all right."

I wrote of these matters as I was employed to do and Charles Colebaugh, the angelic editor of *Collier's*, was pleased but I was not. By now I knew there was a real war on, in these parts, though it was invisible beneath the bright blue water and it seemed tame and boring to report a war without action or eye-witness news. There must be a better way to go about the job.

To justify the *Collier's* expense account, I told myself I might pick up survivors from torpedoed ships or find stashes of supplies for submarines or hidden enemy radio transmitters and anyway, since the war hereabouts was taking place on the sea, obviously I should travel on the sea too. My private dream, which I had the sense to keep to myself, was that I would actually sight a submarine. St Thomas, an American island, was easy to reach by plane from Puerto Rico. After that, formal transportation ceased until the next American base at Antigua, some 275 miles away as I figured on the map. In between was a string of little islands, with delectable names, Tortola, Virgin Gorda, Anguilla, St Martin and St Bartholomew, Saba, St Kitts. Whatever else might come of it, I would see an unknown world.

At St Thomas, I tried to hire a sloop. An old black man, agent for pre-war island trading boats, explained that no one on St Thomas was fool enough to leave port in the hurricane season. Neither he nor any of the locals worried about submarines but worried hard about hurricanes and their Bible, a regional almanac, predicted a bad hurricane this month. When I asked advice of resident whites they asked whether I hadn't heard of the submarines, almost next door in the Anegada Passage. They also said that no white person could travel in the native sloops; I better wait until after the war and hire a yacht like everyone else.

Word of my scheme got around and resulted in a visit from a burly Texas Major in charge of guarding the island. He brought me a miniature pearl-handled silver-plated derringer. It looked just the weapon for a crackpot wearing a négligée trimmed in ostrich feathers who planned to shoot her lover. He gave me four bullets, blunt-nosed 32s, showed me how to load this lethal toy, told me earnestly that it would cut a man in half and not to hesitate to use it. "You don't know what can happen, all alone out there."

I said I could not accept his expensive pistol, had never used a handgun, and was never anxious about my honour. He insisted until finally I thanked him, wrapped the pretty thing in Kleenex, put the bullets in an airmail envelope and the lot at the bottom of my suitcase. Somewhere during the journey, I must have given it away. On this note of comedy, I departed in an ancient motorboat for Tortola, a four-hour trip.

My heart rose like a bird at once. It always did incurably, except in rain, as soon as I felt I had fallen off the map. The motorboat dumped me, soaked by spray and chirpy, at Roadtown, a cluster of unpainted shacks and a single dust street. There were ten white residents on the island and seven thousand blacks, no cars, few bicycles, and one taxi, which was a rowboat. The British Commissioner who also served as doctor, dispensing their small stock of medicines, and magistrate and editor of the mimeographed newspaper, deplored my scheme but passed me on to the local grocer, Mr de Castro, a white-haired dignified black man.

Mr de Castro introduced me to his son Carlton, owner of a potato boat, a thirty-foot sloop called the *Pilot*. A potato boat is an overgrown rowboat, with one sail and a hold for potatoes, which sold its cargo from island to island and returned carrying whatever could be bought en route, preferably rum and tobacco and preferably smuggled back into the home island.

Carlton de Castro was the Tortola glamour boy, aged twenty-five, coffee-coloured, with curling eyelashes, curling sideburns, and gold front teeth. He wore his captain's cap over one ear and had a droll style as if he were a Parisian nightclub Apache playing sailor. His boat, he said, was "clean as fire" but he wasn't crazy about making the trip because of the "hurry-cane." I waved *Collier's* dollar bills under his nose and corrupted him. We would leave the next morning.

In the meantime I shopped since I had to feed myself. Carlton would lay in two casks of water and some stones for ballast; the rest was up to me. I bought the usual sustaining grim assortment of tinned beans, sardines, tea, crackers and an object called Superware Sanitary Pail, made of shining grey enamel, and a large black umbrella to ward off sunburn. The Commissioner generously loaned me two army blankets and a pillow.

Rain then poured down as if here to stay. The sea looked like churned cement. I was marooned in the Social Inn, an inexplicable hostelry—why would anyone come here?—two dirty bedrooms, with beer bottles swept into corners and drifts of cigarette butts, mementoes of survivors off an English ship who had been moved on to Puerto Rico a few days earlier. Rain blew through the shutters and under the door. There was no electric light, hardship for a reader as the only place to perch was beneath the stained mosquito net on the boards of the four-poster bed and I thought I might set fire to the place with a kerosene lamp in that tent. The Social Inn reminded me sadly of the Palace Hotel in Kweilin but there were no bedbugs and one must always be grateful for small mercies. The rain went on and on. I sat amidst my canned goods, eating them from time to time, and read detective stories while the dim daylight lasted.

From time to time I ventured into the downpour under my new

umbrella to call on the only patient in the one-room hospital, a Jewish refugee from Vienna whom I believed to be dying, he was so yellow and so thin, burning with fever. Probably he had malaria and jaundice. Having escaped the Nazi gas chambers, he outlived the Blitz in London as a fire warden. By one of the wild vagaries that mark war, the British government then sent this man, whose original business was the manufacture of perfumes, to Tortola to start a tobacco industry. Of course tobacco could not be grown here and he wanted either to die, as release from the hopeless boredom of the island, or get back to England and join the British Army. He had a clearer idea than anyone else in the area of the reason for this war and a fierce need to take active part in it.

I felt callous leaving him to die there, among kind but uncomprehending strangers. At least he could talk to me, we both knew the Nazis, we had the bond of hatred for them. But when the rain stopped after three days I said goodbye, falsely assuring him of future health. Perhaps a year later, he sent a photograph of a plump smiling man. Christmas cards followed. He had settled on St Thomas, married, was employed in some business connected to perfumery and delighted with his new life. I love happy endings, and specially from that war; there were all too few.

The *Pilot* set sail at seven in the morning, me waving graciously to the public, Mr de Castro Senior and an elderly American whose son was stationed in Australia. The American had shaken my hand in the way one salutes bereaved relatives after a funeral and said, "My dear, I hope you know what you're doing." Having before me two small snapshots, brownish, out of focus, showing the *Pilot* and the crew and me, I understand his farewell-forever manner.

The *Pilot,* pictured upon the sea, looks like the celluloid sailboats children play with in bathtubs. The other photo records me, centre front, dressed in my comfy kit of short shorts, shirt, sandals, surrounded by barefooted black men: Carlton (Cahltin) with a bandana tied about his neck for extra swank, George (Gawge) a lovely giant wearing a felt hat without brim and ragged trousers to mid calf, Walter (Walteh) in dirty singlet and shorts, Voosten bare to the waist and Irvine in a shirt which he wore open and flapping like a coat over underpants. They look villainous. I thought them sweet apart from Carlton who was too vain, and had no qualms about that dubious boat.

The *Pilot* had once been white. The deck sloped downwards without guardrail. The deckhouse was five feet high and five feet square, in which I could neither stand nor lie nor even sit since it was like a sauna. Amidships on the port side a small dinghy was lashed to the deck. You could see worm holes in it and they had one oar; at best it would have held three people before it filled and sank. There were no lifebelts, no sextant, no log, no barometer and no charts. A compass wobbled on the stern by the tiller. The single sail resembled a patchwork quilt.

The dinghy was not as long as I am. Carlton put the hatch cover in it, making a peculiar seating or lying arrangement, a convex curve for two thirds of the length then a drop to a concave curve. I spread the blankets on this surface, placed the pillow at one end, slid my legs under the seat and established myself with umbrella for sunshade. All I had to do was duck when the boom swung over.

The sea looked flat calm, a deception. Long swells moved like muscles under the skin of the water. The *Pilot* dipped and rose, in short jerky movements. Reclining as much as possible in the dinghy, I didn't feel too good but refused to think about it. If this was the *Pilot*'s best behaviour in the best weather, I preferred not to look ahead. Hours later, still sailing along the shores of Tortola, we were accosted by another smaller sailboat.

Carlton called to the passers-by, an old man and his son: "Whatsaysay, Mon, whatsaysay?" shouted Carlton.

The old man shouted, "Oh good, Mon, where you goin?"

"Right roun de globe, boy."

"What you cargo?" asked the son.

"De lady," said Carlton and all men on both boats shrieked with laughter.

Five hours later the crew began to bellow at each other which was the way orders were given and obeyed. It was mid-afternoon and we tied up

to the pier on the beautiful beach at Virgin Gorda because Irvine had to
get money from his wife. "She de cashier," he said. With *Collier's* dollars,
divided according to rank, and their own, each man would buy what he
could and sell where he could; free enterprise trading.

A black man with white hair and moustache, a white topee and rose-
coloured dark glasses received me in the name of His Britannic Majesty.
He was Mr Samuel Flax, the government agent for this island. He gave
me a can opener as I had left mine in the Social Inn and guided me to the
loveliest cove I had seen anywhere in the world. "Oh Moddom the war
is very hard," said Mr Flax. "We don't get no flour and such practically.
And those poor men what gets torpedoed. Yes Moddom we can only
hope the Almighty will watch over us."

The war seemed too far away to be true, no work for the Almighty on
Virgin Gorda, and this cove was a place where nothing had changed since
time began, a half circle of white sand, flanked by huge squarish smooth
rocks, the rocks overlapping to form cool caves and the water turquoise
blue above the furrows of the sandy sea bed. George slashed open some
coconuts for me to drink. Mr Flax warned me against touching the leaves
of the Manchineel tree if my skin was wet because I'd get blisters big as
a two-shilling piece, and they left me to one of the three greatest joys in
life, swimming naked in clean tropical sea.

At ten that night, we sailed. The moon was up, new and clear, and
the sky was soft black, dusted with stars, the sort of sky guaranteed to en-
gender romantic love affairs on cruise ships. We were heading out into
the Anegada Passage, mystical name, and famous as a hunting ground
for submarines. This was the longest lap of the journey, ninety miles between Virgin Gorda and Anguilla. Though feeling a certain distaste for
the hatch cover mattress, I was thrilled by the beauty, the silence, the
great sense of space, and excitement: we were in the real war zone, who
knew what might not happen. Then the rain started and I cowered beneath my umbrella and it was surprisingly cold. The night took on the
most unpleasant quality of nights which is to be long. At sunrise, Virgin

Gorda looked within swimming distance. At noon it was still as close. Wind barely flapped the sail.

The special motion of the *Pilot*, when becalmed, was a bumping jig in one place. Being becalmed sounds like floating on a lilo in a swimming pool. Not so, anyway not so aboard the *Pilot*. Jig isn't exactly right either, the boat bumped and rolled simultaneously.

The day before, with the wind to blow off the smell, I thought the crew's mealtime rough stuff. Gawge, the cook, set up a charcoal brazier alongside the dinghy, doubtless because the dinghy would prevent the brazier and pots and food from sliding off the deck. He then cooked a pan bread called Dumb Johnny Cake, tea, and rice with fish and onions. In the windless heat, sun burning on my umbrella and the brazier burning beside me, the smell of fish and onions added to the rolling jig made me feel excessively queer.

I had not foreseen seasickness and had been actively seasick only twice that I could remember but remembered it well as one of the worst ails that flesh is heir to. I never reached the active stage; I stayed permanently queasy. Numb nausea reduced my hopes to a single aim in life: get off the *Pilot*. This was years before I understood the spiritual and medicinal value of liquor; when alone I carried none.

"George, how long is the longest you've ever been becalmed?"

"'Bout ten days, as I recall."

Already I knew why the survivors in Puerto Rico spoke of men going wacky, wanting to jump out of the lifeboats. How had they endured ten days, eighteen days, with no protection from this cruel sun, adrift in smaller boats, exhausted by ceaseless motion, rations cut or finished, a mouthful of water a day for tormenting thirst?

"George, if we're becalmed five days I'm going overboard. I won't wait ten days."

He laughed. "Doan talk silly, Missus, we ain goin sit heah much more."

"George, are you almost finished cooking?"

"Yes'm. Takin dere dinner to de boys."

But the smell lingered on.

Far to the north, wind clouds streaked across the sky. Three sharp black birds, looking like Dorniers, flew high above us, their wings spread wide and unmoving. I called to Irvine at the tiller, "What birds are those?"

"Doan know de name. We jus calls dem hurry-cane birds."

Usually the men talked among themselves in Caribbean English, an indecipherable tongue. For me they used their version of the King's English. When they talked it sounded as if they were barking at each other and every sentence rose like a question at the end. Now, with the sail not even flapping, they slept in the hold; Irvine nodded over the tiller. I had books and could not read, the ceaseless pitch made letters jump on the page and a cracking headache joined the queasiness. I watched the sea, hoping to see a far-off convoy, a patrol plane, anything to break the monotony, and was cheered by four flying fish.

Towards mid afternoon, I began to be bitten by ants, swarms of tiny translucent red ants which appeared from nowhere. At dawn I had found the squashed body of a very big spider on my pillow and immediately searched the dinghy in vain for its mate; it looked like a junior tarantula, hairy-legged but grey not black. While I could still move, it seemed a good moment to clean up the shipboard insect life, heavy clicking cockroaches in the deckhouse and these infuriating ants. I crawled from the dinghy and staggered to the deckhouse to get Flit; the deckhouse was my storeroom and bathroom, home of the Superware Sanitary Pail and a bucket of sea water for a sloshing shower.

While I was spraying Flit, a moment's breeze, no more than a whisper of wind, picked up my umbrella which I had stupidly left open in the dinghy, and carried it off. I watched it sink, billowing like an old-fashioned lady's bathing suit, and blinked back tears. I might have lost my last friend on earth. On top of queasiness, now I would burn a painful tomato red, blister and peel, the new skin all set to burn again. "Noice umbrella too," George said, with sympathy. Deep in a slough of self-pity, I told myself that the drowned umbrella was too much. Why, why, since I worship the sun hadn't I been born with the right skin? The protest of childhood is, "It's not fair." It's not fair, I thought, aren't ants and nausea and this immovable boat enough? Close to blubbering over my umbrella.

I had no idea a day could last so long. Though different from the endless days in China, it was not inferior to them.

A breeze sprang up in the night. Again the heavens opened to pour rain, but we were moving. The crew took turns resting on stones in the hold. I lay in the dinghy, wet and cold, urging the wind to keep it up, that's a good wind, blow, blow, don't stop for God's sake. Incantations failed. We were out of sight of land in the morning, becalmed again. Carlton was gloomy. I was gloomier but thought it bad for morale if the passenger showed signs of dismay.

"Doan like it," Carlton said.

"Why?"

"Jus doan like it."

"Do you think there's a hurricane starting somewhere?"

"I can't reely tell."

"Then what?"

"Doan know when we'll get dere. Aint hardly moved all night. See de breeze gone down again now?"

I tried to make a half tent with one blanket laid across the dinghy but smothered, drenched in sweat. I thought I'd walk around the deck for a nice change, and nearly went overboard on my unsteady legs. The crew retired in silent boredom to the hold, except for the man at the tiller which wasn't steering us anywhere. I sat on the floor in the deckhouse but hadn't been able to kill all the cockroaches and they revolt me. Back to the dinghy where I brooded on my secret dream for this journey.

Sailing by night in these submarine-infested waters, close to a little island, I would see a periscope rise from the Caribbean, followed by the shark sides of the underwater killer. Submarines had to surface to charge their batteries. (I didn't know then or now what I was talking about.)

They needed fresh water, they would have to send a boat ashore to fill their casks or whatever submarines used. Blind from headache and queasy sick, frying red, I rolled like a sausage on the hatch cover as the *Pilot* rolled, and taunted myself. What had I intended to say when this memorable event took place? *"Guten Abend, Herr Kapitän, wie geht's?"* I hoped a submarine would heave out of the sea and sink us, right now. Only two days and two nights of this and I was a basket case.

Why weren't the gaunt sailor survivors gibbering insane when finally they reached land or were finally picked up at sea? I would have written better of their ordeal after this minor trial on the *Pilot* than I had after meeting them in Puerto Rican bars where I tried but failed to imagine what they had gone through. I guessed that the moment when the torpedo struck would be like a direct hit by heavy artillery on a building. But that was as far as I could follow their stories, only to the actual moment of impact; I knew something about explosions.

My imagination could not feel the aftermath, lifeboats, when survivors compared the number of days they drifted before rescue. Now I could sense those agonizing days and thought it infinitely more terrible to be attacked by a hidden enemy on the sea than anything that happened on land. On land, if still alive, you could crawl or be dug out or carried to help, not wait helplessly for days, weeks on the water, never knowing what the end would be. How many died in the lifeboats from exhaustion, their bodies parched, how many died of untended wounds? The survivors had not spoken of this.

It is true that we need a root of personal experience from which to grow our understanding. Each new experience plants another root; the smallest root will serve.

Irvine, again at the useless tiller, said, "Got to get dere sometime, Missus." He was a kind man.

"I don't believe it."

"Got to. Boun to."

Again at night rain whipped the sea. If drifting in a lifeboat, this rain would seem truly heaven sent, and be collected in anything that held water. After the burning day, it seemed an extra unfairness to shiver under a soaked blanket in wet clothes. But I was past caring, slumped in the lethargy of compounded discomfort and boredom that is the trademark of the genuine horror journey. I could hear the men grumbling and snoring in the hold. The motion of the *Pilot* felt unchanged, roll and bump, roll and bump.

I must have dozed when wind caught the sail and was wakened by Walteh, at the tiller, calling, "Cahltin, come an see! Anguilla dere ahead!" The night was starless black, yet they saw the land, a blacker line against the sea. We weren't going to arrive on Anguilla at speed, but the sight of land restored hope. When we anchored at eight in the morning Carlton said in a solemn voice, like Columbus discovering the New World, "At last we reached." It took three nights and two days to sail ninety miles across the Anegada Passage, that perilous war zone, and for thrills we had three hurry-cane birds and four flying fish.

Carlton's mother-in-law lived on Anguilla. We climbed up a hill which moved beneath my feet and along a rocky path, also heaving gently; I might still have been on the *Pilot*. In the door of a tumbledown shanty an old black woman, wearing wrinkled cotton stockings and a faded cretonne sack fastened by a safety pin, greeted me, welcoming the homeless and sick into her castle. "I am Mother Stoughten," she said. "We are all strangers in a strange land." She sounded as if reading aloud from the Bible, and was lovely. A tin washtub and a bucket of water provided a bath in the spare room. Mother Stoughten sent a child to borrow boards from a neighbour so that I could rest on the spare bed, an empty iron frame. From another neighbour she borrowed eggs and two cups and presently fed us a delicious breakfast of eggs and dry heavy bread and black tea.

"Dear boy," Mother Stoughten said to Carlton, "Do you not know the anxiety which you are causing, knocking about in this month?"

Carlton muttered something.

"It is most reckless."

"Won't have no trouble," Carlton said into his cup.

"Ah well," she sighed. Then, as Carlton came from the great world, Tortola being a centre of civilization compared to Anguilla, she said, "What news is there of the war?" She spoke always with that cultured accent which now sounded more like reciting fine poetry.

"Bout de same," said Carlton.

"Have they reached the Marne as yet?"

"No'm."

"Good-oh," said Mother Stoughten happily.

A magazine photo of Princess Elizabeth and Princess Margaret was tacked to the wall, two blonde little girls with their arms twined about each other, and a correct coloured photograph of the King and Queen in crowns and ermine. "We must hope the war will soon be over," Mother Stoughten said. "For the sake of all the poor people. I trust the Royal Family is keeping well. After you have rested, my dear, our Magistrate will wish to receive you."

I was puzzled as to why Anguilla required a Magistrate. The population seemed to be concentrated in a dozen shacks, similar to Mother Stoughten's, strewn around paths in the immediate greenery. Since there was a Magistrate, protocol demanded a visit. The Magistrate lived in a large bare house on a bare hill and was a black doctor who had trained in Scotland. He was poor in furniture but rich in lithographs of shaggy mountain goats or maybe sheep and bluebells, labelled Glen Nevis, and views of Edinburgh Castle and group photographs of himself as a young man, wearing a Scotch tam o'shanter among white friends in kilts. His sitting-room cried aloud homesickness for that distant cold country.

He invited me to early lunch, warning me it would not be good. Apparently the people here did not grow vegetables, perhaps vegetables had never been part of their diet. For fruit, they had mangoes and bananas which grew themselves. Their constant concern was a shortage of flour. If flour came at all, it came on casual trading sloops like the *Pilot*. When they had meat, it was apt to be local goat and very tough.

We ate goat and rice and, as a special treat, tinned peaches for dessert, while the doctor spoke of Scotland. After lunch, elegantly courteous like Mother Stoughten, he escorted me back to the pier where Carlton waited. Beached alongside the pier lay two lifeboats, a steel craft with motor and an awning arrangement from the American freighter *Thomas McKean*, and a large open rowboat, which is what all old lifeboats were, from an English ship. The Americans had landed here after eight days, bad enough; the English had been drifting on the sea for twenty-three days and the Magistrate-doctor said they were terribly sick men. We looked at the boats in silence. Anguilla was as far out of the world as you could get but the war had washed up on their shore and the effect was dreamlike, fantastic, incredible, as if the sky had rained rocks.

The doctor, when he could tear himself away from loving memories of Scotland, explained a recent political aberration. The French islands, under the Vichy régime, were forbidden to receive strangers. This was an embarrassment to everyone and also caused unpleasant suspicion. Since the French islands were closed, rumours spread; the French islanders were accused of helping the Germans. I had heard such talk on St Thomas. The doctor said it was impossible, he knew the people of St Martin well, they were good people, like the people on Anguilla, like all the people in these small islands. They would never assist the Germans in their cruelty. "Killing innocent sailors," the doctor said as if this was the worst of crimes instead of standard procedure in war.

He gave me a letter to his colleague, the white Mayor of Marigot on the French side of St Martin. Sailing around St Martin, a unique island that is half French, half Dutch, to the Dutch Allied side would take us a long day, if the wind behaved, whereas we could reach the French side opposite Anguilla before nightfall. The Mayor of Marigot was a civilized man and would certainly allow me, though an enemy alien by Vichy law, to land and drive in the taxi to the Dutch side. "It is very stupid and very sad," the doctor said. "We have always lived in friendship in these islands. We have always been welcome amongst each other. We are all human beings and neighbours."

St Martin looked near enough to row to easily. The speedy *Pilot* tacked across in five hours; we anchored just before sunset. An hour earlier, I

observed from my front-row seat in the dinghy a formal ceremony. Walteh, the most soiled of the crew, pulled from his pants pocket a small
creased Union Jack. Carlton had changed into a bizarre costume, possibly
the better to impress the French. It was blue satin lastex bathing trunks,
printed with yellow palm trees and tropical birds. As Captain, standing at
attention, he supervised the hoisting of the flag. When Irvine had completed the job and the flag fluttered from the top of the mast, they looked
up at it with pride.

"Are you all English then?" I asked.

"Yes'm," Irvine said. "De udders change roun. At St Thomas, dey
Americun now. Everybody change but we always de same ole English."

We bumped rather than sailed past the breakwater into the harbour.
A white house with a red roof, a white house with black shutters, a yellow house stood in a row behind the grey stone seawall. Between the seawall and the houses, men were playing boule. Beyond this very French
Mediterranean approach, the single dust street of Marigot was lined by
three-storeyed wood houses, joined together like French town houses,
each with long windows and long shutters on the second-floor balconies,
each decorated with whimsical fretwork. French-Caribbean—Victorian-
New Orleans architecture, I thought, and it couldn't have been prettier,
the houses painted in pastel shades, pink and blue and green and yellow
picked out in white, though the paint was old and scabby. They could live
without paint. Marigot was decaying gracefully.

Outside the town and a few straggling houses dotted along dusty
paths, St Martin was jungle, not the real thing which is hideous, but
great nameless (to me) plumy trees and flamboyantes, magnolias, ceiba,
breadfruit, royal palms, and fringed banana trees, with hibiscus and
bougainvillaea, gone wild and opulent, to splash colour in the rich green.

I felt rotten and looked rotten too in my dirty clothes, my hair
snarled, transparent strips of skin flapping from every part not pimpled
by sun blisters. A porter led me along the main street where superior
Creole ladies fanned themselves on the balconies and chatted from house

to house. Chatting stopped as they stared; children stopped playing in the street. Perhaps they thought I was a new type of female survivor. The porter took me to the police station; despite Vichy, no one was going to fuss about Carlton and his crew, who were fellow islanders; there was a limit to obeying nonsense regulations. If they ordered me back to the *Pilot*, I was prepared to rant or whine, or claim that my long-removed appendix had burst; I was desperate for a bed to lie on until I got my land legs again.

The Chief Gendarme was digging in his garden at the police station. He read the letter from the Anguilla Magistrate. He consulted the Second and Third Gendarmes who were playing dominoes inside the police station. I explained that I only asked to hire the taxi so that I could cross to Phillipsburg on the Dutch side. The taxi could not be granted without permission of the Mayor. The Mayor's telephone was out of order; he lived in some state on his property beyond the town and it was hot. Neither the Second or Third Gendarme nor the porter felt like walking there. Gallic good sense and chivalry triumphed. The Chief Gendarme said, "You had better spend the night here. You can visit the Mayor in the morning. We welcome you with open arms and open hearts. There is no reason why we should not." No reason except the tiresome directives from the Governor of Martinique, a long way off.

The porter, lugging my suitcase, said that the hotel was run by a Basque couple. "Baskey" was what he actually said and I cottoned on when he added that "dey come here after some war dey got in dere own country bout five years pass, near as I recall. Poor people, seems like dey cannot go home. Dey doan talk English good like us."

Mrs Higuera was middle-aged, puffy fat, pale, clearly done in by the change from her brisk native climate. She sat at a table under a hanging kerosene lamp, wearing curlpapers and a kimono and listened to Mr Higuera declaim opinions to the two guests. Mr Higuera sported the idiosyncratic Spanish stubble, grey bristles that remain two days old, never clean-shaven, never longer, a Spanish mystery. His hair was a thick stiff grey upstanding brush. His shirt, meant for a hard collar, fastened with a collar stud; his baggy trousers, greenish black, were held up by braces. He was a solid chunk of man and his opinions were solidly his own.

I had seen thousands like him during the war in Spain; their defeat was mine too. No steadier in my head than on my legs, I said, *"Salud, amigos! Viva la Republica!"* Stuff the Vichy régime and all its despicable works, I would say *"Viva la Republica"* whenever I liked as long as I lived.

Mr and Mrs Higuera rose as one and embraced me, shouting Spanish questions. Yes, I had been in Madrid on the side of the Republic. Yes, in Mexico and Cuba there were many Basques now, among them great *pelotaris*. We were bosom friends within three minutes. The guests watched in astonishment until the Higueras recollected their manners and introduced Monsieur Louis, a young Guadeloupe businessman with Vaselined hair, and Monsieur Jean, a blond French boy in his twenties who, Mr Higuera explained in Spanish, was a good one, he marched himself from France to Martinique when the shameless sons of whores, the German Fascists, took Paris. They were here for a holiday. Outside the five French Caribbean islands, they also had become enemy aliens by fiat, with little choice in travel or transport.

The Higueras's hotel was made to order for one who had spent much daydream time among demoralized castaways in the South Seas. The ground floor was a single room with the adjacent kitchen behind a bead curtain. A large white kerosene icebox stood in one corner but it had been broken for a year. The other furnishings were a loud sewing machine, operated by a hand wheel, four creaking cane rockers and three small dining tables covered by grease and wine-stained checked cloths. The hotel servant, a black man wearing dungarees and drooping straw hat, was setting these tables as if working out a complex jigsaw puzzle. The trimmings were flies, spider webs, insects suiciding on the kerosene lamp, dirty glasses, overflowing ashtrays and kitchen reek. Basques, at home, are noted for their cleanliness. Exile and heat had not altered the open-heartedness of the Spanish poor. We ate swill, lived like pigs, dripped sweat and were delighted with the Higueras's hotel.

I took to my bed. Though pretty bad, it was an improvement on the dinghy. The mattress appeared to have been stuffed with coconut rinds, the sheets and pillowcase indicated both the Higueras's collapse and the shortage of soap; the smell of mildew wafted like incense over all. I clung to the bed which felt like a rocking-horse, and wondered if the good earth would ever stay still again. I had had enough of the *Pilot* but another feature of horror journeys is that once you are on them you cannot change your mind and get off them.

In the morning, the Mayor called for me. He had a fine polished black sedan, a mere six years old; on this island it was like owning the State Coach of England. He was big fair-haired red-faced stout, in his forties, born on St Martin and the local rich man. He drove me to Phillipsburg; the French boy came along to see the unknown world that was Allied. The only boarding house in Phillipsburg belonged to an educated black woman who regretted that she could not take me in. "The place is not fit for a lady just now. We had those thirty-two Dutch survivors here and they drank a lot of punch and smoked a lot of cigarettes, trying to take their minds off things, poor men. I haven't had time to clean up after them."

New survivors everywhere, more ships sunk, German submarines still prowling in their beautiful sea where the rule of life for island people is to give help on the waters, not to kill.

"Poor men," the Mayor said, grieving like his legal enemy, the black Dutch citizen. "I have some extra soap, Mrs Thomas, if you need it for the laundry."

We were silent, driving back, perhaps they too were thinking about the strange war that could not be seen and the sailors who suffered it. Then the Mayor said, speaking French as politeness to the French boy, "I have done my official duty. You cannot stay in Phillipsburg so you must stay in Marigot. No one could expect me to force a lady to leave in that miserable sloop. I have not known many Americans, Madame, but forgive me, is it usual for you to have ideas like travelling in such a boat in wartime? It would be a catastrophe even in peacetime."

"How else could I have visited St Martin?"

"Well yes, that is true. I doubt if there are ten people here who weren't born on the island, but half of us believe we are French and the other half believe they are Dutch. We have no frontier between us and our real language is English. We have lived together in peace for three centuries. I don't think there is any place like it in the world."

"You are lucky," the French boy said. "The island is poor and of no military importance. You can live in peace forever."

"We are lucky," said the Mayor.

Carlton was waiting at the hotel. "No wind," he said. "Looks like de wind gone dead forevah."

"Good-oh," said I, happily, copying Mother Stoughten. "Anyway I don't want to leave. I'd be glad to stay here a month."

"Not me, Missus, I gotta take you fars Antigua, den I goin home. Sooner I get home, de better. I smell hurry-cane somewheres."

With a picnic, water and heavy sandwiches, I set off to explore. St Martin was a magic island. Secret white sand coves indented the shore. I chose one far from town, walled in by thick bush that the rain had polished and framed by swaying royal palms. Under a china-blue sky, I sat naked in the shallows to watch schools of fish, recognizing only silver baby barracudas. And waded out to swim through glass-clear Nile-green water, where you could see below to the sand and more passing fish, into silky deep sapphire sea. And swam back to munch sandwiches in the shade and swam again. The sun was not a torment but the blessing I had always felt it to be, before sailing in the *Pilot*. I forgot the war, it was somebody else's nightmare. I was in that state of grace which can rightly be called happiness, when body and mind rejoice totally together. This occurs, as a divine surprise, in travel; this is why I will never finish travelling.

Time had stopped, I wanted to stay in motionless time, finding new coves, walking in the jungle, and making up stories about the island people. The Higueras had not explained how or why they escaped from Bilbao to Marigot and discretion is a by-product of war too, one does not probe into personal affairs. Nor did I know what revulsion or fear moved the French boy to flee from France. Invented stories were already twining around them. I hadn't felt so carefree since my girlhood travels with a knapsack, discovering Europe.

The wind stayed fair, which is to say dead, for four days. Each day I swam from a lovely cove and wandered in the jungle, finding orchids and flowering lianas, listening to birds and the stories in my head. Happiness had become chronic. Then reality returned in the form of Carlton announcing a useful wind and his impatience to be off. I said *au revoir* sadly and shook hands with most of Marigot and climbed back into the dinghy with a new umbrella.

Our next stop was St Bartholomew, always called St Barts, another French island. We anchored in the harbour of the capital, named Gustavia because St Barts had once been Swedish. The capital was a handful of houses, the school, a church, a tiny shipyard at work on a potato boat, nice smell of new wood, a bar, and a pathetic general store.

Though a very small and destitute island, St Barts was snobbishly proud; more whites than blacks lived here. The white population was the remnant of some ancient Norman seafarers. Having intermarried for centuries, they were poor meagre people with bad teeth and sick-looking ugly faces and often addled brains, but they were certifiably white. Behind the small port, a few sturdy stone houses remained as a legacy of sturdy Swedes, though jungle had crept around them and even into them. I was offered a room in a house left empty for two months by its owner and had to push my way through vines and creepers up rotting wood stairs, and duck and struggle through tight bush to reach the latrine and bathhouse in the back.

St Barts had no Mayor, no Gendarmes, and no red tape. It was even farther from the war than St Martin; the residents were simply not interested. The one sign of changed times was the singing that began and ended the children's day in the school next door to my new home. The songs had been sent and learned by order of the Vichy government. The tunes were merry and the words surely meant nothing to the little black kids. "Save France, Maréchal, we follow you." Before they had sung *"Allons enfants de la Patrie"* and would sing that again after we won the war. I was annoyed by this enforced Maréchal worship, I despised the booby old father-figure who lent his name to collaboration with the Nazis.

When the children sang their traditional lessons in French I listened with pleasure. The teacher chanted the question, in unison squeaky voices chanted the answer. "What are the four elements?" sang the teacher. "The four elements are earth, air, fire and water," sang the children. They sang history, spelling, arithmetic, and literature. It had much charm and surely trained memory to perfection but lasted rather long, six and a half hours daily with a two-hour lunch break. The lessons could be heard everywhere throughout the metropolis of Gustavia.

As I walked the plank from the *Pilot* to the pier, a young Frenchman, also blond, also named Jean, had been there, observing. He took in the onion skins and fish heads left over from lunch on the deck, the shabby hull and sail, the appearance of the crew, not freshly laundered to start and now positively rancid with dirt, and me, peeling less vigorously but a sorry sight. His face showed that he thought us a mess; on the other hand, I roused pity. I had to be in some grave obscure trouble if I was obliged to travel like this. He suggested leading me to a fine cove after I got rid of my suitcase. He was going to fish for lobster with spear and goggles, an enjoyable way to fish though he wasn't intent on fun but on food. Food here was scarce and wretched; he fished from need.

Panting in the heat, I followed him on a narrow track through dark stunted jungle. This was not the radiant greenery of St Martin, this was claustrophobic and instantly remindful of snakes. Each island had its own personality and atmosphere. St Barts was spooky, I don't know why. I felt that the moment we landed, I didn't like the place, I had no desire to linger, no waves of happiness would sweep over me here. The cove was attractive but nothing compared to the lovely enclosed sand crescents of

St Martin. Jean fished with skill and concentration and located lobsters while I swam and hoped for a good wind quick.

We had set out late, walked far, lobster-catching took time, it was dark when we started home. Jean seemed nervous about the time as if he had an appointment. We had asked each other no personal questions, true to war-time form. He spoke of the white inhabitants, saying, *"Ils sont pratiquement gaga, ils ne savent même pas comment se nourrir, ils n'ont pas assez d'intelligence ni d'énergie de cultiver des légumes. Ils passent leur temps en étant fiers d'être blancs comme si c'était un acte de génie."* If he so disliked his neighbours, why stay? But I did not ask. In the dark a little wild cat, barely more than a kitten, leapt out of the choking woods and bounced along the path stiff-legged like a gazelle. It was perfectly camouflaged for its environment, mottled shades of brown. I caught it and held it.

Jean turned off on an invisible track in the jungle, I proceeded with cat to Gustavia where I fed it condensed milk in my musty room so that it became a purring snuggling attached cat. Now I would have company on the *Pilot*. Loving is a habit like another and requires something nearby for daily practice. I loved the cat, the cat appeared to love me. I could face the oncoming days in the dinghy with better heart, having the cat to talk to and play with.

In the morning I broached the subject of weather. When could we leave? I wanted to go to Saba, a Dutch island, which rose before us like a green volcano in the heat haze. Carlton had grown more defeatist every day. Apart from the unreliable wind, I didn't know what was the matter with him. He wouldn't look at me but stood glumly observing his feet.

"They say it takes only four hours to sail to Saba, Carlton."

"More like eight or ten."

"It's twenty-two miles."

"Some say twenty-two, some say forty-five."

"I want very much to go there."

He said nothing.

"What bites you, Carlton?"

"Doan like dis wedder. Saba got no anchorage."

"Let's leave early in the morning. I could see the town and we can come back here for the night if you feel it's unsafe over there."

Carlton was evidently sick of this journey. Paid whenever we reached port, they had done a little business and a little business was enough. On the edge of giving him hell, a foolish operation, I moved along to the end of the pier and sat there smoking to soothe my temper. Jean appeared and sat beside me. Without preamble, he launched into revelations. He came to St Barts originally to get his boat repaired. I gathered he had been frittering away a small inheritance as a boat bum when the war started. He wanted to leave St Barts and join the Free French; he was ashamed to live in safety on this peaceful island when he should be fighting for his country. But he could not leave; he was chained by the voodoo spell of a witch, an added inconvenience being that the witch was his mistress.

Every time he tried to go, he was struck down. On his first attempt to escape, he had lost his boat, a complete shipwreck, and was lucky to get back in the dinghy. Since then, when a rare passerby offered transport, he was always stopped by paralysing illness. He unfolded this weird tale in bright sunshine, while we smoked and swung our legs from the jetty. Assuming he was not a nut, he had been on this spooky island too long. I told him bossily that voodoo spells were rot and he could come with us and make his way to England from Antigua. Bossiness seemed to invigorate him. He would join the good ship *Pilot* but asked that we sail at night and swore me to secrecy lest the witch hear of his plans.

He then took me home, a woven reed hut in the jungle, and I too was impressed by the witch. She was beautiful; tall, lavishly curved, smooth brown skin, thick wavy brown hair to her shoulders and long green eyes: living proof that miscegenation does a power of good. Standing in the doorway, with her hands on her hips, she stared at the peeling blonde visitor with undisguised contempt and dislike. I couldn't think how to respond. Cringe or snub? Jean, apparently sure of himself by daylight, ordered her to bring food. Rice and lobster and fried bananas.

Delicious. Perhaps her cooking compensated for her witchcraft. She moved slowly, graceful as a panther, showing resentment in every gesture. She refused to speak or eat with us.

Not feeling exactly wanted, I returned after lunch to the open harbour front, away from the uneasy woods, and met the schoolteacher, a middle-aged Frenchman married to an island black. He wasn't bubbling over either, and talked about the mistake of marrying a black woman; you sank into their slovenly customs, and fathered litters of noisy stupid half-breed kids. It was senseless to try to teach the schoolchildren. Why would they need the culture of la belle France on St Barts? But he didn't suggest joining my ship to escape. I clambered up to my room and fed my purring cat, the one contented form of life I had met so far.

Carlton was furious over the night departure. "Ain't no reason for it. I doan know dese waters. Stoopid. I gotta tink for de *Pilot.*" I insisted, having promised Jean, and having seen the witch. I'd be jolly glad myself to get away from those baleful green eyes. Around midnight, Jean showed up on the jetty, his teeth chattering in his head, his eyes bloodshot. He was running a high fever; it was all he could do to walk to the harbour to tell me not to wait. Rescue was impossible, he would never be able to leave; he saw his fate with despair. Clearly he believed in black magic but I figured his demon lover could doctor his food with inedible mushrooms, snake venom, cat piss, whatever she found handy and bad for the digestion, every time he acted restless. I urged him to come anyway, sick as he was; perhaps the witch's spell wore out by nautical miles. He wouldn't risk my safety, the weather was uncertain enough without evil incantations.

I thought about him as a tragic figure; I imagined his life chained to the green-eyed sullen witch until she tired of him whereupon she would brew a poisonous spell and do him in. Ten years later, I met Jean again on St Martin. He had a pretty white wife and baby, a real house above a dazzling beach, and a pleasure boat. I dared not ask questions and he offered no information about the witch or his release from her clutches. He looked healthy, happy, and prosperous.

Carlton, informed that we now had no extra passenger, spat with disgust and said he was going to sleep in the hold, he wasn't crazy people, we could leave at dawn. I had a needless night, or half of one, in the dinghy but the little cat was comfortable sharing my pillow. Perhaps the witch, to fix me, arranged the storm. More likely it was the outskirts of a hurricane but storm it was, a wind too big for our patched sail and high foam-capped waves breaking over us. I hadn't known that cats could get seasick; my cat shivered and mewed pitifully and threw up thin yellow streams, then heaved its sides with nothing left to vomit. I felt a monster to have kidnapped the poor little thing from its home and exposed it to such misery and was too busy nursing the cat to notice my own misery, soaked and bruised, as we plunged up and down the waves to Saba.

Saba is in fact the top of a volcano, and there is no harbour on its steep green sides. Closer to land, the wind lessened; perhaps the storm had passed to the north. Walteh balanced on deck and blew a conch shell, making a noise like a weak foghorn. The towering green cliff of Saba remained silent and no one appeared on the immense ladder of steps cut in stone up the cliff-side. I hadn't seen such a stairway since Chungking and doubted whether I'd be able to manage it, with legs like spaghetti.

"Dis here eight faddoms deep," Carlton said accusingly. "In open sea, Missus."

"But the wind is dropping, Carlton. Surely you can anchor until morning. I'll come back right after dawn. I want to give the cat a rest."

Carlton sniffed by way of answer. A Dutch police officer, very hot in gaiters and military collar, had marched down the steps and was waving me ashore from a strip of shingle beach. I paid Carlton the port fare; he had now earned five out of the total seven due on delivery. Irvine and Voosten removed the hatch cover, unlashed the dinghy, lowered it, and Gawge rowed me and the kitten to the pebbles, using one oar astern like gondoliers in Venice. "Goodbye, Missus, I does hope you very happy wid you little cat," said George, the gentle giant.

"Not goodbye, George, just good night." I waited to make sure the dinghy didn't sink before he could get back to the *Pilot*.

The Dutch police officer kindly carried my suitcase though it was beneath his dignity and not his job. I wobbled up the steps behind him, with the crying cat in my arms. Mountain climbing. The village at the top was obviously called Bottom, since it was built on the crater floor of the volcano. Bottom had a dear dinky Dutch charm and felt like a fine September day in a cool country. The streets were neatly laid out in squares and neatly swept. The little houses were made of white clapboard with field stone foundations. White ruffled curtains showed behind sparkling windows. There may have been flower-filled window boxes, I forget.

The black inhabitants appeared better fed than elsewhere, worthy self-respecting citizens in their clean starched clothes. All along, I had been fascinated by the way these Caribbean blacks took on the tone of the ruling colonial power; you would know the nationality of each island without being told as if national genes and chromosomes had been transmitted down from distant European governments. Judging by the looks of the people on Saba and their town, and the brief glimpse of Phillipsburg, the Dutch were the best colonial power in this part of the world as they had been in the Orient, in the Netherlands East Indies.

The Dutch police officer deposited me at the Government Rest House. Being a cleanliness addict, as I have made abundantly clear, I was beside myself with joy. Here you could eat off the floor, if so loopily inclined, and furthermore eat fresh eggs and butter and milk and newly baked bread. There was a real shower bath that ran plentiful water, an authentic twentieth-century toilet, a functioning refrigerator, a sweet-smelling bedroom with a big four-poster and snow-white bed linen and a bedside electric lamp, an immaculate wardrobe complete with clothes hangers. I told the cat that we had fallen on our feet at last. There was also Alberta, the Rest House maid, wearing a starched white dress and Panama hat, aged sixty-four, spry and solicitous and speaking Caribbean-style English with a Dutch accent.

"You from Ammurica, Moddom?"

"Yes, Alberta."

"Oh Moddom what we do widout Ammurica? Ammurica help me every day of my life. So many noice coloured people from Saba goes dere to work and dey send us barrils of cloze and food. God bless Ammurica, Moddom."

I thanked her on behalf of the United States and she asked about the war but before I could answer, she said, "When we hear dey attack in Holland, Moddom, dere warn't a droi oi on de oiland. Let us not speak of de war." I wanted to speak about nourishing food for my cat and get busy on myself with soap and water. I hungered for that beautiful clean bed.

At sunset the rain started and the wind rose in gale force. Acetylene zig-zags of lightning flashed in the sky and thunder roared like artillery fire between the circling mountain walls of the crater. Cold and sleepless with worry for the *Pilot,* I consoled the cat for whom I felt greater guilt every minute. Why had I snatched it from familiar life in the St Barts jungle? What was happening to the crew? Finally I told myself that they were professional sailors, this sea was their home territory, they must know how to cope. And slept uneasily to wake at dawn and hurry down the long steps.

The *Pilot* had disappeared. I dithered in a frenzy, imagining it sunk with all hands, until an old fisherman told me the boat had sailed away as soon as I was out of sight, climbing to Bottom. He said that Saba was no place to anchor in this weather, their own small fishing boats were beached on the opposite side of the island. Carlton and the other men had the *Pilot* and their lives to consider, I didn't blame them, but wished they had at least said goodbye, then remembered that George had done so, nicely. Now I was marooned on Saba. Always be grateful for mercies large and small; how fortunate to be marooned here instead of on grisly St Barts.

The sun shone from a blue and white sky; the green crater walls tempered the wind. It was a fine day and a fine place and I had no complaints. Alberta took a message to the radio operator; would he wire, or whatever he did, St Kitts thirty miles away and ask them to send a motorboat for me. The radio operator told Alberta to report that the storm had put him out of business for the moment but he would signal St Kitts as soon as he could. After an enormous breakfast, I washed my hair. Alberta washed my clothes. I walked around the crater, like strolling in a park. The cat romped around me. I looked at well-groomed cows. I applauded the order and good sense of these people who grew vegetables and tended chickens and cows and made butter and cheese and kept their doll-size houses and gardens pretty. I wondered where on earth you would find such peace as in Bottom.

War is too expensive to waste on useless places. The war had isolated the little islands completely, they were hardly in contact with each other, and unknown in the outside world. All down the Caribbean these small green jewels, pinheads on the map, were blessedly ignored.

Since I was living in perfect comfort and eating good food, I began to fret. Rumblings in the sky might be announcing the much-predicted hurricane; a hurricane would maroon me here indefinitely. There were no companions of the road and no café or bar where I might have sat in a corner and listened. The waves were too high and the air too chill for swimming from the pebble beach. The citizens stayed quietly in their homes at night and the only light in Bottom after nine o'clock was mine. The thoughtful Dutch had put bookshelves in the Rest House sitting-room and books upon the shelves. I had finished my own and with nothing to read I would have been twice as frantic. For I wasn't all that enamoured of peace thirty-four years ago; I was enamoured of surprises and excitement and jokes and risks and odd people and I hurt Alberta's feelings by my eagerness to be gone and annoyed the radio operator by nagging queries.

Alberta woke me on the third morning with a breakfast tray and news. "Dey got a speedboat waitin fo you, Moddom. It costin you sixty dollahs. My goodness!" I gulped the fine breakfast while Alberta packed my small suitcase, kissed her, tipped her, seized the cat and ran down the long steps. The speedboat was a greasy thirty-foot launch with a reeking old engine, named the *Queen Mary*. Its top speed was five knots. The three sailors wore oilskins. The sea looked frightful, endless swaying mountain peaks. I wrapped the cat in my only sweater which might help · it and wouldn't help me and consigned myself to another horror journey. It lasted six hours and was a water version of the truck ride from Shaokwan to the North River. I thought I must have broken my coccyx from banging down so hard where I cowered in the well. Soaked to the skin, frozen, nauseated, I swore that I would never travel by sea again, after I reached Antigua. Sea was for swimming, wonderful for swimming, otherwise I loathed it.

The engine made so much noise, as did the boat, crashing into the trough of waves, that I couldn't hear the tormented wails of the cat, nor feel in the universal wetness its little streams of vomit. I was crouched by a sailor who steered with his foot. In the midst of this hell, he leaned over and shouted, "What you tink of de war sitcheation?"

We docked, they informed me, at Sandy Point. I got out, shaken to pieces, and afraid that my cat had died. My first act was to unwrap the sweater and dry the trembling little body. The harbour master, Mr Williams, a friendly black gentleman, said, "Oh dear, it is against the law to import cats and dogs." I made a speech whose eloquence left me close to tears. Mr Williams was visibly touched. He would telephone the Honourable Treasurer; meantime he invited the cat and me into the comfort of his office.

When Mr Williams reached the Honourable Treasurer, he said, "Sir, there is a female American journalist here with a small cat. She claims this cat always travels with her. She states she never moves without this cat. She is only here in transit, sir, and wishes permission to enter the cat." At the other end of the line the Honourable Treasurer was evidently a sensible man. "Thank you, sir," said Mr. Williams, and turned to me, smiling, nice man, glad to oblige. "The Honourable Treasurer says that it is an exceptional case and the cat may pass freely."

Basseterre is the capital of St Kitts and was so dead that it felt like being buried alive. The hotel and boarding house were long shut, there was no one on the street to question. Whitewashed houses along the sea front were flaking and empty. I couldn't think what else to do so I rang doorbells. A sweet little old lady, with rice powder put hurriedly and crookedly on her face, opened a door. Yes, she would give me a room, but not for money. She wanted it to be very clear that she did not take in boarders, she took in the shipwrecked like me.

She had lived through six hurricanes on the sea front in her over-laden house, bursting with antimacassars and Victorian mahogany and ornamental china in corner cupboards. When young, she sailed to England in a barque, thirty days aboard, too ghastly to contemplate. Now she sat in her drawing-room and listened all day and night to radio news of distant violence. She never listened to anything unless it came over the radio.

I was marooned again in this triste town until the weather quieted. The *Queen Mary* was willing to carry me on a nine-hour stretch of misery to Antigua but not when the barometer was "jumpin roun like a cork in wateh." A sailor would knock me up, that English usage which always convulses Americans, as soon as the barometer steadied.

An article for *Collier's* was overdue. Hardship travel was far from cheap and I had to explain and earn my expenses. But what could I write? No stashes for submarines; no enemy radio transmitters; I had not met, let alone rescued, a single survivor. I sat down and wrote the journey as it was, every inch of it, every person and every conversation. My brain must have been shaken to pieces too in the *Queen Mary*. The maximum length of a *Collier's* article was five thousand words; as near as I can calculate, without counting it page by page, the travelogue I wrote in Basseterre is eleven thousand words long.

Charles Colebaugh took it home to read and laughed himself into a coughing fit. He then passed it around the office where everyone had a good giggle. Much later in New York, Charles said the piece was worth twice the expenses as it had reconciled so many people to staying at their desks where they had to stay anyhow. He said people wanted to travel more than they usually did because the war made travel impossible for them, but after reading me, even when I liked the places, the conditions, the transport, any rational person would think himself lucky to be at home. I pocketed the expense money with thanks and apologies and forgot all about it until I found those yellowing pages among my papers.

Nine hours in the *Queen Mary* was testing for me and almost terminal for the cat but I had the thought of Antigua to sustain hope. The British loaned Antigua for an American base and the Americans whirled up their usual economic hurricane. Money didn't matter, the Americans wanted what they wanted in a hurry—win the war quick and get home to God's country. The island people were drunk on excitement and flowing cash. As danger was limited to ships at sea, life was roaring fun on Antigua. Movies and ice in the drinks and PX cigarettes and a jukebox and splendid types in uniform.

Americans were funnier before America became the most powerful nation on earth. (The British, on the other hand, relieved of Empire, have grown much funnier than they used to be.) I doted on those splendid types in uniform. Badgered by me to talk shop, they allowed as how they were house-cleaning. Four months later all German submarines had been harried from the Caribbean and South American coastal waters, not to return. The sea was again as peaceful as the land.

In Antigua, I picked up the idea for my last *Collier's* article from the Airforce. The wartime system was to hang around and listen until someone said something that sounded like a good line of country. A Southern captain, a bomber pilot, charmed me by his manner and his speech. Off duty, he was a handsome six-foot-two dormouse; I expected him to fall asleep between words or in the middle of chewing gum. "Down theah in Soorienam they got all this stuff, boxxit, y'know, got it in mines aw somethin. You gotta have boxxit foh aloominum an you gotta have aloominum foh ayehplanes so those lil ole kraut subs ah crazy bout ships carryin boxxit, cannot wait tuh sink em. Those lil old kraut subs ah tryin tuh cripple ouah wah effat an we ah tryin to bomb the shit outa them. Can hardly say who's winnin as yet."

Well now, that sounded spiffing. Bauxite, aluminium, threatened ships, war effort. After further questioning, the tall dormouse said, "Yeah we got some lil ole flyin boys down theah an some puah Godfossakin sojers, trampin to and fro defendin the mines aw whatevah it is though that is a tryin an silly job since the krauts got nuthin but subs an they suah as hell doan come outah the wateh." Perfect. I could write about Our Boys on a remote fronter, *Collier's* public was bound to approve. As for me, the name Surinam was enough. I had to see a place with a name like that.

PanAmerican stopped to refuel at Paramaribo, Surinam, on the way down to Rio and I knew there would be cat trouble with PanAmerican, an airline that took the war very seriously and was given to closing the passengers' window curtains whenever you came near a landing field which everyone then saw freely on the ground. I got a big basket and laid on a fall-back position with the Airforce if worst came to worst which it did. The little cat was terrified by the basket prison and scratched and howled and betrayed itself. PanAmerican refused to carry a cat. The Airforce had accompanied me to the plane in case of this wicked act, and received the basket from me, laughing madly and urging me to keep my chin up, war is hell, sacrifice your cat for your country like a man, come on smile kid, we'll look after it like its mother.

They had solemnly sworn to do so but I didn't trust them to remember feeding time or remember consolation for an orphaned cat far from home. I hated PanAmerican, I was in a fury of grief which I know about through reading a heartbroken letter to my mother. Aside from loving the cat and missing it sorely, I had harmed it; the cat deserved better than this uncertain life. The Airforce no doubt thought I was a candidate for a padded cell as I bombarded them with airmail queries about the health and happiness of my abandoned cat.

The quickest way to describe Surinam is to lift a few of the opening sentences from the antique article I wrote for *Collier's*.

"The Dutch, who own Surinam, spent $1,600,000 a year on it and forgot about it. Surinam was just 3,000 square miles of jungle and stale coffee-coloured rivers, with a capital, a very few so-called towns, a strip

of coast more or less chopped free of jungle, 1,900 Europeans who lived
there to administer the colony or make money, 162,000 other folk ranging from amber Javanese to soot-black Bush Negroes, gold mines, bauxite mines, sugar cane and coffee plantations, balata trees, other oddments
in the way of agriculture, small local industries and a climate that you just
about cannot stand but which you finally get used to. It lies, hot, unknown and unimportant, between British and French Guiana, on the
northeast coast of South America. The Atlantic, which is usually grey or
blue or green, stretches along the pancake-flat coast of Surinam and is
pure brown mud for twenty miles out. The inland country was mapped
mostly by guesswork because no one has been able to survey it. Some of
the rivers are navigable for a certain distance into the interior in case
there is any reason to navigate them. There are, in all Surinam, 120 miles
of railroad and since the war 117 miles of road. If you want to get anywhere else you can cut your way through with a machete . . ."

No one else got out of the PanAm plane on the glaring white sand
airfield. No one ever did except by order of the U.S. or Netherlands government. The heat was spectacular. I stood there, blinded and stunned,
and the resident PanAm agent, also stunned to have a passenger on his
hands, said, "You better move off the sand, you'll get chiggers under
your toenails. Some sort of local chigger you have to cut out." I was wearing sandals. When he'd attended to unloading mail and freight and seen
that the refuelling was done, he would give me a lift to Paramaribo. I
should wait in the one-room office.

The Airforce hangars were made of thatch. Alongside them, the U.S.
Base was a collection of barracks and Headquarters, identical wood boxcars. The jungle had been pushed back just behind the burning sand and
looked like a high wall of knotted green ropes. The military boxcars were
linked by anti-chigger duckboards. Men with bath towels around their
waists and stout unlaced boots over bare feet hurried from showers to
barracks; others moved briskly between the buildings, wearing regulation Army trousers scissored into frayed shorts, khaki topees and the

same flapping boots. Nobody stepped off the duckboards. They appeared absurdly young, high-school age, and more absurdly cheerful. By rights they should have been suicidal. Chiggers, sunblindness, and heat-stroke. Not one tree. Not an inch of shade anywhere.

The surface of the new narrow road from the new big airfield was bauxite clay, bright red and streaming dust. After an hour of intense bumping and eating red dust, we arrived in the capital. The PanAm agent mistook my silence, which was speechless gratitude, for shock. "It's pretty rough," he said. "Still, I guess you won't have to stay long." I meant to stay as long as possible. Though I had never heard of Paramaribo or Surinam until two days ago, I felt I had come to a place dreamed of for years.

The town was built along a brown stagnant jungle river. Caribbean-style wood houses, like St Martin but with a comic suggestion of Dutch gables, lined the dust streets. The PanAm agent dropped me at the hotel, saying worriedly, "Hans and Gertie will look after you." Hans and Gertie were young, fair and flabby, as people become in the tropics where it is too hot to rise from a chair, and darlings. The Paramaribo Grand Hotel was three storeys high, with torn matting on the stairs and broken ant-eaten furniture in the rooms. There was an itchy plush sofa in the lobby, cane chairs with holes in the woven seats, and tables covered in smeared linoleum. I loved it: so did everyone else. When the soldiery had two days' leave they came here, as if to weekend in Paris.

I went out immediately to sightsee. The small women of the East, Javanese and Indian, padded about barefoot in sarongs and sarees, wearing their fortunes upon them in gold and silver ornaments. Dutch ladies pedalled by on bikes. Creole women, enormous under starched skirts, balanced baskets on their heads. Girls, triumphant results of blended Malay and Chinese and African blood, flirted along to show off their clothes and hair-dos, copied from the last movie magazine. Black policemen in green uniforms directed the traffic: a staff car, a limousine, the Navy station wagon and scores of bicycles. Government clerks, of different well-miscegenated shades, in smart white suits and briefcases, eyed the women cautiously, as did Dutch and American soldiers properly clad for the city.

The people of Paramaribo were the best sight. But the shops, Javanese, Indian, Dutch, Chinese, were not to be downgraded, the most engaging was Jonas Home Industries where you could buy local products such as preserved tarantulas and native combs, apparently made of filed sharks' teeth.

I was swooning with happiness by five o'clock when I settled on a ruptured cane chair in the lobby to listen to the going gossip. At five o'clock promptly the mosquitoes arrived. "Union mosquitoes," a soldier observed. "They work from 5 p.m. to 5 a.m." They were the biggest mosquitoes I had met anywhere and fearless, they zoomed in to cover one's arms and legs and died feeding while others replaced those you had beaten to death. When the blazing sun went down, the air refused to cool despite nightly rainy season cloudbursts. The rain was lukewarm, encouraged the mosquitoes, turned the streets into quagmires which dried to deep dust a half hour after sunrise. Between five and six in the morning, there was a very faint freshness to breathe.

Within a day, I felt I had been living happily in the Paramaribo Grand Hotel for years, at home in the buzzing local life. Among my new friends were the Singer Sewing Machine Man, who travelled as much as anyone could in this country to collect payments on his merchandise, a Dutch missionary from somewhere in the interior, an English couple on holiday from a distant goldfield. But there was my job, I couldn't simply frolic.

My job was Our Boys and bauxite and the war effort. I went out to the Base. The C.O. was twenty-nine, the Squadron Commander thirty; they were the old men and sometimes called Sir and both were wise and funny and knew how to run this stifling outpost so that the work got done and the men stayed sane and improbably content. The officers lived in the same sort of barracks as the men, the officers' mess was separated from the men's by a sheet curtain that was never closed. The officers' club had ten minimally easy chairs, three worn card tables and a makeshift bar. I came to love the Base too and bought a pair of sneakers as chigger prevention.

When I told the chaps that I meant to write of their noble efforts and bauxite mines, they fell about laughing. They said that if I could write one sentence about a bauxite mine, they would give me a prize, the skin of an eighteen-foot boa constrictor that adorned the enlisted men's club. The barman protested, "You can't do that, it belongs to us." "Balls," said the C.O. "You know you guys would sell your grandmothers. Money, money that's all you think about. What if I offer you fifty dollars?" "Nothing doing," said the barman. "Don't argue," the Airforce Major said. "She's not going to win any prize."

Win or lose, they proposed to send me to the biggest bauxite mine in the Navy crash boat that patrolled the river, much quicker than the launch trip. I thanked them and asked if they would now please explain their noble efforts. The C.O. said that the Airforce was spoiled, no better than weaklings, they could get up in their planes nearly every day and cool off. The Airforce said that the Army lived in shameful safety, think of the awful danger they faced in the sky. "What danger would that be?" asked an Army lieutenant. "The engine might fall out," said the Airforce.

The crash boat sped up a muddy river that wound through walls of jungle. After more than enough of this unvarying scenery it stopped at the river bank, where a lieutenant and driver and jeep waited. We drove a short distance inland. We did the bauxite situation up brown, in no time. He showed me the mine. It looked like an open gravelly field, dug at, chewed, ploughed. The driver gave me some clay, reddish with white streaks in it, which crumbled in my hand. 'That's what we're here for,' the lieutenant said with resignation. The plant to do whatever was done to that clay looked like a cluster of silos and barns, red with dust and silent. A soldier marched steadily around it.

"Interesting?" the lieutenant asked. He didn't seem a day over seventeen.

"Oh, very." We hadn't got out of the jeep.

"I reckon you're ready to go back now," the lieutenant said. "I wouldn't ask a dog to come to my tent for a drink."

"Anyway there's no ice," said the driver. "War is hell." He didn't seem a day over sixteen.

Albina, on the Dutch side of the Marowijne river, was a trading post for gold and balata brought down in native canoes. Gutta percha is made from the latex of balata trees; also useful in war though I don't know why. Arawak Indians and Caribs and blacks lived in villages around Albina. The Caribs were paralysed drunk after a bang-up funeral, you could smell cassava brew all over the place. A Dutch civilian got me across to the penal colony of Saint Laurent in French Guiana, telling the French guard that I was a tourist wishing to buy convict-made trinkets. He had warned me not to speak English so we talked ungrammatical German loudly and satisfied the guard.

French Guiana was a penal colony, Devil's Island being the most infamous prison, and was such a disgrace in the twentieth century that the French ought to have shut up about their *mission civilisatrice*. Now it is abandoned so the French can boast with a better conscience. Convicts, dead-eyed skeletons in red and white striped pyjamas, cut wood in the jungle until they died of exhaustion and disease. One vertical wall of this prison rose from the river, full of piranhas and crocodiles; a ten-foot iron fence, tipped with spikes, closed in the town side. At dusk the fence was patrolled by guards with Mausers; if any prisoner came close to the fence they shot him. The guards' faces suited their work; it was a vile place; I hurried to get out.

Some convicts actually had escaped to Albina chancing the river rather than die surely and slowly in St Laurent. Their dream was to join the Free French in West Africa but there was no transport. They were grateful to the Dutch who treated them like human beings. We sat in the dust smoking American cigarettes, and they told me that, since the Vichy government took over France, the Guiana authorities were trying to wipe out the prisoners by starvation and overwork and punishment. The Vichy French were apt pupils of the Nazis. No man could live more than three months when the punishment started. Half the men, about seven hundred, had died in the prison of St Jean de Maronie; many men were dying every day in St Laurent.

The Dutch officers and non-coms were older and less cheerful than the U.S. contingent, with reason, but the Dutch and Americans got on well, respected each other, accepted amiably their different manners and mannerisms. The Dutch had experienced the war in Holland and their families were still in the occupied homeland. They wrote through the Swiss Red Cross and you could tell it was a bad day by a man's face if he had figured he ought by now to have a letter back and none came. The letters from Holland couldn't say anything but as long as they arrived in familiar handwriting the men knew their families lived and that was enough.

They trained small Javanese and Indian troops on the square in front of the hotel, beginning every morning at five; late at night, lights burned in the Territorial Command offices. Surinam was the last land, except for the tiny Caribbean Dutch islands, where they could raise their own flag.

Having enjoyed myself mightily on this remote frontier, I wrote and mailed off my Surinam article and should have gone home but first I bought a map and was undone. There wasn't much on the map as there wasn't much in Surinam, the capital, a few settlements near the coast and several rivers. This map showed the Saramcoca river weaving from Paramaribo through green then white space, representing green jungle and the white unknown. The river was a blue line up to a small Christian cross where presumably the farthest traveller lay down to die. Beyond the cross, the river was marked by blue dots, suggesting an uncharted course through that big blob of white. The Saramcoca, enticing name, cried out to be explored. How could anyone expect me to miss such an opportunity; besides why need anyone know what I was doing? Exploring was a brand-new type of travel.

A black city slicker presented himself as guide, interpreter, and organizer. I don't remember how this character entered my life. Perhaps through the owner of Jonas Home Industries to whom I had been talking about his merchandise; probably I said I wanted to go upriver and see for myself whence came these lovely bottled snakes, giant centipedes, and monkey-skull rattles. The city slicker claimed that his name was Harold; I never met anyone less like a Harold. For me, he was Mr Slicker. He wore such dark glasses that he looked eyeless, and a red bow tie and a sweat-stained crushed Homburg hat and a suit in the same state. I was sure he was syphilitic, heaven knows why. He was smarmy and generally repulsive.

Unless off my rocker from heat, I can think of no explanation for venturing into the unknown with him as sole companion. Not that I would have wanted to involve a friend, not after China, but the cat would have been a great comfort. Mr Slicker was responsible for all equipment and provisions. I packed necessities like cigarettes and books in a basket, kept my room, and announced that I was going to visit friends for a while. It did not seem best to talk about exploring until after I had passed the burial cross on the map, and returned.

Mr Slicker and I set off in a taxi for a few hours, then embarked on the river in a hollowed-out tree trunk paddled by three blacks wearing loincloths and knitting needles stuck in their hair. I was miffed by the knitting needles. Couldn't they tell the difference between a tourist out for local colour and a budding explorer? Mr Slicker, surprised by my disobliging remarks about the knitting needles, said these fellows always wore them, why did I think they'd bother to earn money if not to buy pretty hair pins? I was hauled aboard to sit on my hump of tent and mosquito net and we proceeded upriver.

Paddling is not speedy and the current was against us. Very slowly, we moved along the river, wide and brown like all rivers here and blocked in by jungle so dense you could see nothing except a high dusty green barrier on both sides of lifeless water. I heard some sort of birds making unpleasant squawks, but never saw them. Mr Slicker was full of dire instructions. I must not dip my hands in the river or they would be bitten off. I wasn't hankering to dip my hands into what seemed like thick hot mud but didn't believe him. To entertain the rich lunatic they were paid to paddle, the crew threw some mushy grub they had been eating into the water which at once boiled. The food was yanked below and the river flowed smoothly on, with all its charms hidden. I kept my hands to myself and wondered if these tree trunks ever capsized. Unwilling to admit it, I was less interested in exploring after the first day.

Mr Slicker spotted a place where the jungle had receded a few yards and there we camped for the night. Fussy and again dire, Mr Slicker told me to wriggle into my pup tent at sunset because of mosquitoes.

"I haven't been jumping under my mosquito net in Paramaribo at sunset and there are millions of mosquitoes. Look at my arms." My arms looked like measles.

"These here are badder, believe me, Moddom, they make you sick."

"What do you think they do in Paramaribo? Half the place has malaria." This week the Consul was laid low, last week the Censor had been shivering and shaking; the regular choice of disease was malaria or an indigenous dysentery.

"No, badder than malaria, believe me Moddom."

Well hell, I didn't want to sit by him, shrouded in smoke from the fire he had lit as mosquito repellent. It was hot enough without that. I couldn't read anywhere. Hard ground was better than the hatch cover, but I wasn't sure where I stood on the different merits of being rain-wet and cold or sweat-wet and suffocating. Mr Slicker hummed by the smoking fire. The knitting-needle boys, with whom I couldn't exchange a word as they spoke a language of their own, must have dossed down in the hollow tree trunk. I was back in the well-known long nights.

Next day I was saved from staring blankly at jungle by a river village of blacks. They had hacked away a homeland and lived in pointed thatched huts, starkers, but greased and glistening and also stinking with rancid coconut butter, the local Elizabeth Arden skin cream. Mr Slicker explained that skin was the first attraction of a woman and I could see why since the ladies were mainly huge bottoms, like carrying your own pillow, and pendulous breasts. Little leather pouches, containing charms against evil spirits, hung between all breasts. A few of the men wore a brown cotton bag to hold their privates. I was surprised that a naked black man does not looked naked to a white-oriented eye. The men's bodies were muscular and strong to the waist, from canoe paddling, with spindly legs. The village received me with much pinching, patting, tweaking, and howls of laughter; they treated me like a circus sideshow not an explorer.

The ancestors of these blacks, brought here as slaves, escaped to liberty in the bush. For two hundred years they had paid tribute to no government, obeyed no rulers except their own and lived independent of the white man. Nothing had changed except transplantation from African bush to South American bush. They didn't even go in for knitting needles. It was not my cuppa, I was sickened by the circumambient body odour, but they seemed happy living as they liked in their own style, as they always had. Just freedom was enough.

Mr Slicker was deep in conversation with the Chief and didn't notice my increasingly urgent signals for departure. I was tired of painful pinches and about to shout at him when he came over; every time I looked at his face I got a shock from those black holes instead of eyes. "The Chief says you tell Missy Wilhelmina he is sorry to hear she cannot go home."

"Missy Wilhelmina?"

"You know, the Queen."

"Right, I'll tell her the next time I see her. Come on, I want to get out quick."

Now a river launch passed us, bearing a load of camera-strung waving Americans, the men in those shirts printed with tropical flowers, the ladies in hair-nets and plastic curlers against the destructive damp. I cannot remember who they were or how they got there. Can they have been a holiday group from the bauxite managerial set? We caught up with them at a large opening in the jungle where a jetty led to a primitive board bungalow. A white couple lived here, a middle-aged paunchy hairy American and a young girl. The man was fulsome about the joys of living in sin far from the idiocy of the modern world. The girl, a forerunner by decades of her present hippy sisters, seemed like someone who is whistling in the dark. A few blacks appeared and stamped around in a shambling dance. The tourists were noisily excited, clicking their cameras at the noble savages.

I thought both tourists and white couple loony. By that process which has to do with not seeing the mote in one's own eye, I failed to consider that tourists and white couple might think me and my tree trunk gang too loony to believe.

Again we camped, again at sunset I retired to my tent, unable to read, finding the ground hard and the night extremely long. Mr Slicker kept assuring me we were near the Christian cross marked on the map; he might as well have assured me we were near Paris France.

The third day we reached another river village, everybody well greased and smelling to high heaven of that fashionable rancid coconut butter. I made Chinese politenesses with the aged Chief until I heard piercing screams, a body in torment. I demanded to know what was happening and got flat silence from all the residents and from Mr Slicker. The screams were a woman's; I rushed around the village and located the sounds coming from a closed thatched hut. Get her out, I began to scream too, what are you doing, do something! Stop torturing her, I shouted, what is this, help her! Issuing orders in a fury: someone had to stop the screams.

The black folk had drawn back from me and wore expressions of frozen anger. Mr Slicker, gauging the situation whatever it was, seized my arm and pulled me away, protesting. He hustled me into the hollow tree trunk and our crew paddled smartly off at full speed, to a badly aimed hail of stones from the village younger element. I couldn't prise a sensible explanation of these goings-on from Mr Slicker. Either he didn't know or wouldn't tell but I had interfered in bush business and Mr Slicker was thankful we got out undamaged.

In all the intervening years I have had no reason to report that episode to anyone. This summer, since I was delving in my memory, I told it to a friend while we sat on her terrace in Switzerland, drinking wine and watching the beautiful sunset view down the cleft of green hills to the Rhone valley and across to the jagged snow mountains beyond. I was admiring the view, which is one I love with fervour, and talked absent-mindedly, saying, "I never understood what the uproar was about."

"Perhaps she was having a baby," said my friend.

It had not occurred to me and of course was the answer. Of course. They would shut a woman off alone in a hut and let her scream it out by herself, the coconut butter savages, and as it had to be an ancient rite, their custom for childbirth from time immemorial, they would be frightened as well as insulted by my interference. I saw that Mr Slicker had done me a real service; I could imagine a well-aimed stoning if he hadn't been so fast on his feet.

Perhaps later that childbirth day, or the following day, we came on a lumber camp. Three sweating amiable white men directed a black labour force in felling trees: rare wood, I suppose, as this small operation couldn't be worthwhile for wood pulp or average building material. I was pleased to hear I hadn't lost my voice if nothing more. Mr Slicker was as useless as Mr Ma for information and lacked Mr Ma's charm. We travelled in silence. The lumbermen must have explained about their trees but information is something I constantly seek and forget first. A black child ran up a four-storey tree trunk, outdoing any monkey and scaring me badly; I thought he was showing off and would fall to his death, I provoked loud hilarity in my fellow whites, not due to witty remarks but due to being there, with my ridiculous expedition.

By the fifth or sixth day I was ready to leave exploring to explorers whom I now revered for their endurance but felt must be a special brand of insane.

I couldn't tell where we were, maybe we had passed the burial cross, maybe it lay weeks ahead. Failure of an enterprise: itching from insect bites, cramped in pup tent and tree trunk, dirty, thirsting for cold water, sick of everyone's smell including my own, sunk in the true horror journey boredom. We turned around. I was looking forward to the flesh pots of civilization in Paramaribo.

Then the fever hit me. I thought it was malaria but malaria, though a shocker, is not even close to what the Saramcoca produced. My bones felt broken, I whimpered with pain when I moved and finally I couldn't. I was carried ashore to sleep, and could only crawl, whimpering, beside the tent, modest to my last breath about the inevitable calls of nature. Mr Slicker shook me, shouting "Moddom! Moddom!" like a butler announcing that the house is on fire. "Wake up Moddom! You are talking and crying!"

"What?" The man was crazy; I had been asleep.

"Drink some tea, Moddom, it helps the pains. I told you these mosquitoes are badder."

"What?" I couldn't raise myself to drink. Mr Slicker had to handle me like a hospital nurse. He had taken off his black glasses to reveal orange-red eyes, like the yolks of Chinese thousand-year eggs. His breath was bad too. He was in a great turmoil, perhaps fearing I would die, a weak white woman, and leave him to explain matters to the authorities in Paramaribo. I wished he would stop breathing on me and go away.

I was unjust to Mr Slicker. It wasn't his fault that I decided to explore the Saramcoca. He did his job well and got more than he bargained for. The knitting-needle boys made a sort of stretcher from vines. Mr Slicker got me aboard and kept the canoe paddling like a boat race from dawn without stops until dusk. The return trip is dim, it can't have lasted more than two or three days. Mr Slicker delivered me to the hotel where I crept up the stairs to my room on all fours, unseen, and lay there, not thinking to ask Gertie for a doctor. I am not sure about this: was I too sick to think straight or too ashamed to admit where and how I got so sick. Later, my own doctor diagnosed this dread disease as dengue, commonly and well named break-bone fever. It is supposed to recur but never did.

The fever dropped by itself in a few days. I told Gertie face-saving (my face) lies: I had an allergy which often caused these bouts of fever, I didn't want to see any of Our Boys, as I couldn't bear the sorrow and awkwardness of farewells. Though the fever was gone or at least diminished, acute pain in all joints remained: I told Gertie that I would disappear quietly on the next plane north.

"Did you have a nice time with your friends?" Gertie asked.

"Lovely." Mr Slicker, the blacks et al. Even reaching for a cigarette hurt so much I wanted to cry. On the final day in Paramaribo, trying to lift myself from a chair by my arms because my legs wouldn't do the job, I slipped and fell on my wrist, fracturing it. It was only a sharper pain in the other diverse pains. I sent for adhesive tape, strapped the wrist and shuffled to the plane, a wreck of an unsuccessful explorer.

The plane was deliciously cold and as we flew unpressurized high in the sky, by miracle or by chilling, my bones became normal though the wrist ached worse. When I returned to my happy home, everyone gave me a nice welcome-back kiss and asked why I was wearing that grubby adhesive tape, but they were too busy to listen to travellers' tales.

Money, not war, destroyed the old life of the islands. War only fed in the first big dose of money. I am thankful that I knew the sleepy lovely little islands all through the Caribbean before the dollars poured over them. At first the wintering wealthy arrived, then the reduced-rate summer tourists. Now they're coining money everywhere the year round. It's a success story; it's Progress.

The last time I saw that beautiful cove on Virgin Gorda it was full of suntanned bodies and ringed by boats, from swan yachts to rubber Zodiacs, and there were bottles and plastic debris on the seabed and picnic litter on the sand for the rich are as disgusting as the poor in their carelessness of the natural world. The Social Inn on Tortola is incredible prehistory where now you book months ahead to reserve rooms in ten hotels, or buy a luxury condominium residence; the *Pilot* is unthinkable in the two stylish marinas. St Martin, which I loved first and most, is a thriving blighted area. A great runway on the Dutch side receives jets.

Phillipsburg and Marigot are boom towns. Handsome houses of foreigners dot the hills. There are grand hotels and crummy motels, casinos and boutiques, supermarkets and launderettes, snack bars and robber restaurants, throngs of visitors and plentiful muck on the beaches. And the island, once a green bouquet of trees, looks bald. Progress uses space and is more valuable than trees.

It is ridiculous to repine for a past simplicity and quiet and loveliness when I can live where I choose while the islanders are anchored where they are, and probably mad about Progress. Seeing them, I don't believe that they profit from its advertised benefits. They used to be short of cash but never hungry, never crowded, or hurried. They worked when they had to and not a minute more. Free of nuisance government, they lived in a close community, as content as mortals can possibly be. If they wanted adventure or consumer goods, they went off as sailors or emigrated for dollars but all of them returned to visit or drowse through old age, and knew they could return to what they had left: home didn't change, home was safe. Now they work for the foreigners on their islands and though they have more money than ever before they feel poor by contrast and they are no longer the sure, idle, chatty, easy people I remember. In another ten years they may be as bitter as the blacks in Harlem.

Between planes, this winter, I hired a glittering Mercedes taxi at Phillipsburg airport because the owner-driver had grey hair and would have known St Martin before it turned into a gold mine. He had driven visitors from the North so long that he sounded American. "Well, Madam, everybody's got good work and lotsa money, see all these new little houses the people built for themselves? Got everything they want inside, fine things. Got money in the bank. Everybody's doing very well on St Martin. But the old harmony is gone, it's gone for good."

The Caribbean has become a resort and is a world lost. This cuts me deeply in my feelings, as Mr Ma would say, because I loved that world, its looks, its climate, its aimless harmless life, and it was the best anywhere for a solitary swimmer. I don't like resorts and I can't afford them.

Grumetti Serengeti Tanzania, early 1970s

Four

INTO AFRICA

Three thousand unexpected dollars fell into my lap from the sale of a short story to television. Slowly it dawned on me that I could blow this money, I could pay my own way to Africa. No editors would send me in spite of repeated suggestions for riveting articles; I was not an old Africa hand. You must be an expert first though how do you become an expert if you can't get there. I have read haphazardly about darkest Africa all my life but cannot remember what I read or how I made such a simple picture of that central slice of the continent. It was a vast lion-coloured plain, ringed by blue mountains. Beautiful wild animals roamed across the land and the sky went up forever. There were no people in this picture, no Africans or anyone else. I craved to see the country and the animals and now with this money I could do it. Travel for pleasure, the most daring idea yet.

A nice young woman, a travel agent, came for a drink. We got out the Encyclopedia Atlas and looked at the map. I thought it might be a good idea to cross Africa from West to East along the Equator. Douala in Cameroun was the nearest place I could see to the Equator line on the west coast; neither of us had ever heard of it but she promised to make inquiries and arrange a ticket. That took care of travel plans.

She called up shortly to say that I needed yellow fever and smallpox vaccinations according to Air France who flew the route from Paris. My GP had been stationed in Nigeria with the RAF during the war; his feeling about Africa amounted to morbid disturbance of the brain. The whole place was beyond words hideous and to go there of one's own free will was certifiable. The diseases were revolting and inescapable. If I insisted on this mad venture, he would shoot me full of every known antitoxin for everything he could think of.

His war career just about did me in. On top of smallpox and yellow fever, I got shots against typhoid, plague, cholera, polio and tetanus; pills for dysentery, diarrhoea and malaria; unguents and powders to heal sores and skin infections. He implored me never under any circumstances to drink anything except bottled water and better check where it came from too; and be sure to use disinfectant in washing water. The bugs in water were worse than those in food. Every insect was poisonous and there was no end to their number and variety. He advised me to buy a snake-bite kit but I refused, saying I would die of fear anyway if a snake sank its fangs in me and besides didn't he expect me to be dead of disease without help from snakes. I felt very ill due to all this preventive medicine and unable to concentrate on the journey.

With only a week left, I had an attack of nerves; I really must collect some useful information. This led me to telephone two friends who had been in Africa. One told me to buy khaki trousers and shirts and comfortable boots in London, to stock up most heavily for the dysentery branch of sickness, to call on the R. and W. King Company Traders when I got to Cameroun, they'd look after me, the insects were indeed a trial but as I liked heat I would have a wonderful time. The other friend said not to bother buying anything here, I could get what I needed in Africa, and it was cold at night, she had found that a hot water bottle came in handy and take at least one heavy sweater and when I got to Nairobi call on Ker and Downey Ltd, they'd look after me, and wouldn't I be a bit lonely, Africa was so big, but I was bound to have a marvellous trip.

They were talking of two Africas, West and East, and assumed that everyone knew the difference. Africa was Africa to me, about as clever as thinking New York and California would be the same. Always glad to postpone shopping, I compromised by buying a hot water bottle. And set off to cross the continent with a brand new Boots' hot water bottle, wool trousers and heavy sweater, three cotton dresses, two pairs of city shoes, and a large Spanish fisherman's straw hat. Since I knew nobody anywhere and expected to be gone nearly three months, I was more interested in amusements.

These were tubes of acrylic paint, as I was in an ardent phase of Sunday painting, tiny cards for solitaire, the only card game I know, fine binoculars to gaze upon elephants and giraffes, my particular passion, a rotten little portable typewriter for writing short stories in my ample leisure time and books, ranging from *War and Peace,* for nourishing length, and Jane Austen and Shirer on the Third Reich to paperback thrillers. Luggage being a proven misery, I took only one suitcase and a cosmetics case for medicines but I was worried about books. Solitude is all right with books, awful without.

On 23 January 1962, I left London, both arms throbbing hotly, switched planes in Paris and spent the next thirteen hours overnight, jammed in the increasingly squalid tourist section of the plane together with a bunch of young European mothers and their small children and babies, all heading for the Congo where a war was going on. That took the edge off any sense of risk at charging into Africa.

In the early morning, coming down to land at Douala, Africa presented itself as grey-green jungle swamp. Muddy snaking rivers and mosquito lakes broke up the jungle. Uninhabited and uninhabitable, except no doubt for reptiles. The rivers washed out into the Atlantic making a wide band, it looked miles wide, of dirty brown water against the blue. I couldn't believe my eyes. Where were the golden plains and the mountains? Sick from medical care, sick from sleepless exhaustion, I tottered off the plane into a kind of raging heat such as I had felt only in Rangoon before the rains. All I could think of was my hot water bottle which caused me to laugh loudly while the few other arriving passengers stared and drew away.

I can report in detail on part of that long African journey because I found a complete diary, Douala to Khartoum, which I do not remember writing. What I do remember is the summer months, after this trip, in a Pension on the Adriatic outside Trieste, writing copiously about East Africa, with notes to shore up my memory. I was searching for that manuscript of which no scrap remains when instead I came across this West African true life story. It's just as well; I remember West Africa the way one remembers pain, as an incident but never the precise sensations.

January 24: First act on African soil: the eager native porter dropped my heavy cosmetics case on the foot of the Air France stewardess. She hopped about saying *"Crétin!"* Porter grinned and shrugged. Health inspector, studying my vaccination documents upside down, had diagonal tribal scars on his cheeks and a nose like a gorilla; unsmiling. Taxi boys crowded, jostled, screamed, grabbed luggage. Price dropped from 300 to 100 francs, but at the hotel the driver simply kept 300 francs and sped away. The hotel belongs to Air France and is the best in Cameroun, though there is hardly any competition. These international cement packing cases for people fall apart fast; it's a consolation. My room has walls lined with dark wood which has not been dusted or polished for far too long; whole place is just not clean, wearing out. But the air conditioning is at deep freeze pitch and the bathroom works.

Outside the window is a garden, gravelled paths, lawn, flowers, trees, and a swimming pool. The sky is grey-white, very low; a small wind moves the trees. The sun is like a fried egg, Israeli fried egg to be exact, with that specially pale yolk. Beyond the swimming pool the jungle begins again and is cut by a wide, slow, brown river. The garden looks as if everything was struggling to grow in the wrong climate; an incongruous European oasis on the matted west coast of Africa.

Sleep that knits up the ravelled sleeve of the air traveller.

The local French are having an aperitif or cocktail party on the roof terrace. Perhaps thirty men in business suits and four dressy wives, who end up sitting together, alone at a table. It looks deadly. The common folk must use the bar this evening; it has air conditioning, a wall tank of gold-fish, all the modern conveniences. The clientele is petit bourgeois white, in shirt sleeves, except for one African guest, very fat, wearing an Italian silk suit, whom I heard called effusively, by his countrymen at the air-port, *"Monsieur le Ministre."*

Dining-room on roof; also European copy, with exposed goodies, from smoked salmon to pastries; head-waiter, waiters, the works. Young French wives wear highest possible beehive hair-dos and shortest possi-ble skirts, all learned from Paris magazines and quite well done.

Dreamed in the night that Peter Sellers was my doctor, tenderly ex-amining my arms, sore from shots. I was half pleased and half aware of being mocked, when an alarming noise broke in. It sounded as if a phonograph needle was stuck on a record, saying in a loud ugly voice, "Dig *me,* Dig *me."* Still part asleep I wondered what on earth the neigh-bours were up to. Instead it was tree frogs, in the encircling jungle.

January 25: White skin is horrid. Along the edge of the pool lie the fish-belly bodies, the ladies in the least of bikinis, the gentlemen in their "slips." Does this fried-egg sun not darken the skin? Only one who looks nice is a lean, light brown Camerounian.

A tiny white boy is being looked after by a black manservant, who moves as if his joints were rubber, without noise or effort, always near the child but not insistently. The French mother calls the child; at once there are nerves and fuss; the child now falls and hurts itself, howls. Within minutes the baby is returned to the black man and all is peace and hap-piness again.

An elderly Frenchman, who seems to be the hotel manager, spoke to me. No, you cannot drive between here and Yaoundé, or from here to the ex-British Cameroun, unless you go in two cars and well armed. That way, you will have no trouble with bandits. They attack cars, one never knows when, it is like roulette; burn the cars, steal—weapons preferred—and murder the whites. Then they eat those organs which give strength, such as brain, heart, and liver. I see at once that I am going to have hell's own time knowing what to believe in Africa; though I had heard in London that this area, inland from the coast, was unsafe, there being no government control over it.

Cannot buy any khaki clothes or shoes; now limping around with blister on my heel. If I could go barefoot and wear a *pagne*—a long length of brilliant, often beautifully printed cotton material, wrapped around from breast to ankles and passing over the head like a veil—I would be handsomely dressed.

Douala is shabby, sprawling, and hideous. There is a huge cement church, little rows of shops, empty spaces, more shops. Worse, this is not strange and exciting; I've seen it all before, only much more attractive, in the Caribbean. The natives look like Caribbean blacks and are dressed in the odd scraps which are apparently the lot of poor black people who live anywhere near whites. But the scrappily dressed blacks have an agreeable air of going nowhere in particular at their own time and enjoying it; they seem eccentric and free. They are also very pleasant, unlike African Americans who have plenty of reason to be surly and usually are. These Africans are after all at home, and bosses in their own house, and though it looks a very cheesy house to me, hereabouts, still no one with a white skin can push them around just because of having a white skin.

Poor countries can be as expensive as rich ones. $4 for a wretched lunch. $10 for hotel room (same for instance as the splendid Edwardian luxury and super bathroom at the Bellevue in Berne).

January 26: In the kindergarten across the road the children scream and shout steadily, not just at recess, like a babies' riot. The town is full of schools. The French teach people to speak their language, which they rightly regard as a boon. One can get on very well with French, though the blacks talk pidgin among themselves. This is a heavenly tongue, a most comic version of English. Thus, when wishing to say that a woman is pregnant, one says: he gottum bell. All animals are beef. Dangerous animals would be: dat beef too bad. I wish I could speak it.

Rereading Isak Dinesen's *Out of Africa.* It bears no relation to this part of the continent. This is obviously *Heart of Darkness* country. The power of *Out of Africa* is her self-possession. The charm of the writing is an archaic and quaint elegance—the idiom not quite right. But she worries me on God; as if she knew that He and she were both well born.

The taxis drift around with a chum or two chums in the front seat beside the driver. This afternoon, passing the cement church, the chum said, "The biggest sinners and worst men everywhere are Catholics." He is a Catholic.

I am getting out of here tomorrow, flying in the early morning to the capital, Yaoundé. Africa is there, somewhere; I only have to find it.

January 27: On the plane sat next to a gum-chewing American youth, of the utmost physical and mental pallor, who was the U.S. courier. He came from Frankfurt, or somewhere in Germany, carrying a thin canvas bag of diplomatic correspondence for the U.S. Embassy in Yaoundé. This made me think hard about the posters in English wartime railway stations: a stern face, an accusing pointed finger, and the query, "Is your journey really necessary?" What can they have here as top secrets? Perhaps hot news on the organ-eating Communists in the bush between Douala and Yaoundé.

Yaoundé looked more hopeful from the air, pimple hills, a town straggling and nestling, red dirt roads. But the same low milky sky, and the muffled scalding sun. The locals are awfully pleased about being grown-ups on their own, and crazed with pleasure over their bureaucracy. You have to fill out a landing card, name, age, occupation, motive of trip etc. etc., which is such a bore and waste of good trees, at every stop here, not just when crossing frontiers. All formalities, health, customs, are again repeated.

The taxi ran all right for a bit, since we were coasting downhill; after that I could have passed it at a walk. My blessed friend, who told me to take my troubles to the R. and W. King Co, Traders, will receive her crown in heaven. My luggage was deposited in front of the R. and W. King godown, in a dusty compound of warehouses and a one-storey office building, and I asked for the manager.

The manager, a Frenchman of perhaps thirty-three or four, was very tall, good bright greenish eyes, thin as string, grey-white in colour and worth making the trip for. It is one of the best treats in life to find someone that you can laugh with, immediately. I had plenty of troubles. My heel was infecting; I was greasy with sweat; there was no room in the Yaoundé hotel; I did not know where or how to proceed, and something mysterious was going wrong with me, in that my feet and ankles, hands, face and middle area were swelling as if a bicycle pump had been applied, I was acquiring spots on my face, and felt both poisoned and suffocated. It seemed unfairly soon to be mowed down by Africa. I must have been a tasty sight in my rumpled and sweaty cotton dress, my fisherman's hat, limping and frenzied. C. took this all with ease and apparently with pleasure. He asked me to stay at his house; he asked if I would like to go for the weekend to friends in the bush, he sent me off with his driver to buy shoes.

The shoes were a pair of men's sandals, with crêpe rubber soles, made by Bata, coarse, ugly, comfortable and costing $10. I keep noting the prices because they so astonish me; but I suppose one is paying for the transport, not the object. I got a pair of men's cotton khaki socks, equally repellent, and a pair of men's khaki trousers and shirt; and am now equipped with the clothing that the blacks buy, if they have the money.

C.'s house is a bungalow at the edge of town, darkened and cool, with the impersonal comfort of bachelors' quarters, a view over near hills topped with feathery pepper trees, and my own bathroom. After lunch we separated for the chloroformed sleep which strikes one down in this climate. In the late afternoon we set off for M'Balmayo.

This is Conrad's Africa, not the one I had longed for, but authentic. The road was bad and thick with dust; when passing the few cars, we rolled up the windows fast, so as not to choke on the floating red cloud. There were villages—a straggle of shacks—at the edge of the road, with jungle behind. The trees are immensely tall and skinny, like all jungle trees, and no one knows the names of any of them. I recognized only what I took to be ceiba. This pushing, twisting, grappling mass of vines, trunks, bushes is as ominous as prison walls. The blacks drifted around their villages and along the road, dressed in faded calico; bathed in stagnant jungle pools; chatted. One could not see how they lived. (C. has explained to me that I must not say *nègre*, which is an offensive word here; one speaks of *les blancs* and *les noirs*, the acceptable usage.)

Conversation in the car: C. has been here fourteen years and is addicted to Africa. Worked for years at the R. and W. King station in M'Balmayo. Says nothing about own past or background; natural reserve which is not snubbing or paralysing as the English can be. Immediate sense of his being very sane, very wise, very tolerant.

He says (remembered in a jumble): In Africa you have to know how to play bridge, a life saver; there is no conversation and since one cannot always read, one must find some means of being with others painlessly. I imagine they all know each other both too well and too little, like jailmates. American Embassy is second biggest building in Yaoundé; Americans contriving their usual golden ghetto; Embassy and its dependent houses divided into flats (nice-looking) for staff. Though wood is the main visible product of Cameroun, and everyone else has locally made furniture, they have shipped from the U.S. every piece of their furniture, including for the least of secretaries. Also their food. They give some official parties where plainly they are unhappy; but what they do is stick together, always. Hardly seen by other European residents. No Americans in Cameroun except them, and I think no U.S. business interests. The English diplomatic staff who wind up affairs of British Cameroun are two people. Size and grandeur of U.S. outfit produces wry, jeering distaste.

France gives large subsidy to Cameroun. Why? French still here, were never landowners or farmers. Civil Servants, military, traders, professional men. All went easily in granting independence—I should say because no French financial interests harmed. Compare with the muck of Algeria.

Local product at this season is peanuts; traders buy from natives;

small traders go from village to village, then sell to bigger trading company. R. and W. King has outposts and travellers. Women cultivate peanut crop, simplest primitive agriculture. R. and W. King imports anything anyone wants and can pay for.

President Ahidjo has nine cars (very little road to use them on). Lives in palace of French Governor-General; lovely tropical kind of White House. Formerly avenue lined with fine trees; now cut down (so you can see the splendour) and avenue lined with those awful street lamps newly erected in London, neon band on a metal pole. There's a regular item in the national budget for graft. Seems sensible when one thinks of it, providing it's enforced. Graft inevitable, therefore allow for it but limit it.

Most discouraging; plenty of water and no place to swim. River through Yaoundé, forming lake; water filthy; can't use. Water always filthy (disease) or full of something that bites or eats you.

M'Balmayo; an opening in the bush and not a big one. The entrance to the home of C.'s friends is just behind the gas station; squalid. Immediately changes, after coming through their gate. A low small white house, with a living room that reminds me of Cuernavaca; beams, a fireplace (incredible; when used?), sofas, basket chairs, nice plain dark wood tables, messed with books, bits and pieces; evident signs of taste. No electricity, shower is a bucket with holes in the bottom. Brilliant, simple object available in local hardware stores; a string releases a shutter over the holes; the bucket goes up and down, to be filled, on a pulley.

The Kolars have a green lawn, fenced in, and a big tree for shade (of the amate species I think.) Their servants—cook and boy—live in a little house behind theirs. It is primitive, attractive, and comfortable. The Kolars see no charm in it.

Their story: they are in their early thirties, Czech refugees. She looks like a Parisienne, small, slender, well-built, golden skin, pretty face, chic high hair-do, blonde peroxided hair, good makeup. She was wearing white tennis shorts and shirt as she keeps her body in shape with great care, during the exile here—exercise and sunbathing (heroic act to go voluntarily into the furnace). He is tall, romantic dark good looks, fashionably dressed in the sort of clothes men wear along the Mediterranean, pastel-colour linen trousers and matching sport shirt. They would fit into the international smart set anywhere in Europe, by appearance.

He escaped from Czecho about twelve years ago—they have been in Africa twelve years—by holding up a Czech airliner in mid-flight and forcing the pilot to land it in France. She married a mutual friend, a foreigner, purely as a form, in order to get out and join him; that first chaste marriage annulled. They are both devout Roman Catholics.

They grew up under the Nazi occupation of Czecho. By birth both of them (I sense) were well-off upper middle class. Instead of leading that sort of life—Aya would have studied art or music or done nothing much, like a pretty young lady; Jean would have gone to university, probably abroad—the Germans fixed things differently. The Czechs, it is to be remembered, were regarded as a slave race and ultimately were to be sterilized into extinction; Czecho was to become part of the Greater Reich. So this slave race, when young and under German domination, was not allowed to enjoy higher education and all had to learn a useful trade. I don't know what Jean did; Aya became a pharmacist, and this is the first good turn I ever heard of the Nazis doing for anyone.

Because now, they own the pharmacy in M'Balmayo; Aya is the technician and Jean manages the business. There are no local doctors; Aya practically operates as one. Amazingly, this tiny shack of a shop, in the African bush, provides them so rich a living that they can spend half the year in Paris, where they have a flat. Jean is a writer; he sold his first novel, in French, to the movies. That windfall is allowing them to build a house in Corsica. But the pharmacy is the gold mine. The reason for this economic miracle is the blacks' passion for medicines.

They have no children and seem perfectly suited to each other.

We sat in the garden and drank whisky and soda. I can hardly swallow anything, and look as if suffering from hunger oedema. Jean's conversation at first startled me; my main impression was that a man so young could hardly talk such trite die-hard Tory stuff. Then I began to think what he knew of the world: the Nazi occupation of his country, and a lack of heroic resistance to it by his people; the Communist occupation and again a lack of resistance; and his escape from that into postwar France where democracy can hardly have been said to shine at its brightest. I keep forgetting the limitations and impoverishment of the experience of the young, especially the Central European young. When you think of it, it is amazing that they can believe in anything, considering what they have seen, none of which was likely to arouse faith. It is not, on the other hand, surprising that these two, who are intelligent and concerned people, should have put their faith where it is safe, because it cannot be disproved, and has a quality of timelessness: in the doctrine and ritual of the Catholic religion.

Both Jean and Aya have had Africa; they are sick to death of it. Though full of contempt for the blacks, intellectually, they get on with the blacks easily and nicely, in practice. They have become French citizens and have the love of the converted or the adopted; great reverence for France as "civilization." They consider the white race infinitely superior, and think all the blacks will do on their own is destroy whatever civilization the whites brought them, and revert to their natural savagery. I have no impression that the whites have brought much civilization myself; I feel the whites have brought a certain number of modern conveniences for themselves, have restrained the blacks from a certain amount of mayhem, again for white safety and comfort; and have made money. The missionaries are something else; their object has not been to make money, but I am suspicious of them, mainly because I look at our white world and cannot see that nearly 2,000 years of Christianity has cured our savagery. So it seems conceited to foist off our notions of religion, which we have never practised, on to people whose savagery is after all disorganized, personal and small-scale compared to ours. Missionary schools and hospitals are another matter.

Jean wanted to know about books and writers; Aya about fashions, plays, the Twist. My memory has really gone to pot. I can remember nothing about Europe, scarcely believe it exists; and find it so irrelevant to everything here that it has no interest.

These two are spellbinding when they talk local lore. None of us knows enough to speculate well, and one finds the mind turning ashy with large issues and generalizations. Thus I particularly remember their news on the blacks' passion for medicines. It seems that all the natives, who can afford it, take castor oil constantly and colonic irrigations three times a week. They showed me a picture of a colonic being given to a tiny baby by a large black woman: simple system, the woman spits water up the child's anus. The blacks adore injections, that feared hypodermic needle, and especially adore anything which gives a violent reaction—pain, swelling and fever.

Black medicine is mysterious; a boy was crushed between a wall and a truck, Aya and Jean gave him up for dead, too many broken bones, too much loss of blood. They wanted to take him to hospital (but the blacks do not like hospitals; they like buying their stuff at the pharmacy); his family carried the shattered and unconscious boy away and the witch doctor and herb woman got busy. The Kolars do not know what is done but believe it is herbs, leaves, applied to the body, and unimaginable concoctions to drink. Anyhow the boy returned, walking, in three months.

More: the blacks are all becoming drunkards. They used to drink a homemade beer; having more money they switched to cheap French (or Algerian?) red wine: *pinard,* as one says. With more money, to rum; the richest now drink whisky. They drink compulsively; having started a bottle it must be finished at one go.

The blacks begin their sex life at about the age of twelve. By twenty, young men are impotent and come to the pharmacy asking for aphrodisiacs. They also use native ones. A young man cannot marry because a wife costs 150,000 francs, a fortune. The result is that older men can afford a wife or wives. No woman is faithful; syphilis is general. If a man is caught as an adulterer, he must pay the injured husband a fee for the use of the deceitful wife: tribal courts attend to this. The blacks like children, and illegitimacy is no sin or shame, and the children mooch around contentedly in a general family huddle. It sounds rather nice and cosy

and easygoing. The syphilis part is no good though, and perhaps explains some of the deformity I have seen, bad eyes, etc.

The Kolars insist that the blacks have no real feelings of personal af-
fection, individual love, loyalty. They are attached to their family; they
belong in it and would be helpless without it. There are also family customs of hospitality, which put the kibosh forever on individual effort.
Any relative (and everyone must have dozens and dozens) can come and
park on a richer relative, gratis, thus literally eating him out of house
and home. No one may refuse this burden or burdens (if richer, more relatives settle in). For if you do refuse you are socially outcast, a swine in
the eyes of all; and also, if in need yourself one day, you would not find
a single helping hand. There is not much use in getting ahead, acquiring
the goods of this world, on the level of the average tribal black (maybe it
does not work like this in the higher echelons—a very thin slice of higher
echelon exists anyhow). The relatives will hear about prosperity all too
soon.

We ate dinner around a blazing fire, outdoors; glorious sausages and
rolls and pickles and potatoes roasted in the coals. I would not have believed, after the airless heat of the day—it is like being wrapped in a
damp blanket from top to toe and like being slugged—that a fire would
be possible; and not only that but a sweater over one's shoulders for the
part not exposed to the flames.

Tomtoms began to beat in the jungle. Very loud, very insistent, and
curiously frightening. I cannot describe their beat, which was varied;
sometimes it gave the impression of a voice screaming a warning and
sometimes of a voice mourning. The Kolars said it was just news being
sent around; a wedding, a funeral, whatever was going. The blacks talk
all day long, endlessly, to each other, about nothing: exact, trivial bits of
information. At night, they continue to do so with drums. I see the point,
though. If any country could make people frantic to keep in touch, it's
this one. You sense that the land is hostile and wants no one on it; it feels
dark all the time. A kind of panic must be inborn, and people usually nat-

ter when afraid—until the point where fear is so great that it produces choked silence.

I should say at once and get it over with that I hate mosquito nets, both for themselves and for what they imply. And dread wriggling myself somehow inside and somehow tucked in and then, hot and stifled, realizing, in the dark, that something else is in with me—what?—a spider, an unknown flying or crawling insect, the insomnia-making mosquito? That's my first and last report on mosquito nets; otherwise I'd talk of them daily.

January 28: This is the 9th Annual World Day of the Lepers. I saw a notice to that effect in the Yaoundé post office, and Jean knows all about it. There is a handy Leprosarium; Africa apparently swarms with these wretched people. At 9.30 a.m.—which is late in the morning—we arrived at the leper colony. We turned off the main dust road on to a dust track and after a few minutes were in a small clearing in the bush. Around a central dust square, the lepers have their houses, square mud shacks with thatched roofs, crumbling. I think there were twenty such huts in all, though I went into a state of shock at the beginning and failed to see well throughout. We had missed the Mayor and other notables (who can they have been?) who made speeches in honour of the day; no one was left except the resident lepers and their visiting families. Apart from small children, everyone was drunk, cheerful to roaring.

Aya wore high-heeled white sandals and a pretty sleeveless cotton bouffant dress, suitable for a garden party. Jean and she know many lepers well; they are clients of the pharmacy. (Lepers move about freely; no quarantine.) My hosts called greetings and shook hands. I was filled with a despicable cowardice; had worn my khaki socks, to keep my feet protected, and now could not touch anyone. I smiled and smiled, it must have looked like a jack o'lantern afflicted with the horrors, and bowed and began to feel that I was not really here, some disembodied part of me was moving around this fearfully hot and abominably smelling place. The lepers were in high spirits, and their visiting families showed no signs of disgust, dismay, nerves (contagion); they might have been at a party or reunion in a normal village.

The band sat in the shade of some matting held up on poles; four musicians as I remember. (No good going on with how blurred it all is.) Their instruments were hollowed-out sections of tree trunk, made into drums, and a small home-made wooden xylophone. On these, they beat such drumming as I have never heard, every sound different, very fast, very complex. (The musicians were tight too.) The special feature was that some of them had no fingers at all, but only stumps of thumbs; one, I seem to think, beat with the stumps of his wrists, being handless.

To this wild music, in the glare of this sun (veiled always in the oppressive white sky, but still bright and boiling), the leper ladies danced. The Grand Guignol never thought up anything like this. They were dancing the Twist. So here is where it comes from, traced to the source. They do it of course far better than the half-witted whites who now revel in it, and their music is infinitely better and more compulsive. The motion is the same, except that they also writhe and shake their upper bodies, when so inclined. They scream, howl, laugh, jerk, twist. They danced alone, facing us, the newcomers, *les blancs,* the audience.

There were old women, hags—no adequate word exists that I know of—with rouge dabbed in flat brilliant red circles on their cheeks, beat-up straw hats on their shaved black fuzz, and the shapeless dirty printed calico dresses which must be the missionaries' legacy to African womanhood. Naked under these dresses, obviously; long flat breasts could be seen to bounce and flap beneath the clothes; when they turned round the protuberant native buttocks squirmed—but the buttocks look hard as iron unlike the breasts. Toothless mouths opened to shriek. They were as drunk as skunks. I could not look closely enough to see how leprosy had affected them, except for the too obvious ones—those without noses, just holes to draw breath in.

There were also little girls, dancing in this awful gathering. I saw no signs of disease on them; either they were visitors, or uninfected children of lepers. One little girl was lovely; I think she was four years old, round face, baby fat arms, tiny turquoises in her ears, a narrow blue ribbon tied around her shaved head and a short blue dress, a proper western kiddie's dress. She danced the Twist faultlessly, deadpan, torso steady, not sweating, solemn, and competent.

I felt faint from the smell, aside from the sight. Jean pointed out several men with a withered stump instead of a foot; more without hands, noses. I think these must all have been arrested cases, though I don't know, but I saw no sores, bandages, blood; and no leonine faces (at what stage does that occur?).

Beyond the dancers, arrayed in an impressive row on the ground, were about eighty bottles of red wine—for continuing the celebration. Jean said they would drink, eat and dance themselves into unconsciousness, as the day wore on. But if you have leprosy, my God what could be better than to dance and drink oneself into unconsciousness as often as possible? I very much hope that charitable funds, contributed throughout the world for the care of lepers, went into buying the booze.

Wringing wet (I was), we left. There is no moving air; even in the car the false wind is hot. I thought that I smelled myself now, and smelled as the blacks do. I spoke of this, still deeply ashamed. It seems at once sissy and inhuman to be so violently affected. Aya and Jean said one never got used to it; you just put up with it, learned control or something. I said that if they smelled so revolting to us, it stood to reason that we must smell in some disgusting way to them. Yes, said Aya, they say we have the "stale odour of corpses;" they find it sickening. This cheers me; fair's fair; I don't feel so mean-minded and soft. But I still think no one has yet sufficiently considered this aspect of the fact that all men are not brothers. All men, I think, could hardly be more different, alien, hostile; we are one biological genus, since any of us can cohabit with any of the opposite sex and produce offspring. But I don't believe we are of one species; the definition is too simple.

We drove from the lepers to the Catholics. A priest, called Père Moll, has created this world and it is imposing. He has been architect and chief builder (literally, physically) of a large brick church, a hospital, a convent, a girl's boarding school, and a day school. With such parishioners as he could collect, he cleared the jungle himself, and goes on doing so now, for their crops. It is a little kingdom, seized from the jungle, and created by will and sweat.

Mass was taking place; we stood at the door of the more than half empty church. Females on one side, with their heads properly covered; males on the other, properly dressed in shirts and long trousers. The choir was nice. Père Moll, invisible at that distance, preached the sermon which I made out vaguely through the echoes: he was telling them some story from the life of Christ and drawing a moral. It sounded rather like the lecturing I remember from Girl Scout days, but with an added, supernatural sanction. I am allergic to church-going when I can understand the words, so Jean and I moved off to the priest's quarters, with Aya and C. coming after us.

They made themselves at home in the shabby little room that Père Moll and his adjutant priest use for home. It was furnished with a few worn leather chairs, a table with a dusty lace doily, and magazines, photographs of something religious on the walls. No one could suggest that these men live in luxury.

The adjutant priest, a big, stout, red-faced, quiet, beaming Dutchman, came in. They wear white robes and sandals and topees; I do not know what their order is. He was teased by my friends, who are on terms of great intimacy with the two priests and call them *"tu;"* what was he doing ambling around, not working on a Sunday morning, and furthermore joining us in a drink (which the Kolars had ordered, without ceremony, from the priests' affable black boy). He had been taking mass since 6 a.m. and had been up before then; now Père Moll arrived, High Mass being over.

Père Moll is tall, lean to emaciation, with sunken cheeks and a beautiful vertical line down them, very bright grey eyes, thick, wiry, short-cut grey hair. He is a handsome man, aged fifty and an Alsatian peasant. He must be made of solid muscle and is unlike any priest I have ever before seen; his most striking quality is his tough maleness. The conversation was entirely joking; Père Moll's Alsatian accent is a treat. I am perplexed by the clergy; do not know the right tone; and besides I now feel so rotten that I could hardly be good company with anyone. We drank whisky and soda (surely madness in this heat), and departed. That evening the two priests were to come to the Czechs' house, as usual, for their weekly bridge game.

After a delicious lunch, we separated for naps; I fell into a dazed sick heavy sleep. It was cool in the late afternoon, and again we sat under the tree, chatting. Jean is too dogmatic for me; this is because I am dogmatic myself. I have a sudden notion of why history is such a mess: humans do not live long enough. We only learn from experience and have no time to use it in a continuous and sensible way. Thus I know the thirties and forties of this century, but have only been peeking at the fifties and sixties. Jean starts where I leave off. Naturally our conclusions, based on our experiences, are radically different. It is as if the human race was constantly making new road maps, unable to guide itself due to changing directions. Jean has given up hope for his country and his countrymen, finally, since the behaviour of Czecho during the Hungarian revolt in 1956. C. does not speak of himself at all; I have no idea where he came from, what his life was before Africa; and why Africa and the career of a trader. He listens marvellously, the sort of listener who makes everyone talk better and whose laugh is a reward.

We waited for the priests and a last drink before driving back to Yaoundé. The natives had told Jean of a gorilla, living nearby (place-names mean nothing to me) in the jungle. The said gorilla had kidnapped two girls, at different times. The first was dead when found, the second lived long enough to say that the gorilla had been *"très tendre,"* had built her a nest in the trees and brought her bananas, but he "broke her" and she died of it. I said flatly that I did not believe it; Jean believes it absolutely. I said what nonsense; it's against nature. Père Moll, grave for once, said, *"C'est contre tout."* (Did he mean God's plan?) Jean insisted. (N.B. Months later, I asked Solly Zuckerman about this. He roared with laughter. "Do you know how big a gorilla is?" He held up his pointer finger. "A gorilla has hardly enough energy for a lady gorilla, let alone strange black girls.")

Père Moll began talking of medicine and the blacks. Their stories are unlimited. The blacks, for unknown reasons, believe that gasoline is a splendid cure-all, taken internally. A boy asked Père Moll's permission to give some gasoline to a man with fever. Père Moll naturally refused. The boy stole it; the sick man swallowed it happily and died. This apparently is not infrequent.

Schweitzer is not regarded locally as a hero and great thinker. His medicine is thought to be backward and his life not unique, or saintly, but only highly publicized. The feeling is that others, unknown and unsung, do better and harder jobs.

Jean showed me an elephant's tooth; I wish I had seen more of their trinkets. I cannot judge weight and size but I'd say this one tooth weighed at least three pounds and was four inches square. It made me realize the size of elephants more than anything else has.

They all advise me to go north, where there are wild animals and real natives, the naked pagans, the Kirdis.

In the darkness one cannot see the dust on the road, but only choke on it. C. and I dined and talked a bit. He knows a great deal about the blacks, from observation, but says no white understands them. He himself has an infinite capacity for patience, and treats the blacks with quiet, slow good humour. I think he is a man who does not judge; combined with intelligence and gaiety, this makes a rare creature.

In the night, the sickness, which has been building in me from my first day in Africa, exploded like a fierce intestinal storm. I have decided to call it ptomaine poisoning, for the comfort of a known name and known ailment, but it passes in violence any previous attack. Pain, aches throughout, insides turned to water, sleepless night. I am in despair with myself; imagine caving in, so quickly. Am I simply not going to be up to Africa, appalled by the heat, smells, dirt, and now sick?

January 29: Up at dawn, no breakfast, do not dare even drink water, since I have to sit on the plane to Garua for a couple of hours. C. saw me off and found another R. and W. King representative, bearded, stout, young, a travelling inspector or some such, at the airport; consigned me to him as a precious package. Plane journey hot, unpleasant with muffled thunder in my stomach and shooting pains. The airport at Garua is modern and elegant, a false front for the town. There is even a cement highway from the airport to the centre. But once in Garua, Africa has come closer than at Yaoundé.

There is one hotel, a collection of *bucaroos* (the native hut—round, thatched roof) improved for European use which is to say with cement floors, screens on the windows, and a bathroom. The huts are dirty, the central building—eating place, kitchen, and lounge—is dirty; and there was no room. I half reclined in the shaded lounge from morning until about 2 p.m. longing for a bed or death. At last the proprietor, a loud, bullying-to-blacks, smarmy-to-whites, mixed-up character gave me a bucaroo. Huge spider in the loo, which loo fills by pouring water into it from a pitcher; cement floor under shower slimy; all vile, all stifling, but a bed.

Now R. and W. King again enters my life; I regard that company as guardian angel and owe them, it, undying gratitude. The local manager, a fair slender young man, not at all C.'s type, called on me; very kind, indecisive, solemn. The problem was to rent a car to go farther north, to Waza, the game park, and to the hill villages of the Kirdis. I called on the game warden, large easygoing man whose house looks as if he was moving a collection of secondhand furniture either out or in; it occurs to me that the French do not *live* in these parts of Africa, no matter how long they actually do live here. They do not settle, take trouble, own, beautify; they do not send down roots. They are all going back one day to France.

The game warden had a panther, aged one and a half months, as a kitten. It was adorable, friendly, soft, cuddly, and with a blue eye that warned how dangerous this little house pet was going to become. In his dusty backyard, he has a small private zoo ranging from crocodiles to antelopes. The natives know he loves animals and bring them for sale.

The game warden said he was going to Waza himself tomorrow and would see me there, he sketched out a journey for me, and though I waited hopefully for him to offer me a ride, he did not do so. (C. was an exception.) Though polite and helpful, I doubt if the French are any cosier here than in France; hardly cosy to each other; and never ones to say come and have dinner, or come along on the trip.

January 30: Half the day spent on acquiring a car. Finally, I had to take what I can get (three are available); a huge Citroën sedan, worth its weight in gold obviously. In the course of this hot and rather muddled dickering, I saw Garua: two short streets of shops and warehouses, and a native village enclosed behind high red adobe walls, with pointed thatched roofs showing above the wall. Very handsome and absolutely off limits. Natives sell vegetables, fruits, odds and ends, alongside this wall. The blacks here are a new kind, and a pleasure; the Fulbé (Fulani) is the predominant tribe; they are Moslems and must have Arab blood, judging from their features. They are a handsome race, with smaller noses and mouths and larger eyes than the coastal blacks. The men wear white, striped or coloured *djellibahs* and skull caps, the women wear a flowing *pagne,* like a sari, in brilliant printed cotton, with a gold ring through one nostril. The clothes that absolutely do not suit the blacks, and degrade them—as bad cheap copies are always degrading—are white western clothes. The only ones who look right in anything belonging to us are the boys and young men, naked except for ragged khaki shorts.

The river here is navigable during the rainy season and Garua is a port; the river is now a wide shallow stream flowing between sandbanks, very picture-book tropics. Peanuts and cotton are shipped from here. I spent some time at the R. and W. King office, listening to the peanut business being transacted. A notable (i.e. rich man) or chief arrives, very large and very stout (are these certain signs of wealth and power?), wearing wonderful garments—one chief looked like a miraculous male bride, in immense white embroidered robes and a beautiful turban, made of a fine white material with white design, which was the size of a pumpkin and intricately wrapped on his head. He had delicate hands, a voice of girlish softness and shyness, a café-au-lait face, and I took him to be about seventy years of age. He was in his forties, a chief and a member of parliament. These gentlemen sat down, in turn, and talked to the R. and W. King manager who adapted his manner to theirs; thus jocose with one, quiet and formal with another; but always in perfect humour and with no sign of impatience, seeming to enjoy the visit and the deal, as they did.

They were discussing the price of peanuts and the amount each notable would guarantee to have delivered to the R. and W. King warehouses. The price seemed to be open to discussion, and the amount (in tons, in what?) equally so. I inferred that these great men got the order; their underlings then went from village to village and collected and delivered the goods. I would like to know what the humble grower got out of the deal, finally; and how the workers (the wives) were rewarded, if at all. For the first time in my life, it occurred to me that there was glamour in business; previously I had only thought business was a dreary way to make money.

The R. and W. King warehouses covered sand dunes, mountains, of fresh shelled peanuts. Impossible to believe; the source of peanut butter, American childhood's pet fattener. Peanuts look lovely in pale beige drifts like that, and smell lovely too. Blacks were sweeping the peanuts back up into a tighter space. The highest peanut-dune must have been twenty feet high. Being a trader now seems to me a romantic life. One of them told me about buying the pagnes, the printed dress material which comes in a regulation length, so that each dress, or sari, is a completed pattern with a border of solid colour around the design. It is necessary to know what next year's fashion in pagnes will be. How this can be discovered, I am unable to guess. One year the black ladies will prefer blue to any other shade, or red or purple; it changes. Sometimes birds and leaves, sometimes flowers, sometimes a rather abstract design find more favour. The trader, who is an importer as well as exporter, has to be on his toes to lure the ladies' fancy. What fun. Buying for Neimann Marcus or Selfridge's, on the other hand, would seem to me a crashing bore.

I had to send a cable home, giving my future address; I feel that I have been far off and lost for months; you might think I was hiking through really darkest Africa in Livingstone's time. The post office was crowded, as usual, and the black petty bureaucrats have adopted the French manner in post offices; to wit, nasty. They are just as rude as the French, whom one always wants to murder as they write away with their squeaking pens and pale ink, but they are far less efficient. Somewhere in the post office a white always lurks, tactful and rarely seen, to keep this inferior machinery running at all. The black clerk could not find out in what country London was located. I suggested *Grande Bretagne*. He was angry and said sullenly, *"Mais oui. Londres est très connu."* Then he began to read slowly down the long long line of microscopic print, the names of all the countries in the world. I wanted to help, impatient, and again harassed by the smell of my black brethren all around me.

The King manager restrained me, with a smile, not a word. The unwritten law is not to offend by impatience, which impatience is the clearest possible way of saying: you are a fool. Impatience is the emotion that comes most easily and is hardest to govern. Also, one must not laugh at incompetence or bone-headedness; one must wait. Finally the clerk located London; it took forty-five minutes to send a cable of ten words.

Turning away from the counter, I nearly fell over a leper who was crouching by me on the floor, one stump of leg bound with a bloody bandage. He raised his hand for alms, a hand without fingers, a ridged stump, half healed, half bleeding. You stick a coin in a ridge, trying not to look or touch. It is tragic and revolting. *"Un lèpre,"* said the King manager. *"Il y en a toujours dans les bureaux de poste."*

By three o'clock in the afternoon, I was ready to go. An R. and W. King driver had produced a friend off the street to be my driver, no one knew him nor knew whether he could drive (we are casual hereabouts). He is a slender, fine-looking, fine-featured, pale brown Fulani youth, wearing a clean apricot-coloured djellibah and a little embroidered round orange cap. No painful body odour, too good to be true. The working of the Citroën, which I also do not know, was explained to him; he drove once round the block with the garage-owner; and we were off.

The road gave out almost immediately and became dust ruts and rocks. It was hot to begin with and got hotter. This is a different kind of heat: dry, and worse. Sweat evaporates quickly, my skin feels as if it were cracking, tight and scalded. After a while, the heat seems to come from inside.

Ibrahim is a good driver and reserved; he sits silent in front and chews a native gum, which he must swallow eventually; I have not seen him spit but occasionally have seen him gnaw off something invisible. I tried to make conversation; having thought he was seventeen, I learn that he is twenty-three, married, and has a child. That is all I can find out about him. I think he speaks very little French, aside from being a non-talker. We eat dust.

I do feel that I am in Africa now, and it is oppressive. The sky is higher here and a very pale blue, cloudless. One cannot see far distances (what am I dreaming of? visions from a mountain top?) but what one sees is arid emptiness, with dead yellow grass and some scrub trees. We pass native villages, walled with adobe or with rush mats, the pointed thatched roofs showing. (Are they walled to keep out wild animals at night?) Natives roam about near them, on the road, across this uninviting country. The adults are half naked, the children naked. From the rear it is impossible to tell a man and woman apart; equally tall, square-shouldered, narrow-hipped, shaved heads. The women wear a dirty dark-coloured sarong, the size of a small bath towel, the men are variously covered. Nose rings now appear; bullet heads, flat noses, big mouths; not Fulanis. The people are very thin, often with swollen bellies. Breasts are soon gone; the old women have perfectly flat pieces of skin hanging on their chests, sometimes there is nothing of a breast except a jutting nipple. Ruptured navels make their ugly bump on all the children's bellies. Everyone has flat feet; so much for the myth, derived partly from Pocahontas, partly from Isadora Duncan, of bare feet, never cramped by shoes, growing beautiful and high-arched. On the other hand these people can walk on anything without pain and walk endlessly, which is again confusing. Perhaps, as in all else, Africans are different; I don't recall that the shoeless Chinese peasants were flat-footed.

The children are charming and dark skin always looks more alive and healthier than white but as to features and body, no one could say this is a beautiful race. Still, they give an impression—which I cannot remember anywhere else on my travels—of being at ease, no that's not right: of taking life by the minute as it comes, without anxiety. What am I trying to say? That, if they have enough to eat, I think they are much better off as they are than they will be if our civilization gets hold of them.

The sunset is red across an immense sky. The little mountains and huge massed boulders of volcanic rock are black against the light. Twinkling fires shine in the villages. Towards Marua, the rocks take on strange shapes—a great ape god, a Buddha—and there is no sound except the car and no one to be seen. I feel that man is a brief event on this continent; no place has ever felt older to me, less touched or affected by the human race. But the blacks and the wild animals belong here. In the mud huts that any rain will wash away, or behind their mat walls that any wind will knock down, the blacks have lasted and know their place in the land, and fit. No one else does; and I doubt if civilization, our kind, ever will.

January 31: Last night, the R. and W. King young man (again different from my previous guardians; more like a charming Etonian who chose hardship) led me to the local inn; modern bucaroos, very fresh and swank. Brand new too, and I wonder what they are here for. A great pleasure, after that slum in Garua. The burning dry heat of the day is followed by a too cold night; this is not a climate in which you can win. It is also cold in the early morning; gets light at 6.15 a.m.

To note: it takes time, great determination and a lot of money to escape civilization. To note further: there, one is really alone. This has nothing to do with the familiar being alone—lighting on a hotel in a strange city or village in Europe, travelling by oneself, having no friends, working, reading, looking. This is solitude: the difference and distance between me and these blacks is too great to cross; it almost makes one feel blind and deaf, so complete is the isolation.

I bought an assortment (scant and untempting) of tinned foods, for Waza, where you feed yourself, and Ibrahim and I set off. The heat was now on the way to becoming intense, at about 9 a.m. We drove through the usual dust, over the usual road; but the Citroën is a beautifully sprung car and though I do not think its life will be long, it cushions one well. Driving is rather like riding a roller-coaster, hour after hour. Due to heat or dust or something, I am already getting blasé about the remote ancient life of these people in their villages. Nothing about them dismays me except their smell. Otherwise I regard them as right and at home—and a world apart, which I am no more apt to enter than I am apt to enter the domain of wild animals.

Around 1 p.m., we got to the back gate of the Waza game reserve. First sight, inside the park, was two Kirdi women, as tall as very tall men, looking like men except for the extraneous pendulous breasts, tattooed, tending goats. Then we began to see birds and animals; a great flock of crested cranes, all standing in the same way and facing the same direction, like a division at ease. After this, I got my first glimpse of giraffes; everything is not as foreseen. The giraffes here are pale, creamy, scarcely marked, and they move like shadows among the thorn trees. They are very shy and yet inquisitive. Above a thorn tree, a head turns towards the noise of the car; ears out, the large heavily lashed eyes bewildered, the mouth like the toothless old. They look the gentlest of animals and the strangest. Their kick, with the front feet, is apparently fatal, but is only used for self defence. Lions attack young giraffes. Judging from the glimpses I got of them, family life means a lot to giraffes. They have delicious gestures, rubbing their necks tenderly together, seeming to kiss; and the young ones run—in that adorable lolloping way—to Mum, when a noise disturbs them.

There were huge herds of antelope; don't know their names; some with brown faces, some white and black. Male and female keep company.

A family of warthogs, father, mother and three young, galloped across the road with their tails erect as radio antennae. They are very neatly formed and look like much bigger animals, like boar perhaps; except their smooth haunches are like toy horses. Now more giraffe and crushing heat. The animals move in the blazing midday sun to get water. One cannot see far; this is tree and brush country—not jungle, bush—a flat land, with a high pale blue burning sky.

The *campement* for visitors to the game park is made of bucaroos, as usual, and a communal dining room. Also communal toilet for several bucaroos, which does not work. Very primitive altogether, but on a height and therefore catches a slight breeze. You take your tinned food to the dining room and a cheerful and incompetent black opens the tins and heats whatever is inside to a lukewarm temperature. The only reason to eat is from necessity, to keep up one's strength as we always say of drink; I long for iced water.

After the usual stunned afternoon sleep, I set out with Ibrahim and a Mandara tribesman called Ali. Ali's people were a fisherman tribe on Lake Tchad; I don't know how Ali got down this way on to dry land, but consider it a mistake. He is tall, filthy, his whole face lined with tattooed scars, his eyes red, wearing very short blue shorts, a singlet and a black velvet cap like Nehru's white one. At 5 p.m., after failing to find anything much on the tracks (which are no pleasure to ride, and the heat is still suffocating) Ali went off, leaving me and Ibrahim under a tree, beside a pond, and near some enormous elephant droppings. We could hear the elephants tearing down trees for their dinner, in the bush. Ali reappeared about half an hour later and suggested that I follow him on foot, into that high bush, to look at a herd of six elephants, which was feeding some six kilometres away. I doubt if he knows anything about distance; but I know that night falls at 6 p.m. I said *quelle bêtise*, crossly, and thought really the French were daft, why didn't they train their guides better.

On the way back to the *campement* we saw a hunting lioness, moving fast and flat through the long grass; it was the same tawny sunburned colour as the grass and looked extremely dangerous. Ali was so excited that he screamed in a high voice, whereupon the lioness made off.

Now that it is somewhat cooler (or perhaps now that the lions are hunting), the animals are on the move. I saw running giraffes, a slow long rocking movement of shapes among the trees; running gazelle, too lovely for words, like flying. Families of warthogs were galloping away as if on some private racetrack. Occasionally we cross mountainous elephant droppings and torn trees. Jackals look like dogs and run the same way. There were two amazing birds, white and black bodies, bigger than storks, with red beaks and red, yellow, and blue marking about their eyes. "What are those birds, Ali?" "Birds," said he. I could not believe that the anthills really were anthills, though they had to be, but they were much bigger, higher, and solider than I had imagined, so I asked Ali what they were, too. "They have always been like that," he answered. I'm not going to learn much nature lore from him.

This reserve is claustrophobic, and not my dream picture of how the animals live in Africa. The bush creeps up to the track, the animals disappear into it. Sense of tremendous goings-on, invisible and silent, hidden by the high grass. The heat is like a punishment.

My intestinal tract is cause for complaint, if that's the source of the trouble. Starting to swell again, from the feet up. Tired and disappointed. I feel as if there were a barrier like glass between me and Africa; I have not found whatever it is that I am seeking.

February 1: Six other whites, French people, are staying here. I saw them last night in the communal dining room. They are very gay, on holiday from whatever their city jobs are. The shops in towns are still owned and run by whites, and there is always a white in the background, at the garages, hotels, in the government, tactfully holding together such civilization (oh that loose word) as exists. These people might be tradesmen or civil servants, with their wives. Weirdly dressed, according to my preconceptions from movies and books; ladies in tiny shorts, gents in city shoes and bits and pieces of outdoor clothing—more like beachwear than animal-watching. They are well equipped with food, as for an extended picnic.

It is not to be imagined that whites, because so few and far between, fall upon each other, especially upon strangers, with cries of welcome and delight. The French party did not notice me and I did not think it correct to make overtures.

I spoke to the game warden, who was dining well and alone, about Ali; very affably of course, but pointing out that it was hardly sound to suggest venturing into the bush, unarmed, after elephants. I had read that in the game parks in East Africa one was never allowed to get out of one's car, or go off the track without permission. The car smell (petrol, oil) muffles the human smell and the animals have not yet put two and two together; also one can get away quick in a car. The game warden said, "Oh no, one must always have confidence in the guides." (*"Il faut toujours faire confiance aux pisteurs."*) "They know the animals well, and the terrain. You are safe with them." I still did not agree with this, but felt I was being cowardly, and after all the game warden must know his business.

This morning, Ali and Ibrahim turned up an hour late; Ali's fault; Ibrahim, left to himself, is a most reliable boy. We were too late to get to a mirador above a drinking pond, before dawn, to watch the elephants come for their morning splash. I was furious and Ibrahim was miserable; he had not slept all night, due to the bedbugs in Ali's hut. He looked dirty, unlike him, and very unhappy. We drove futilely, as the sun rose higher, and saw nothing; I was conscious of time lost and costly kilometres. We arrived at a dead end of track where another, older guide was setting off with three French people, a peroxided lady in peacock blue trousers and little white ballet slippers, two men just as oddly clad. Ali and their guide talked excitedly; Ali explained there were elephants in the bush, and urged me to follow. Filled with doubt, I tailed along behind.

The Frenchmen made jokes in their usual voices. I remembered two rules about proper bush behaviour: (1) Wear no bright colours. (2) Do not speak. Elephants have bad eyesight and are alleged to see nothing more than twenty feet away; but have fine hearing and an acute sense of smell. The older guide and Ali were both busy being very Red Indian, noting twigs, droppings, sifting dust to see how the wind blew. I thought them theatrical for our benefit. We walked single file deeper and deeper into the grass which was higher than my head. I doubted that this undertaking was well advised.

We heard a tree crash, some distance ahead, and Ali cavorted with excitement. On we went until we saw, at a reasonable distance, an enormous bull elephant silently eating the tasty top of a thorn tree. I focused my binoculars, had a good look and felt no urge whatever to proceed. The French, innocent and unafraid, city people to their ballet slippers and the toes of their pointed shoes, pushed on. I told Ali we would go back.

He led me on another track; I had lost all sense of direction as soon as we got into the bush; trees look alike, you see a few feet ahead of you on the narrow beaten path. I heard in the grass to my left a lion; have never heard one before, but knew at once what this snarling, coughing sound was. I was badly shocked and whispered to Ali, *"Un lion."* *"Oui,"* he said. *"Où?"* "Where?" when referring to a lion, is not the sort of question you expect from a game park guide; it did the exact opposite of inspire confidence. But it was not the lion that had frozen Ali and made his eyes roll: in front of us, some twenty yards away, silent as stone, stood elephants—we had come on a little clearing. There were two females and a big bull, motionless. Fortunately I did not see the two baby elephants behind the females, or my panic would have been greater.

I focused my binoculars with clumsy hands, terrified, and there sprang into view, far too close, an enormous still head, with small suspicious eyes under old drooping lids, looking into mine. The last thing in life I had ever wanted was to be face to face with elephants, on foot, in the bush, accompanied by an imbecile. Ali was desperately lighting matches and sifting dust; too late, I thought, if we are downwind they'd have charged us by now. The elephant fears no animal except man, with cause; and is incensed by the human smell. At this point there was a crunch to our right and behold, much nearer, a much bigger bull elephant was gently pulling off bits from a tree top with his trunk.

Ali, his eyes rolling, whispered, *"Beaucoup éléphant."* I was too alarmed to speak, but pushed him, to indicate that we should get a move on. He went ahead, walking fast and silently. I followed trying not to make a sound, and when he stopped, I raised my eyes from the path and saw that he had brought us, in a half circle, even closer to the elephants. The two baby elephants now all too visible. I was rooted to the spot with fear, an expression I have often read but never experienced. I was also beside myself with anger, furious with the game warden, furious with Ali; imagine being in this Charlie Chaplin situation of the greatest peril, because the whole lot of them were bloody fools. The elephants, again soundlessly, lifted their ears, which stood out like tremendous swaying leaves, and silently turned to face us.

Ali began to take me, respectfully, by the bottom, to urge me away, his eyes were wide, staring, his mouth open in shock. I slapped him smartly on the shoulder and hissed, *"Cours! Je te suis."* He ran, leaping on his huge flat feet, and I ran after him; I would not have believed that I could run so fast and so silently. I decided not to think about the lion in the grass; better just not to think of it. After some distance, Ali slowed down; we were still however in an odious fix, able to see nothing over the grass. *"Bon maintenant,"* Ali announced a bit breathlessly. It did not look *bon* to me.

We went on walking; the heat was the least of my concerns. Finally Ali came to a broad dust track, which he recognized. He stamped this with his bare foot, laughed, and said idiotically, *"D'accord."* I have never so wanted to hit anyone, but I never have hit anyone and it's too late to start. Ali now turned and said smugly, *"Ali bon type. Blanc veut voir éléphant. Ali trouve éléphant toujours. Toujours."* It seemed futile to point out that the elephants had found us, if anything; and that he was a menace to life and it would be a frosty day in Waza before I ventured into the bush with him again.

Ibrahim was waiting by the car. I said furiously that I was hot and wanted to go back to the *campement*. On the way Ali boasted of his exploits to Ibrahim while I sat behind, seething. We saw ostriches, an untidy weird bird, with an upper thigh like a ballet dancer and feet like high-laced black shoes. Their walk and run are prissy and feminine and incredibly fast. We stopped at a water hole to watch a tribe of brown antelope—there must have been several hundred—crowded together like sheep, horns and heads clear against the sky, queuing for their turn at a drink and a wash. The water hole was lined with drinking and wading and rolling bodies; when the occupants were finished they moved off, still in that close silent formation and were lost under the trees, while newcomers took their place. The organization and amity of this communal life was astonishing; the silence and the beauty were heart-lifting.

I saw a tree full of birds that looked like eagles, and a couple of grey monkeys; useless to ask Ali for nature lore; besides I was still too angry to talk to him. The heat had become intolerable, and I decided I'd had enough of Waza, French game parks were not my dish; I meant to look at animals with love, not in mortal terror, and hoped to find someone who would explain them to me. I paid Ali off, and told Ibrahim that we would leave after I had had some breakfast.

Left at 10 a.m. for Mora, the main town of the Kirdi country. The road climbs and is bad as always. Mora has a French resident, like a district commissioner I think, but it's a native town with a market, the Sultan's palace, and the small jammed dwellings of the blacks. The market was poor, main interest being the beads, which are brilliant, cheap (is there a great bead industry for black consumers?), and coveted by the Kirdi ladies who wear nothing else.

My pressing problem was to open a tin of ham for lunch, without a tin opener. We drove around to the Sultan's palace and found the old gentleman sitting in the street, under a tree outside the gateway to the royal compound. He sat on a chair surrounded by sons, ranging in age from naked pot-bellied babies of three to adolescents. The babies wore *gri-gris*, magic objects of some sort for warding off evil, in little leather pouches around their necks; otherwise they wore nothing; the youths wore trousers. The Sultan was robed and benign. One of his elder sons translated. (I think the multiple wife system must be fun for the children; a child is sure of having numerous little brothers and sisters of his own age to play with.)

The Sultan sent for a tinted photograph of himself, looking like a bad job done at the beginning of the century. Framed in gold. A memento of his journey to Paris. I asked politely if he liked Paris and he replied that he liked it better here. Did I not like best where I was born? Answer is no, and moreover I don't like any place permanently, but that was too complex. The Sultan ordered my tin of ham opened, having sent for a knife. Clasping my greasy lunch, I bade him farewell. He seemed a nice old man, and I think his people will hardly find themselves catapulted into the twentieth century under his rule. The local potentates—sultans, chiefs—are the absolute rulers of their surrounding tribes; this must be the last living sample of the Middle Ages.

On to Ondjila, a Kirdi village in the hills. A huge stalwart man of thirty-five is the chief of this tribe who live in specially small and tall round mud huts with thatched roofs, nestling in the rocks of the mountainside. The chief does not speak French but a fourteen-year-old brother does. The Chief is accustomed to showing *les blancs* his palace, for a tip. In the porch—a thatched loggia with mud benches down the sides—the fifteen wives of the chief sat doing bead-work. They buy the long strings of beads at the market and work them into fancy wear, for their necks and waists, their only clothing. The youngest wife looked about fourteen. The chief has eleven children thus far; he cannot have put his heart into the job. His mother was also there; the old women are the worst advertisement for primitive life as they all look shrivelled and shrunken and bitter. I haven't yet seen a happy old woman's face; same is not true of old men.

Each wife has a bedroom hut and two huts to store millet, her private granary or larder. The bedroom hut contains her bed, a smooth piece of wood with rounded edges, rather like a surfboard, which is raised by adobe bricks so that the head is higher than the feet. She also has a petrol tin for water, a stone for grinding millet and a little fireplace, very easy to make; two medium-sized stones are laid on the mud floor and that's the fireplace. No one has thought of a chimney. (Also the wheel was never thought of in these parts.) No clothes of course, no blanket. Presumably living conditions here are the best in the village; early Red Indians were sophisticated, artistic and luxurious in comparison.

The chief and a swarm of young brothers took me up to a hillside to see a stone house they had built (stone storage shack), their communal granary. Below this steep hill, the land dropped away to a cultivated valley. The chief made a sweeping gesture, his face alight with pride. His kingdom, worked by the women and children. Each year they have three months of feasting and parties; they then drink all the millet beer and have a lovely time. After that the women get to work again.

I asked the fourteen-year-old brother how long the chief had reigned; he misunderstood me and thought I'd asked how long chiefs had been reigning here. *"Depuis le commencement de Dieu,"* since the beginning of God, he said, amazed at my stupid question.

I gave the Chief 1,000 francs, having no smaller bill; I was nervous about tipping a king but he took it with grace and satisfaction.

Down the mountainside from them (these are small mountains, which look as if they were full size, the way a warthog looks like a boar) there is a missionary. I went to call on him, out of curiosity. The old Sultan in Mora is (by dress) a Moslem; I can see that Islam, which is so permissive about wives and so forgiving generally, if you just say your prayers, and warlike, would appeal to these people; but I cannot understand what Christianity could mean to them. The priest had just returned in his Citroën tin-lizzy from somewhere or other; he was a young bearded man, wearing khaki shorts and shirt and spectacles, and like Père Moll he is a new breed to me. All muscle, lean, tough, much more one's idea of an explorer than a priest. Père Sylvestre, he is called, and his order (name forgotten) stems from Provence which is also his home.

Père Sylvestre had built his house with his own hands, a bucaroo much better constructed than the blacks' are, though they have been making these round huts for centuries, and the priest only used his eyes and figured out improvements. He has a dispensary hut too, and his chapel, made of stone, with a tiny stained glass window; all his love and skill have been lavished on this chapel of which he is touchingly proud. He thinks that within ten years he may make a few converts.

He is bone poor, and alone, and when he finds he is going round the bend *(tournant en rond)*, he goes off to see some brother priests forty kilometres away—a long journey on these roads—and talks to them until he's sure of himself again; then returns to these pagans. He likes the pagans very much (and they like him); infinitely prefers them to Moslems, and says they have a deep religious sense and a unique god, whose name is the same word as for sky. He is learning the language from children, who all day long squat around his hut and stare at him. The language is of course not written; he writes it phonetically and hopes to master it in time. The language has no, repeat no, abstract words. I think it will take quite a bit more than ten years to convert these Kirdi. They've been managing without abstract words or ideas for untold centuries. Like everyone else, he practises medicine as much as he can; people in France send him gifts of money and he spends it on medicines. One could hardly go very wrong, there are no doctors anywhere around.

We talked at length; I will put down what I mainly remember, translating literally. "From the human point of view, we have no right to touch these people. From the supernatural point of view, it is our duty to teach them about Jesus Christ." "They are happy; they are not demanding; they do not want or need unnecessary things; they are familiar with their dead; they have much that we have lost." I cannot remember how we got on to the subject of women, perhaps through the chief's fifteen wives. I had been doing simple arithmetic and figured that if the chief was fair and spent a night with each he could visit each wife twice a month, which might not be adequate. The missionary doubted very much whether the chief satisfied his wives. "Do you believe that they occupy themselves with the pleasure of the woman? *Eh bien, moi, je trouve ça humainement dégoutant.* (Well, I find that humanly disgusting.)" I never thought to hear such words from a priest and was astounded. I also wondered if he imagined that all white men were sufficiently informed or concerned to occupy themselves with the pleasure of their women; and was startled to find that his anger on behalf of the women was greater than mine.

I felt more indignant about the heavy work the women do, while the gentlemen tend herds which isn't too bad, or loll. All the time we were talking, young girls and women passed downhill to a valley in front of his house and climbed laboriously back with large water jars on their heads. Does the female sway-back, which is universal, come from this; the young spine bent by these weights? The result is an ugly body, with a deep curve from shoulder to buttocks, and the stomach pushed out. The resultant walk—steady head and shoulders, swinging hips—is fine; but not the deformation of the back. Père Sylvestre said that the men, when choosing a woman, looked at her skin and her jewelry, not at her face and figure, "as with us." His pity for the women contradicted his saying that the Kirdis were happy. Though the men might well be happy as larks.

On the face of it, missionaries here are a doomed lot. They have been in Africa for over a hundred years and even if conversion to Christianity is merely a head count, I doubt that they are a roaring success. I wouldn't preach anything to the blacks, not anything at all. If they want our kind of medical care, it should be given to them, but ideally by trained black doctors, though that may disturb the Darwinian balance of their world and their lives. A child is born each year; the hardiest live. The survivors have to be strong enough to endure this appalling climate and land. Much better to teach the women birth control. But I think nothing will be taught or learned for a very long time, and I do not consider this a disaster by any means. Who are we to teach? Leave them alone is my cry; let them find their own answers. We cannot understand them and the answers we have found haven't been anything to cheer about, for look at us . . .

I had lunched in the priest's hut, off my ham and heavy bread bought at Mora. The priest gave me sacramental wine, all he had; it tasted like red ink but he did have cool water. (I travel with two bottles of Evian bumping beside me on the seat; their temperature is not quite suitable for hot water bottles but almost.) Now the chief appeared, Père Sylvestre said he expected him. Whenever Père Sylvestre returns from a journey the chief shows up to hear the news. The passion of the blacks for talk, gossip is understandable; they live entirely by word of mouth, and my imagination cannot grasp a life which never, generation after generation, needs the printed page. The radio is unknown and there are few travellers and their own trips are made on foot and limited. They do not visualize the whole of their country; Yaoundé would be another world; and of course nothing at all really exists beyond their own tribal land.

I gave the priest 1,000 francs for medicines; it seemed only right after giving the chief 1,000 francs which I hope he will spend on beads for wives. Ibrahim and I set off in the heat and dust. Ibrahim is growing thinner before my eyes.

The road to Mokolo, over the mountains, is a backbreaking surface and the view is the best yet. It is dark land, with outcroppings of volcanic rock and then the mountains start behaving well and merging and flowing into each other, and one can see a long way. There are little clumps of huts, stuck away on the hillsides. The Kirdis run out to raise their right arms high in a salute and/or to scream and laugh. They seem to have no pubic hair; they must be a generally un-hairy race, the women's legs and arms are smooth as are the men's faces. Black penises don't look naked, nor do female pudenda (on the contrary, very small and neat like little girls'). The women haul water and wood along the paths, but seem cheerful about it, and I doubt if they do more than the necessary each day. Men can be seen sitting or lying naked on rocks, at ease; time passes. This century has nothing to do with these people.

On the road, we saw a collection of European buildings; a church, a house, another big building that might have been a school, all very neat, gardened, made of stone. We stopped and immediately a white man and woman rushed out; they were in their forties I would think. German Swiss, and Protestant missionaries. The woman has been here five years, the man has spent ten years in Africa. They are very thin, very white, very ill-looking (really suffering ill), lined and dried: classical missionary appearance, from literature. When they came, they said, the "poor people" were wretched, living in fear of the conquering and marauding Fulbé tribe, and hiding in the hills. They had no clothes, didn't know how to do anything, and were sick. Now look, said the missionaries, with pride; but what was there to see—a girl, covered with a pagne, knitting a narrow strip of red wool (whatever for?). And a few schoolboys.

They began to murmur what sounded like an insane incantation or as if they were talking in a trance, over and over, again and again—Jesus Christ, who died for our sins, if we can teach that, then these people are saved. As they droned these words, like self-hypnotism, I was embarrassed and frightened, as with the mad. I excused myself from visiting the mission, said I would think of them when next in Berne or Lucerne or wherever it was, and fled.

Arrived at the Hotel Flamboyante at Mokolo; a large fairly tidy room for eating, with a bar; local meeting place, I assume; and a single-storey row of bedrooms. I wondered at the lack of a mosquito net and was told there were no insects at this season, all dead from the dryness and the heat. A very nice young Frenchwoman, of the lower middle class, and her mechanic husband run this hotel which is also the garage and gasoline pump. She has been here for twelve years; in another year and a half they mean to return to France, as they cannot stick the new black régime. I gather that this revulsion is due to *"pagaille"*—disorder, not knowing where one stands, sudden taxes, etc.—rather than to colour prejudice.

We talked about missionaries, my latest puzzlement. Madame says the Catholic priest has been here for twelve years and he believes that when he leaves it will be amazing if two blacks remain Christians. Madame thinks all missions are idiotic; these people *"demandent pas mieux que d'être laissés en paix."* Furthermore, their happiness is their own, we don't understand them or anything about their lives and they never talk openly to a white. There is a smallpox epidemic in the region, and much leprosy. Some years there is famine, and then the people are really miserable. Otherwise they are quite content, living in the present and accepting whatever happens to them.

Madame had to leave as local customers arrived, two French couples for their evening card game. How many nights have they been doing this? They slap each card down on the table very hard, but scarcely speak. No one is the least interested in talking to me; I am too shy to butt in. It occurs to me that—in my Yaoundé trousers and general dustiness—I must look very unappetizing; also it is unheard of for a white woman to travel around the country alone. I don't imagine they have any sinister ideas about me, but probably think I am dotty. No one is ever eager to chum up with the unbalanced.

February 2: Mokolo market is poor and pitiful too; the naked Matakam Kirdi women obviously come for fun and chat rather than gain. (I should say here that there are some 200 tribes in the Cameroun and some 122 different dialects; they've got Europe beat on this kind of division, hostility, and barriers. The country is a bit larger than Japan with a population of about 3,200,000.) The naked women bring a few handfuls of withered-looking vegetables for sale, but spend more time visiting with each other than attending to business. Their clothing consists in a leather thong around the waist from which hangs a metal *cache-sexe,* wide leather anklets which stop circulation, and same sort of bracelets around the upper arm which cut into skin, a narrow leather band around shaved head. For jewelry, they wear a silver pin like a toothpick, jutting from the under side of the lower lip (how does it stay in?), and in the large holes in their ear lobes they wear either wooden plugs like a spool or peanuts. Over one shoulder hangs a strip of earth-coloured cotton, which I think is what they use to carry the vegetables to market. They are uniformly hideous, of all ages; not a body that isn't lamentable.

These people apparently make nothing themselves except the women's jewelry and cache-sexes, and their primitive tools. For tilling the soil, they use a long hook; it is about a foot and a half long, a straight handle, with a small curved hook at the end; that's all. The metal is silvered—don't know what it is—and has a simple design of dots.

Today we have to get back to Garua as President Tubman of Liberia is coming to town with President Ahidjo of the Cameroun for a state visit, and my dusty Citroën (whose rear doors will not now open) is required for the presidential cortège from the airport.

All day there was no shade anywhere, and the heat began to have the power of noise. No sweating, but burning skin and insatiable thirst. I drank from my hot Evian bottles, and five minutes later my mouth felt swollen and sandy. One blows up, as if the heat had been swallowed.

The scenery is rocks, starved dying skinny trees and few of them, rocky mountains and the strange reddish needle formation of the Kapsicki range. I don't think the moon can look any worse than this.

At the village of Rhumsiki, which huddles under sharp granite peaks, a little boy led me over the path to the huts. An older boy of about seventeen, a real layabout type, followed us; it appeared they were brothers, but only the little one knew French. At the entrance to their congeries of bucaroos, a naked crone was sitting in the dust; she was the older boy's mother. He did not speak to her or notice her; she had the usual expression of old women, a depressing and baleful bitterness. The little boy said proudly that his brother (the older one) had seven wives, which if true is not bad for his age. A wife costs a mere 20,000 francs among this lot, less than $100. *"La femme s'achète avec les arachides,"* said the little boy. Literally, a woman is bought with peanuts, which I found delightful. A wife is a fine thing really; she takes the place of a work animal, she is a cook, she produces children who have great value, in that the boy can be a big shot and the girl brings in her bride money, and finally the wife is handy for what Jean had described as the main native occupation: sex.

We stopped in to call on a wife, a dark shadow in her tiny mud igloo. She was smiling, pretty and young; I had not realized they cannot even stand upright in their homes. One begins to be impatient with them for their own sakes, quite apart from any impatience one might feel on one's own behalf. Her husband, the adolescent oaf, spoke and was given food. He offered me some which I rapidly declined. This is the famous millet, basic staple of life. It looks like a wet paste made of whitish sand; it is a rough flour kneaded with water and dipped in ground peanuts, the African hamburger, I take it. Her bed was made of mud, covered with a mat. These Kirdis are poorer than Père Sylvestre's friends.

There was loud noise, as of quarrelling, from lower down in the village, where the men were gathered in the meeting room for their morning chat. We ambled down that way and saw all the gents, sitting under a roof of mats, busy as beavers, talking, some spinning wool—like winding yarn on to a stick—some heating a jug over coals, and apparently all had drink taken, but specially the chief, who was staggering drunk and in a temper. He lurched out of the porch, shouting over his shoulder to the other chaps, said *"Bonjour Madame"* to me without surprise or interest, and reeled off to the well where the naked women were washing themselves.

I gave money to the little boy; the oaf also asked for some but I said a man who was rich enough to buy seven wives should not beg; and as we left I saw the older one take the money from the little one, as his by right.

We passed a pond of stagnant water where some ten Kirdi women were having an uproarious bath, bouncing and splashing each other. They all leaped out of the water and came to the car. Ibrahim speaks a little of their language. Their cache-sexes were made of fresh leaves; it's very pretty to see them walking along, with the greenery bobbing in front. Their instinctive gesture, when a stranger passes or when talking to me, is to place a protecting hand over these leaves. Modesty is certainly a weird and various human quality. These ladies lined up alongside the car and at first I could not imagine what they were doing. They squatted, pointed, wriggled, stared and shook with laughter. Then I understood that they were looking at themselves in the dusty side of the Citröen, which was apparently the first mirror they had ever seen.

They couldn't get over it, they thought themselves so funny; gales of giggles. Scoffing at each other. Never saw a jollier group. They are tattooed on the belly, shoulders and the face; raised black welts about a half inch long, forming a design; must be extremely painful when it is being done. One of them had good breasts, so I took her to be between thirteen and fifteen, and as yet childless; they said she had just been married. I asked her age. Three, they said happily. I pointed to a woman with breasts like narrow saddle bags and asked her age: nine, she said. How restful to have no idea of time, nor your own place in it. At a certain age, nature indicates that you are ready for marriage. At a certain age you can no longer bear children. Then you are old and in due course you die. No more detailed timetable is needed.

We passed a school where uniformed children were doing some sort of gymnastics and, farther along, a sand dune of peanuts waiting by the roadside to be collected. I wanted to ask about the school; the teacher was reclining on the peanuts. He was a Sahara tribesman, a Moslem from Chad, with one eye blind and its lid stuck shut with yellow gug, tattoo marks on his face, a shirt, trousers, and black velvet Moslem cap. A very ugly man and as it proved an intelligent realist. He wanted to go down the road to the market at Bourha so I gave him a lift. He talked facts and sense, and I felt no strangeness with him; but I wonder how many are like him.

He got his wife, to live with him, after seven years of marriage; all this time he was paying off her bride money—140,000 francs in his tribe, a fortune. He had three children by the time they were finally able to live together. Before that he worked, went on visits to her, begat children, saw them a few years later. He says the question of the *dot* (the bride money) is terrible; it is their curse, but their great-grandchildren will solve it, not before. A girl is ripe at eighteen (I should have thought sooner and perhaps he was being careful of me); she has no husband because no one can afford to pay for her; she sleeps with someone, anyone, even many; she gets venereal disease; then she is married off as a virgin and is sterile.

"Nous sommes pourris des maladies vénériennes." We are rotten with venereal disease. He said this with fervour. (Did that explain his blind eye?) They are ashamed to admit that they have such diseases; they dare

not go to hospital because someone always sees and everyone talks; so the disease is not treated and eats them more and more, and is spread. In marriage, a girl has no choice of her husband; it is her father's right to arrange the marriage and collect the bride money. But if she insists on marrying her choice, the father gets no *dot* and if the husband is brutal to her, the girl gets no protection from her family; hence girls do not insist on marrying for love, but marry as is the tradition, in the secure way.

The government (obviously the French) built his school which is *"très beau,"* and everything is free including books. In seven years his school has given no *"certificat"*—this would be a passing grade in a stage less than our grammar school. Down the road, another school has existed for eleven years and been able to award only two certificats. A little boy he had pointed out at the peanut mountain had been in the first grade at his school for six years; the child enjoys school but cannot learn. Parents do not want their children to go to school; after school the children are *"déracinés"* and changed and do not wish to stay in the bush and work the land. Also, not going to school, or not staying at school, is sometimes the fault of the teachers who beat the children to make them learn. Neither parents nor children approve of beating. (These people appear to be very kind and easygoing with children, who are allowed to roll and tumble and play about like puppies; you seldom hear them crying.)

Missions are useful—they teach a lot. But many of the people do not like them and wish the missionaries would go. *"Quand on vit parmi les blancs, on a toujours les ennuis."* When one lives among whites, one always has troubles. He is twenty-four years old and has been teaching since he was seventeen. He knows that he is too old now to do the studying he would need to go on to better jobs, teaching in higher education. He is resigned to this, and he loves to teach; he has the soul of a teacher. But he is a realist and he thinks there will be very few changes here for a very long time.

He took me through Bourha market; this market is held on a little slope (why here and not somewhere else?) once a week. There are travelling merchants with their stalls and the natives come from the neighbourhood to buy and sell and talk. All the food was awful to behold and to smell; the rest of the market goods was bits and pieces, some plastic ware, some shoelaces, some matches, salt, very little. A strong odour of smoked fish hung over all; I passed up the pleasure of walking through the meat stalls, due to the flies and stench.

Here the Kirdi women were even more astounding; they had gone in for cosmetics. Makeup consists in covering one's skin and hair with oiled red earth. Their colour was very queer indeed; this is pancake makeup to the nth degree. Also their hair was done in tiny short braids, like flat worms on their heads, and solid with red mud. The silver toothpick, jutting from the lower lip, is now adorned with a green ball, like a plastic grape, at its end. These Kirdis, the schoolteacher told me, worship a magic mountain in the vicinity; it has a crater lake and the water changes colour every minute, from white to violet to orange to green to red to blue. He claims to have seen this. On the great annual religious day, they carry a lamb around the base of the mountain; it starts as a lamb and by the end of the journey (a few hours later) it is a full-grown sheep. He has also seen this. He himself worships Allah. (Baffling.)

Across the road from the market is an open place, jammed with happy people; this is the beer market. (No one stared at me or laughed; wonderful manners.) Since there is so much poisoning, the beer buyer makes the beer woman, who sells, drink first from the calabash of beer. Poisoning? Oh yes, they kill each other *"comme ça,"* for anything. For what? Jealousy, envy, because they believe they have been insulted; for any little thing.

We parted with expressions of mutual esteem; I meant it. I thought him an interesting companion; and I agree with his conclusions. Change will be very slow; the answers, if any, will be found by their great-grandchildren; *on a toujours les ennuis si on vit parmi les blancs;* this is their show absolutely, they have to swim on their own and where and how they swim is also their business.

Ibrahim and I were driving along, sick with thirst and silent from misery, when I saw in the road a man with two large horns growing out of his chest. I thought maybe I'd gone off my head and told Ibrahim to stop. No by golly, he did have two large horns, just above his nipples; they were made of leather and this must be the ancient art of cupping to cure sickness. The countryside was emptied in the blazing afternoon; not only the insects die, but all life is beaten down.

I gave Ibrahim one of my Evian bottles; he took it without a word, same as he had previously taken bread, and an advance on his salary. I feel I have treated Ibrahim badly, from ignorance; I do not know how to treat him. The Citroën's owner told me to lock the car at night and keep the key; Ibrahim has a small cotton blanket, no other possession. I have not worried about his living arrangements on the grounds that he must know, better than I, how to manage in Africa. He is punctual and he can drive and he looks after the car (or else he doesn't and it is running without oil or water and the tyres are either too flat or too full). But now he looks gaunt, hollow-cheeked, grim.

We stopped in a village to rest in the shade for a minute; Ibrahim threw away the precious, costly Evian, took the bottle off to a well, drank, and came back with it filled with mucky brown water. He does not speak enough French for me to talk to him; I sense that he dislikes me and feels abused. I know I am not behaving properly but what is properly? I can only be polite and pay him what he asks. Whites, though this is what is resented, do look after blacks; and blacks, though they clamoured for independence, expect it. Benevolent paternalism. I don't know how to look after myself, let alone a native on his native heath.

Late in the afternoon, we reached the airport road at Garua. Here the chiefs and their retinues—convoked from hundreds of kilometres around—were already drawn up in a dress rehearsal for the arrival tomorrow morning of President Tubman. They had sat in the sun all afternoon and they lined the road from the airport to town. Each chief sat on his horse (the horses were small, scraggy and enduring), surrounded by his principal warriors, mounted and on foot, and his musicians and servants or bodyguard. The horses were as ornately adorned as the horsemen; some beasts being caparisoned as for medieval tournaments, in padded calico, some wearing red or blue brocaded and fringed trousers on their front legs, with long trains falling over the haunches; some had multicoloured, wool-tasselled headdresses; bridles and saddles were heavily trimmed with silver or brass (maybe gold, for all I know); some wore plumes.

The chiefs and their cohorts were also fantastically clad: horsemen in chain mail and helmets like the Crusaders, horsemen in immense robes and immense turbans; a metal casque fringed with ostrich plumes and a sort of mobile on top; lances, swords; bodyguards in brilliant tunics; musicians with drums and long trumpets. It was the strangest sight I have ever seen; not a bit dress-up party (so much the happy impression one gets in London for state turn-outs). These people were wearing their tribal clothes and looked what they were: barbaric, remote, sure of themselves, and extremely tough. The faces were unsmiling under the terrible beating of the sun, and you felt they could take any kind of physical hardship and despise it. It was an exhibition of strength; their own kind of strength. No use against modern weapons, but deadly otherwise. I would hate to rouse the anger of these hard and alien men.

Every so often there would be a burst of sound, from drums and the fluting trumpets; horses would rear, horsemen galloped to change position in the ceremonial ranks. No one knows or cares who President Tubman is: he is black and a President and he is coming with their black President and this is an occasion.

In Garua, banners across the main street say: Long Live to President Tubman.

Back in my filthy bucaroo in the Garua hotel, I listened to the drums in the night. The visiting chiefs and tribesmen are camping all around the town. The drumbeat is monotonous and untiring and merges finally with the steady grinding of the insects; the trumpets sound like reedy flutes and make a music like that of Indian snake charmers, but the tune is always the same. In the dining room, the gramophone plays a record of a French crooner.

I lay under the mosquito net and thought white people were boobs.

Africa has nothing to do with us and never will have. I also thought of politics: Cameroun has a black gentleman in European clothes representing his nation at the UN in New York. The naked pagans and the barbaric chiefs will be spoken for, in French, by an African who has learned the European tricks, and will be a black copy of the other gentlemen gathered in that glass palace on the East River. African politicians, outside Africa, must represent their people even less than politicians generally do; or else they represent how their people might be a hundred years from now.

It is all mad and a joke. We are fools; we believe in words, not reality which the words are supposed to describe. Politics—the bungling management of the affairs of men—is a game played among themselves by a breed of professionals. What has politics to do with real daily life, as real people live it?

February 3: At 8 a.m. the chiefs and their bands are filing to their appointed places, along a narrow road which runs behind my bucaroo. The music now sounds rather like bagpipes, again the same tune and drumbeat endlessly. There was a band of archers preceding one chief, with huge bows, clad in purple tunics and trousers; their sergeant-major wore turquoise blue. Very beautiful; very wild.

Financial news: the car cost $55 a day, and I travelled, in four days, a total of 214 miles and it was bone-breaking hard work.

The toilet in this bucaroo is too eccentric; it ejects water at the sides. One needs Equanil here too, not only in our white urban civilization: tranquillizers against impatience, against the hysteria induced by heat, and the disgust at dirt.

At 11 a.m. I got a ride to the airport, to be on hand for the arrival of the two Presidents. This event was pure Waugh and sublimely funny: the reason for its being a cause of concealed and supercilious white giggles was that today the blacks were putting on a show copied from the whites, and when they copy they are absurd. (Since 8 a.m. the chiefs and retainers had been waiting, immobile, on the road to the airport.) At the airport, always under this sun, in the burning dry still air, the Jeunesse

Camerounaise was lined up in ranks. Boys and girls, dressed in a uniform of orange and green calico, printed with the Cameroun flag and the portrait of President Ahidjo; their clothes were the first treat, and to see them being serried, "scoots, clin in taught, word and did," was hilarious. The tarmac of the airfield looked as if it would bubble and boil any minute. Important chiefs sat under black cotton umbrellas, near the airport building; masses of the superior gentry stood in the sun between the Jeunesse Camerounaise and the chiefs; there were some uniformed soldiers, a guard of honour. The whites of the town were all present, wearing jackets and ties; ladies also nattily gotten up in hats and gloves. The bar did a roaring business in anything wet and cold.

One hour late, the Presidential plane (naturally flown by a French crew) landed. The two great men and their staffs, in business suits with briefcases, descended. They started to walk across the frying tarmac, to salute the guard of honour. Halfway there, one feels by accident, the band struck up the national anthems of Liberia and Cameroun. These are both very long, tunes pinched from bad light opera, of an indistinguishable mediocrity. During this ordeal by music, the Presidents stood, Tubman bareheaded with hat over heart, Ahidjo, being a lucky Moslem, able to keep on his little white round embroidered cap. The sun hammered down on them.

Clearly relieved by the end of this sunstroke nationalism, they were at last able to move. President Tubman was heavenly; he beamed at the Jeunesse Camerounaise who shouted slogans in unison. Alas for all political youth movements and shame on the grown-ups who direct them. When he reached the massed but privileged public, he began shaking hands like Nixon himself, with a will; hands stretched over heads, hands thrust at knee level; he shook and shook them all, finishing up with the standing chiefs. It took a long time. Everyone was delighted; the performance was proceeding with a fine democratic dignity, fit for any western newsreel camera.

Finally, the two Presidents took a well-earned rest in two comfortable chairs, inside the airport. They had nothing to say to each other. President

Ahidjo is a large young man, lineless, pale café-au-lait, with a politician's face; amiable, bland, and shrewd. He wore loose fresh white robes and his Moslem cap. President Tubman is small, solemn, very black, dressed like a prosperous Southern undertaker (he looks highly American), smoking a cigar in a gold holder. Then the Presidents entered a big open American car and, followed by their dignitaries in all the available cars (my Citroën, sketchily dusted, was used by some lower-downs with briefcases), the cortège whizzed off. They passed the line of chiefs at forty miles an hour; not kosher, they slipped up there; the Queen of England, the President of the United States would never have made such a disdainful gaffe. The rest of us got out of the blazing heat as best we could. What, I wonder, is this jamboree in favour of; what politics bring these two great men to the distant northern Cameroun; what fences are being mended?

It would be self-indulgence to describe the food we are served; enough to say that I'd put this place high on the list of ptomaine centres and only need drives one to eat at all. At lunch, a young American spoke to me; he was a Jew, whose family came from the Sudan—he has relatives through the whole Middle East and Italy and Spain. He is a big nice-looking boy and the crown prince of a great leather business. He was given a leather factory in northern Nigeria by his papa and is now learning the business from the ground up, and loving it. He is first-generation American and adores the U.S. and is as patriotic and devoted to the American way of free enterprise as any pure WASP of long standing. Yet he learns everything here, the language, the customs, and is surely more adaptable than most Americans; and hardship and dirt do not dismay him. His life and background are interesting, he is not; but I'm getting used to that in far-off lands where every foreigner leads a singular life and ought therefore to be a singular person. It does not work this way at all.

After the usual deathlike sleep of the afternoon (I have about enough energy for five hours of living per day), I walked to the Hôtel de Ville, to see the festivities in honour of the Presidents. It is a curious sensation to be alone, the only white on foot, in a great African crowd. They ignore me, do not stare or laugh; I feel that I am a non-person.

The Hôtel de Ville has a terrace; on this the notables were seated and here the Presidents, in due course, would watch the charge of the chiefs and their retinues, a charge up the main street, with a salute to the Presidents as the mounted men thundered by. Too early for that; no Presidents in sight, but at the edge of the street there were dancing groups and semicircles of spectators. One group was depicting hunters; the men were old, heavily clad, with monkey tails sewed to the back of their clothes. They circled in a crouch and sprang; again and again. Another set wore beards of monkey fur and made jerking movements of their heads, while three boys stood alongside holding folded black umbrellas. No idea what that was about.

Far down in the town, away from the grand people on the Hôtel de Ville terrace, there was a real dance. The dancers were young Kirdis, young men and girls. The girls wore little white woven aprons, size of pocket handkerchiefs, as cache-sexe, and strips of leather between their legs; the boys wore ragged homemade shorts. There were no drums. Suddenly, the boys would leap into a circle; they made a sound which at first I thought was the copy of a barking dog, but then decided was the sound (their very own) of a man panting in the act of love. They slapped their bent left arms hard against their sides; this was the music; it was also the sound of two bodies striking each other in a fiercer kind of sex than we know. They leapt, jumped, panted—barked, bucked, slapped their arms against their sides. Then a girl attached herself to one man, behind him, touching his shoulder with her hand and swaying her body, or danced in front of him. The girls' dance was thrusting sexual motions of the pelvis, and gestures of the hands showing how the belly will swell with child. They were very handsome blacks, and their dance was a most direct sexual statement. It was exciting to watch, and I began to imagine what the three months' drinking and dancing and fornicating orgies of the Kirdis must be like.

Time for the horsemen. These people, who had been travelling for days to get here, had been stuck in the sun for two days—first to practise, then to receive the Presidents—and ignored for their pains, made their final gesture towards the great men, and neither President was there on the terrace. Each chief, at the head of his own band, galloped his horse at top speed up the cement of the main street, lance on high, dipped it to the absent Presidents, swerved his horse and galloped off to the side of the Hôtel de Ville until he could rein in. They rode as though joined to the horse, and they rode very fast, and were an imposing sight.

The local authorities however, in what I now regard as par-for-the-course lack of foresight, had allowed cars to be parked where the horsemen were to pass, alongside the Hôtel de Ville. No one told the horsemen. I watched the first wave, at full gallop, come straight on to the backs of the parked limousines; and held my breath; they managed to pull their horses up standing. No one moved the cars; the horsemen had to adapt themselves. Evidently here, as everywhere, the city slickers rule and win; the country boys get the dirty end of the stick. The country boys are the ones for me, though; they look terrific and their own men. The others, who have a thin patina of western civilization, set my teeth on edge; they are like a conceited but untalented amateur theatrical company, putting on a stupid play in the mistaken impression that they've got the lines and gestures right, just like the whites.

Tonight there is a reception for President Tubman at the house of the French Resident. I don't understand what the role of the French civil servants is, now; as advisers? Anyhow, that house would obviously be the grand place, so there the party is to be. The R. and W. King (or "Le Keeng" as called throughout Cameroun) manager tried to get me invited; he was tactful, not mentioning the subject again when he could not swing it. I am too insignificant. It is another angle; not the Quiet American, not the Ugly American: the Unknown American. I found this pleasing and took my weary bones to bed; but the tam-tams (drums) beat all night; and I waked to the same music. The horsemen were passing my bucaroo again, for the last time, on their way home to the bush.

February 4: President Tubman's visit brought many strangers to town and two days ago at the hotel bar I saw two French women who filled me with shame for my sex. They looked more slovenly and old than their age, which I'd put in the early 40s. They were drunk on bar stools, one with her hair falling down, one with gluey eyes; a horrid sight. I steered clear of these ladies until this morning, when my transport to the Pitoa market—some ten kilometres out of town—failed. They were going in a Landrover with a Cameroun official, and offered me a ride. I learned that the drunkenness was an error and due, they said, to their inexperience of booze. But what a queer pair, even sober.

One of the ladies is an old Cameroun hand; she introduced herself as *"ethnologue, sociologue et avocat."* She is a compulsive talker and braggart, without a shred of humour or self-consciousness, and she evidently knows a great deal about the blacks and this country. She wore very short aquamarine shorts, a blouse with lace, and canvas leggings over sneakers. She has the sloppily pinned-up unwashed hair that only a certain kind of French concierge would be caught dead with. Her chum is a peroxide blonde, pale, with glaucous eyes, a simpering manner, but restfully clad in a dress. The blonde sat in front with the driver and our host, her arm along the seat back, her head too close to the African official, whispering. The word "avid" might safely be used, as description. The ethnologist etc. said her friend had lost her job after seven months and now she was waiting. For what? A black protector?

On Sunday the tribes from all around walk to Pitoa market; it is a big market and richer than any other native market I have seen. The things on sale—specially repellent fish, vegetables, salt, cloth, cattle—were not interesting; the people were.

The Bororo are a nomadic tribe, herdsmen, and the handsomest yet encountered. The women wear sarongs and are extremely thin and narrow-bodied, with fine bony faces like ancient Egyptian sculpture or like beautiful Jews. (But then Akhenaton the Great looks exactly like a Jew.) They are copiously tattooed on the face; they have wide eyes. Their hair is dressed in the most complicated way, braided with coloured wool, yarn, and somehow laced around their heads. Their men are very tall, also with these wonderful Semitic faces, wearing embroidered caps, robes and swords.

The Fali are a Kirdi tribe (i.e. naked pagans) and the women wear a fringed leather *cache-sexe*, bands of something that looks uncomfortably like horsehair between their legs, ending in a brush behind, like a chopped-off tail. Their jewelry is the most painful to date: silver buttons on the outside of the nostrils, a large (silver dollar size) round stone ornament, like dull mother of pearl, set into and jutting out the lower lip, and holes all around their ears for silver rings. They dress their hair in braids with oiled red earth, so that they seem to be growing dozens of pieces of dark red macaroni or little sausages.

We wandered among these people and the *ethnologue* pointed, discussed, lectured, with lofty condescension. I felt miserably embarrassed by this arrogant performance. She told me that the black women know herbs to use for abortions, and do so constantly. She said that once, in the bush, she had been ill and taken native medicines and thought she would die of it; she concluded that their intestinal arrangements are quite different from ours. I wondered whether the locals hadn't tried to poison her.

Meantime the Fulbé women moved gracefully around the place, covered in their elegant pagnes (does clothing induce grace; the naked women have none). The Fulbés are on the whole the most attractive, and have the most lovely eyes. Their language—the language of the conquerors—is the nearest to a lingua franca in this tribe-divided land.

At the edge of the market were the barbers. The barber squats on his heels, the customer squats opposite him. And then, with a sure hand and a razor-edged knife, he shaves the inside of the customer's nostrils. A terrifying feat.

I caught the plane at lunchtime for Fort Lamy in Chad. By local standards, Fort Lamy is a big city and I was looking forward to a clean room and, by God's will, air conditioning. I also had romantic dreams about Chad, though all I knew about it was its name which appealed to me from childhood. It was boiling hot, even in the plane, and for half an hour before reaching Fort Lamy we flew over poison green swamp. Horrible country. In this swamp there were small islands with a clump of trees; then the endless scum and craters in the scum. I began to feel depressed about Chad.

There is one good hotel, the Chari, on the river of that name, which bounds the town—a wide stream in a flat land. This hotel was full. I went to the Grand Hotel, in town, and suffered complete despair. The squalor is even greater than in Garua, and here there are mosquitoes to boot. The dirty dark little room stinks of DDT and is littered with mosquito corpses. One dares not open a drawer or a cupboard, to see the relics of the other guests. There is one toilet for the whole hotel. The hotel keepers themselves are like something out of a bad play about Africa; a poor obese young man with open sores on his face and arms, and dirty clothes, a sluttish dark woman. It is appalling.

I went to the bar to take to drink (but they had nothing that one could swallow except beer) and there my acquaintance was made by an elderly muscular Frenchman who began to attack me, as an American. It was the fault of America that all these black countries demanded and got their independence; France had brought civilization, France should fight to keep her colonies and etc. etc. I asked him if he was a member of the OAS, said that I hadn't seen enough civilization to sneeze at, noble talk tired me, I thought whites were fools ever to have come to these god-awful places in the first place and if they stayed it was obviously to make money and not spread civilization which no one wanted or could use, and though normally I disagreed with my country's politics, on principle, if we really were responsible for getting the blacks' independence, which I doubted, we were on the right track. Also considering what a waste of life and money Algeria had been, it was demented to suggest more fighting for people who didn't want you. The French had better be chummy with the blacks and go on making money, if anyone could in these unbearable places. With that I flounced off to the U.S. Embassy, hoping to find some mail—I had given the Embassy as my forwarding address, knowing no other—and hoping someone would ask me to stay the night so I could get out of that ghastly hotel.

There was mail but no warm-hearted invitations to come on home. The famous American talent for hospitality, as I have noted often before, is lacking in the U.S. Foreign Service; but I suppose that's self-preservation. And the other thing is: whites do not cluster round newcomers, with smiling welcomes, in Africa. They keep themselves to themselves, much more carefully than in New York or London. Rarity has no special value in these parts.

I roamed, ate a foul meal somewhere, and came back to that despairful hotel room when I was too tired to care any more.

February 5: The horrors of the Grand Hotel exchanged for the horrors of the Parc Hotel. Cigarette butts in the corners of the room, the last tenant's sheets, a filthy bathroom with a cracked cement floor; but a toilet of one's own. Sartre should have seen these places so as to get the stage set absolutely right for his hotel room in hell. The privilege of residing in these sewers costs $12.50 a day; two inedible courses for lunch cost $4.40. It is no wonder that people find it strange not to say suspicious that I am travelling in Africa for pleasure.

Added to which, these hotels are in the centre of town, and with their small shuttered windows the rooms might as well be on the airshaft of a Times Square hotel. Not that there is any view in Fort Lamy; it is perfectly flat and suburban. The place name is full of romance; the place looks like an ill-kempt "garden city." Straight streets run to roundabouts, whence diagonal streets cut off—there must have been a plan at some time. There are trees and flowers and grass and it is cooler than in the northern Cameroun; but dull. The shopping street is short, with offices, shops, and the U.S. Information Service reading room, in one-storey buildings.

Outside the Grand Hotel, the natives display their tourist wares on the pavement; the beasts of the bush carved in wood; some well done, some badly done, but all done alike—yet this is not factory work, and the same design for every antelope, every elephant, is proof of a wanting imagination in the craftsmen. However, this is the first time I have seen any handicrafts for sale; there are also daggers and baskets and ugly brass work. The pavement merchants have a curious notion of business: they expect bargaining but when there are *no* tourists and *no* sales, the prices rise—the idea being that you have to make more money when you sell less.

I returned to the U.S. Embassy; proof of being at the end of my rope. I am not an Embassy-category traveller and do not expect help from our embassies or consulates. We have an Ambassador in Chad, because we are a rich and foolish nation. The work could be done by a Consul and a stenographer, and they would have time on their hands. An Ambassador immediately brings into operation Parkinson's Law; he needs a staff commensurate with his rank. The Ambassador was away on a hunting trip, and the staff was turning over papers; Parkinson's Law demands that people make work for each other. They have a visitor's book with four names in it, to which I added mine.

By luck, the First Secretary knew someone in my family. Owing to this personal (not duty-to-the-public) bond, I was quite well received and asked to lunch the next day. My object is to get out of Fort Lamy and see Chad but this is a grand undertaking. There are practically no roads in a country which is three and a half times the size of France, and mostly desert. Due to this year's floods, the few roads are mainly impassable. Further, there are almost no cars to hire and those will not be rented for travel on the roads, which ruins them. (Only for use in the town and environs.) It is impossible to get to Lake Chad, a body of water larger than Lake Michigan when the rains swell it, otherwise a swampy mass, with approach only by river boat. River boats are not passenger boats, but trading vessels; they go when they go, and plod around the lake villages for a couple of weeks; rather be shot than stay here a couple of weeks.

The French military are in control of whatever the independent Chadian government does not control, and control seems the order of the day. The French have an Army and Airforce Commandant here, and their combined permission is needed to go to the Tibesti, the strange country on the northeastern frontier adjoining the Sudan. The Tibesti is desert, with curious rock formations, and oases, and is alleged to be fascinating. The only other place to go is south, to Fort Archambault, where there is reputed to be much game and the biggest elephants in the world. Planes fly about once a week to each of these areas.

I spent the morning with the U.S. cultural attaché (I think he is that), a very nice man, half black, who no doubt was selected for this job to prove to African blacks that all men are equal in the U.S. Mr X. has about as much relation to the Chadian blacks as I have to Einstein. He speaks careful correct French, and is courtesy itself, and patient; hand in hand, we went to the Chad Ministry of Information, since one must check in here as in a dictatorship or country at war. (More and more convinced that the whole place operates on Parkinson's Law.) There we met a nervous thin young black, second in command, who was doing his best to run a Ministry of Information, according to notions received from whites or from reading, when there is no information to give and no one to ask for it. He was cordial, upon being told that I was "a distinguished American writer," and suggested a dinner party for me on my return to Fort Lamy from wherever I was going.

We moved on to the Mayor, whose permission was needed to go to the Tibesti. His Honour was large, cross, and not up to his job. A small, infinitely discreet Frenchman stood at his elbow, while His Honour was unable to make head or tail of my passport, my wishes, or what he was meant to do about it. Still with great tact, the Frenchman got us out to his office, a hole in the wall, and did the necessary writing on my passport. I wonder whether His Honour can read or write? Out of a population of three million, there are three Chadian university graduates, none of whom live in Chad.

The futile and dreary day wore on. I was sitting in the patio (at least shady) of my loathsome hotel when a young American came to call. This youth is aged twenty-two and on loan from a midwestern university to help the Chadians with their mobile film unit, the said truck and camera equipment being a U.S. gift. He's nice, if as unfinished as the foetus in the womb, and has a general right idea; he lives in the native section of town, with an "Arab" family—i.e. a black family of the same general race as the Fulbé, distant Arabic descent and the Moslem religion—he speaks the local Arabic dialect and perfect French. He's adventurous, and untroubled (lucky chap) by any need for hygiene.

We talked French literature to my headaching disbelief; I doubt if I've had such a conversation since college but then he is just out of college. We also talked about Life; a subject of which I am increasingly unsure with every year. We agreed to go south together; he knows an odd couple at Fort Archambault who run a hotel, which he describes with enthusiastic romanticism—there we would surely find transport to get to the big game country.

I wrote letters until 1 a.m., again seeking the fatigue which would blot out the filth of my surroundings; and watched my ankles swelling, and with weary dismay realized that I was getting ready for another bout of ptomaine or whatever it is.

February 6: Up at 6 a.m. in the fresh grey morning. As soon as possible (offices open at 7 a.m.) I went off with our First Secretary to call on the French Army. We visited the Infantry Colonel, who saw no reason for me not to go to the Tibesti (and equally no reason for me to go); and proceeded to the air base, to get the okay of the Airforce Commandant, Colonel Bienaimé, and to learn when an army plane was going and if I could have a place on it.

The Colonel is a man of thirty-five, I should guess, tall, dark, with shining dark eyes and an early morning stubble of beard, clad in the remarkable uniform of French soldiery hereabouts, the shortest possible khaki shorts displaying hairy legs down to ankle boots, and a leather windbreaker with fake fur collar (it is cold before the sun rises). He received us with splendid teasing ceremony, always addressing my chaperon as *Monsieur le Chargé d'Affaires des États-Unis.* He asked to what he owed the extreme honour of this visit. He then telephoned to a military chum and colleague whom he must have seen the night before if not that morning. With the same beautiful stateliness he began, *"Mon*

Colonel, je profite de l'occasion de vous rendre mes hommages respectueux,"
and went on to outline the situation: *une dame Américaine de haute dis-
tinction* wanted to fly on one of their planes to the Tibesti. It appeared
this could be done. The fare was discussed, far from cheap; the plane
would not be going for four days, and one had to take another plane back
within two days or be stuck in the desert for over a week. It all began to
seem more trouble than it was worth.

Evidently the Americans do not mix with the French, and there is
some bad blood because the Americans think the two swimming pools—
one belonging to the French infantry and one to the French Airforce—
are breeding grounds for polio. This is taken as a reflection on French
standards of hygiene. American officialdom is usually resented. It has far
more money than anyone else and clings to its golden ghetto and its ex-
clusiveness irritates. I'd have given anything to spend the day laughing
with Colonel Bienaimé but I was under the wrong auspices.

I lunched at the house of the First Secretary. It is quite pretty, a modest bungalow with five rooms, furnished in imported American interior
decoration style, cool and clean. This wee dwelling belongs to a coony
Chadian who soaks the U.S. taxpayer $15,000 a year rent for it. It can-
not have cost more than $5,000 to build if that.

In the afternoon, in a hired car, I drove about with young H. of the
mobile film unit. He adores this place but then he is too young to have
seen a great deal of the world. He took me to the market, where the large
array of foodstuffs, spices, bleeding meat etc. was nicely covered with
flies. He eats everything local and takes his dysentery as it comes. All the
blacks are dressed here and not nearly as interesting or varied as the natives of Cameroun. The women wear a long sarong from breast to ankles
and a gold ring in one nostril. They do their hair in short braids, plaited
from the crown of the head, so that they seem to be wearing a cap of
dusty wool fringe.

We visited H.'s home; he lives with his chauffeur's family, in an
adobe compound. He has two rooms, off the mud courtyard, the family
has the other huts—these are square and like Mexican Indians' houses.

He is very fond of this black family (several generations of it) and they of him. He covets his chauffeur's wife, whom he thinks a beauty, but honour forbids his lifting a finger. Honour has not however kept him away from all black girls, and he thinks it's great.

Moved to the Hotel du Chari, and it changes my outlook to have a clean room and view over the wide sand-banked river.

February 7: First day of Ramadan. For a month, all Moslems will be gloomy by day, from hunger, and happy as bird-dogs after sundown when they can feast.

Local politics seem to be about the usual; there's an election for the government, hand in hand with the granting of independence. The President then takes over and gradually removes those people who are not of his tribe (main point) and party. Here President Tombelbaye (delicious name) has invented a sweet touch; those who are booted out are "foreigners," not native hundred-percent Chadians. I think all these countries will have one election, supervised by the retiring colonial power, and that the President then elected will stay in for life, unless (until?) there's a palace putsch or assassination; and I do not see how it could be otherwise.

The use of the word democracy in these parts is more of our passion for self-deception and lust for the word rather than the fact. The blacks know no native form of government except the traditional absolute rule of the chiefs; the President is the super-chief, that's all. They cannot read (not enough of them to mention) and the jolly first election is done with symbols; vote for the elephant or the hippo or whatever pleases your fancy. After that a ruling clique will emerge everywhere, but power cannot be too obnoxious here because communications are so bad—hard to catch the "enemies of the régime." The tiniest possible proportion of the people in these new "republics" must be engaged in politics anyhow; corruption and graft are nearly private enterprise.

To cheer myself up, I painted a giraffe with love from memory, washed clothes and played solitaire. Ah Africa, land of romance and adventure.

February 8: Tidbit to add to many others. When H. leaves, which will be soon, he expects the mobile film unit to survive him by a few months. The car is American made and spare parts have to be ordered from the U.S.—first you have to know what you need and then find it in a technical catalogue. The car is also not built for these roads. No car is built for African roads which are not suitable for four-wheeled, power-driven transport, but the Landrover, being the nearest thing in an automobile to a tank, is probably the best bet. Then the locals will not be able to care for, repair, or even use the fine camera equipment. End of story.

All the whites (except H.) object to this place, but they have unworried, unlined faces. They may be bored but not harassed. *"C'est l'Afrique"* replaces *"C'est la vie."* It is not an exhilarating spot, this Fort Lamy.

Late afternoon, H. appeared to announce that he cannot go south. His landlord, the mobile film unit chauffeur, is diagnosed as having galloping consumption and must be bundled off to hospital at once. The rest of the compound has to be found (the wife has gone away to visit her mother) and everyone has to be tested for TB including H. He is now their nanny, a role whites do find themselves in. Also a child in the family cut off its toe last night on a broken teapot. H. beside himself, with these new physical and moral responsibilities.

I am sick of Fort Lamy and indeed of West Africa. I want to get out. Desperately. This feeling of being clamped in a boredom as acute as pain, and as solid as prison walls, is something I've felt before—in China. There's a plane to the frontier at Abeshé day after tomorrow. I can hardly bear to think of the day's wait.

February 9: To do something, to pass the blind time, I hired the Mairie launch and went on the Logone river, which joins the Chari here. We steamed mildly up the stream to Kousseri. The houses were of adobe, built like baby forts. In the market, Mandara women (the tribe of Ali, the Elephant King) wore myriad short braids on their heads and deeply incised scars on their faces and nothing much else. A young girl had a scar—a narrow black welt—running straight between her brows on to her nose, thus achieving a look of hideous anxiety which a lifetime would, with bad luck, leave on any of us. The Banana women (another tribe) are the ugliest to date, almost too ugly to look at, with anthropoid features, and lip and nostril plugs, and shocking bodies.

The French part of the village looks like movies of the Foreign Legion with the Commandant's house, the fort and the Mairie, crumbling, white, isolated under the dull white sky, shrouded in dust, the end of the world.

All along the river the blacks sit. They are capable of doing this for hours, without moving a muscle. The young men are given to exhibitionism and have lovely bodies to exhibit—naked, gleaming black against the golden sandbanks. Modesty must be an instinct with women only; the men do not bother to move from a crouch, while defecating, no matter who passes.

Farther up, the villages are made of rush mats, bound together loosely. These people must be as poor as it is possible to be, and with as few needs as wild animals. No one is fat.

In the evening a French archaeologist came to have a drink with me at the hotel. He was another type; quick, lively, absorbed in his work. Possibly he keeps this fine intellectual tone by living over half the year in Paris. He startled me by calling a waiter and telling him to empty the ashtray, and bring a fresh cloth for the table, before serving the drinks. It would not have occurred to me to make such huge demands; I'd gloomily go on taking the squalor.

The archaeologist told me that his assistants, all blacks, would be talking both merrily and intelligently, but when a white man (not himself, he is in their confidence) came in, they would shut up and look and act like stupid wooden images. It is clear that schizophrenia operates with the blacks; and their mistrust of the whites makes them behave in just the way which infuriates the whites—to wit, like mute goops. My answer to this is: let the whites get out, let the blacks see how they can run the show by themselves, let them feel at home until such time as they'll learn to be themselves and not to have whatever complexes they have now. But of course that won't be done as the blacks, who know enough to have needs, need what the white man has brought with him: all our modern aids-to-living, from electric light to telephones to cars, planes, fridges, and the amusements of the mind too, including archaeology.

They cannot dominate modern machinery, and I wonder when they will be able to. I think it would take a brilliant intelligence to learn—from scratch—the things any American boy seems to know easily, almost by instinct, simply because he has been brought up with, surrounded by, machinery. But how very complex a gramophone would seem, if one were alive in the seventeenth century and suddenly given one. So I suppose the whites will stick around, grudgingly and sullenly required, for quite some time. The whites in turn will linger on either because they have Africa in their bones and really love it and cannot imagine another life, or plainly for pay.

Lebeuf, the man who digs, told me that the oldest human cranium had been found in Chad, but surely Leakey found it in Tanganyika. He also said that the Sao culture here dates from the tenth century. I'd like to know if there have been many changes since that time, outside of the towns.

February 10: This day will go down in memory with days in China, in the special chamber of horrors kept for such memories. But I feel proud to have survived.

I was called at 3 a.m.—one half-hour late—with fifteen minutes to pack, dress, swallow tea, and leave for the plane. Frantic: my one wish is to get out and if I missed the plane it would be days before another left. Downstairs I found the air crew, they also had been called late. No one protested; it is not worthwhile.

We took off at 4 a.m. in the dark. A handsome grey-haired man sat next to me; he proved to be the invisible Frenchman who keeps telecommunications running. He has lived in Africa for twenty years and loves it; he cannot think of living elsewhere. He said that expensive and complicated telephone switchboards arrived from France (France is fairy godmother to Chad as well as to Cameroun) and these were either broken almost at once, or unused because there was no black personnel to work them. He says this without heat, shrugging.

There must be some reason, which I am unable to see, for continuing this charade—African independence, whites behind the scenes keeping whatever does run still running. Why bother? Why have telecommunications? For whom? When and if the blacks learn to handle these white toys, let them buy them and use them; possibly the blacks would be happy enough without them; very few ever have contact with our sort of equipment anyhow. I don't see it. But this have-your-cake-and-eat-it performance keeps Mr Goy, my companion, in Africa; and he is content.

As the sun rose, we came to Largeau. Real desert and the first I've seen. The sand is reddish gold in this light, beautiful beyond words (so that I understand all the Englishmen who have fallen in love with this landscape), driven by the wind into symmetrical shapes. The wind forces the sand into a curve, with hollowed centre; all these great waves of sand face the same way. I do not think it can be described, painted or photographed so that the impression of untouched, harmonious elegance would come across. Largeau is an oasis with hundreds and hundreds of royal palms, and whitewashed huts and houses clustered under them. Surrounded by the desert, it is the one splendour I have seen, finer than anything before in Africa. I am filled with regret that I did not stay here instead of in Fort Lamy—and no one in Fort Lamy has either seen or felt this wonder, since Largeau was spoken of disparagingly as nothing much.

The air, at this hour, is wildly exciting, clean and cold; feels like high mountains. We walked across the field to the officers' mess, to try to scrounge breakfast. The officers' mess is a small hangar; broken bottles were being swept up, like snow, by a languid black; a small anti-tank gun was parked inside the door. The officers and gentlemen looked a frowsy lot (the French do not dress for dinner or any other meal, in the wilderness), dirty and inhospitable. We transit passengers sat on benches at one end of the long board table while the officers sat at the other, and drank hot coffee and ate thick slabs of bread. It turned out that I needn't have been so hesitant about coming in, so polite about intruding; we were charged for breakfast and that was that.

On to Abeshé, where we arrived at 10 a.m. My arrangements had been made by telephone. I was to be met and taken from here in a Landrover by Mr Kabbabé, a Lebanese. The distance between Abeshé, near the Chad frontier, and El Geneina, the first village inside the Sudan, is 123 miles. At El Geneina, tomorrow, I am to take the Sudan Airways plane to Khartoum. My Landrover ride to El Geneina cost $80—I thought that stiff for 123 miles but was in no position to argue. If you want to go on your way, in Africa, you take whatever transport you can get and pay what is asked.

Mr Kabbabé's son-in-law met me at the airport and drove me to the Kabbabé residence and shop, adjoining the market. Abeshé is flat and boiling hot. It is on the pilgrim's route to Mecca, and a caravan centre; the most alluring sight was the camel park, where—instead of cars—are massed camels, looking long-lashed, dusty, and resigned in a well-bred way. The market is large, malodorous, and the natives are again tattooed, semi-naked.

Mr Kabbabé does not live here all year round; his daughter and son-in-law (and their child) are the resident managers of the family business. These people are very rich, having made a fortune out of this kind of small-time trading. The accumulation of money is the ruling interest in their lives. They do not notice the ugliness and discomfort of their home, and seem perfectly content. Family ties are sufficient for the private emotions, and the money rolls in, penny by penny. Western whites would be out of their minds in no time in such a place, not the Lebanese Kabbabés.

They had decided to make an outing of my journey; Mr Kabbabé, his "boy" (an old, very intelligent black), his daughter and a French peroxided lady friend came along for the ride. We were tightly packed in—we three ladies in the back seat—and off we went, with a picnic lunch, at 11 a.m.

Very soon, I decided that Mr Kabbabé was going to earn every cent of his $80. He is a bad driver, of the sort who goes fast for a bit (only a short bit, no more was possible) and brakes suddenly at the edge of a deep hole lined with stones. There may be worse roads in the world, but I do not know them. We braced with our feet against the constant jolting, and clung to the sides of the Landrover to keep from breaking our necks at the sudden stops or when negotiating potholes. The heat was what could be expected, only more so, and wet; we were soaked, with dust caked on us, and I was dead tired by one o'clock.

The Kabbabé daughter and her chum were gallant and cheerful and made potty female conversation and laughed like idiot babes at each spine-cracking jolt. When it looked as if even the four-wheel drive would not get us up the sandy sides of the dry wadis, I suggested that the ladies walk; this was also life insurance. Mr Kabbabé did not inspire trust; but he would not let the black man drive. Yet all day long, the black man warned him of the road, pointing out—with marvellous vision—the pit-falls ahead. Mr Kabbabé has a will of iron, he can't be a day under sixty-five, and he's fat and soft, and it was a punishing journey.

We stopped in the shade, of which there was not much—this is scrub country, dry as a bone, with wizened thorn trees and brush—to eat lunch. Now Mlle Kabbabé (don't know her married name) showed a facet of her nature, no doubt both inherited and cultivated, which explains how the Kabbabés have become rich: she is a miser. She could hardly bear to part with the ample lunch she had brought; every bit was offered tentatively, alert to withdraw it; thus she managed not to give us enough. She was stingy with the water, of which we had plenty. Since I could not get through my bread, nothing much to spread on it, and little water to help it down, she saved the crust, saying she could not throw away bread.

We passed camels munching thorn trees and, in the dry wadis, black Moslems lying in the shade, too weary to be interested in us; they are fasting, and to drink no water from sunrise to sunset in this heat must be a severe strain. We passed one car all day; the Kabbabés knew the occu-pants. No one would willingly go on this road twice. Not a road, a mur-derous camel track.

At Adré, we had to go through Chadian customs. The black official was shouting with rage—the ill-humoured defensiveness of the black officials is universal. They are not up to their jobs, they fear mockery, they behave like brutes. A man who may have been a Syrian, not white and not black, was here the tactful *éminence grise*—he got us through. The black official was in such a temper, what with us and a young German couple arriving in the country, and all these passports in different languages, that I feared he was going to throw us out and close the frontier in a pet. One neither argues nor explains, above all one does not smile; one takes it.

The frontier post at El Geneina was closed for the night by the time we arrived, but Mr Kabbabé knows everyone and someone was sent to rout out the customs officer. Meanwhile two tall pale-black men in robes appeared, Sudanese officials. They were pleased by my compliments on the station compound, which looks like nothing in Chad—it is white-washed, pretty with bougainvillea, neatly laid out. They were calm and agreeable, sure of themselves, speaking correct English, and altogether an advertisement both for the Sudan and for the British as colonial nanny. But there are always vast numbers of papers to fill in; the blacks have copied our bureaucratic foolery with enthusiasm, and added to it. Patience is the first requirement for travellers in Africa.

Eventually we arrived at the resthouse at the airport—it was now 8.45 at night. My day had gone on too long, seventeen hours and forty-five minutes. I was nearly crazy with fatigue. There was no room at the resthouse. The President of the German Parliament (a short man who resembled an irritated warthog) and two subservient underlings had got there first; they have been travelling around West Africa offering German money for something or other, and they look as if they hated life by now. The other rooms were used by the Sudan Airways crew.

Mr Kabbabé suggested that I give a tip to the head boy and something would be fixed for me. I thanked Mr Kabbabé who had earned his money the hardest way, and promised to look up another daughter in Khartoum. The head boy brought a cot into the customs room; this was a large room filled with counters for examining luggage (too odd; luggage-laden passengers here?) with three doors and four windows; a scruffy goldfish bowl. My cot had a paper-thin mattress and for sheet and blanket a soiled cotton brocade tablecloth. There was only a weak kerosene lamp, and by careful positioning, I could undress in privacy and not notice my new home.

The bathroom was another horror. I stood in the filthy tub and dipped water out of a bucket with a thermos cup, to give myself a shower. The latrine broke my lion heart. For dinner I had a bottle of tepid beer, two Equanils and a sleeping pill; the intention being to pass out as fast as possible.

In the night, I was very cold and woke and had to go to the loo. The latrine was more than I could face so I wandered out in my nightgown, on to the sand. And saw, drugged with sleep and shivering, the great African sky which I have been seeking—a riot of stars, velvet black, felt as an arch, and the air seeming to glint with starshine. I just managed to attend to my needs in time; out of nowhere black shapes rose—the Ramadan feasters were not all asleep. I crept back to my cot and thought what a price I had paid for that one glimpse of a perfect sky.

February 11: Shortly after eight in the morning, the English crew appeared and walked to the plane. They were shaved and wearing spotless white shirts and shorts; cheerful and serene. I do admire the English. To keep up this appearance is a superb act of will, an affirmation of self-respect in the face of all odds.

It was hot in the plane and hotter on the ground. We landed at Nyala, El Fasher, and El Obeid, and arrived at Khartoum at 4.35 in the afternoon. A wearing weary day.

The land is desert but not pure sand; the earth is brown, hard-baked, cracking, spotted with an acne of scrub and lined with dry stream beds. How or why anyone lives here beats me. El Fasher is a big cattle and horse trading centre, lashed by a hot wind. We ate lunch in the airport building, abominable greasy food, and afterwards I waited in the lounge, which was occupied by two heavy Britishers, drinking beer. One was a

Scot, the other working-class English—he spoke uneducated English and fluent Arabic. These men, in their forties, are engineers, stuck in this hole to help the Sudanese build dams to catch the rains in the wadis. I can perfectly understand the remote life where nature is welcoming but regard this sort of man as a mad hero.

The Sudanese are all glum from Ramadan fasting. Their officials wear clean starched khaki uniforms, exact copies of British tropical army gear; they look natty; one has a feeling of greater tidiness and pride here.

The Khartoum airport is a fine modern building, and to be avoided. *Pagaille* reigns. Perhaps the fasting has made everyone more surly and incompetent than usual. I waited endlessly where my luggage was supposed to arrive and finally found it sitting outside on the pavement. Meanwhile I watched a touching scene. On our plane there had been a black mother with four beautifully behaved small children. At the airport, their father met them. The children raced to him; he kissed them all, but his favourite was the littlest girl; he could not get enough of her. They sat on a bench, waiting for who knows what, and it was a picture of family love and happiness and tenderness. Whites say that the blacks have no real personal affections and I doubt that very much indeed.

Men, meeting each other, put their left hands on each other's shoulders and shake hands; it is a noble-seeming gesture. This race is deformed by tribal scars too, but tall and well-made with handsome round heads.

I had been dreaming of the Grand Hotel; one must not dream of hotels in Africa. Upon arriving there I was flattened by misery. From the outside the hotel is a long and attractive-looking building which faces the Blue Nile. Inside, it is like a big English hotel on the seaside, gone to seed. No English hotel by the seaside is good enough as a start. I was given a room, exactly like an eighth-rate English hotel room, with dark blue rep curtains and dark varnished cupboard and washbowl and hard bed, and the use of the public toilet and bath, both filthy. The food was inedible English, too.

This is Khartoum, at the junction of the two Niles, fabled in song and story, the scene of Gordon's Last Stand. Only a firm resolve to live in imagination and literature would make it bearable. My heart sinks like a stone.

I give up. I am getting out to East Africa. Camping in game parks and watching animals cannot be as dreadful as all this. I hoped to go by boat up the Nile and land at Entebbe, but the Sudanese government has declared the upper Nile a military zone (whatever next) and I cannot face any more paperwork, squalor, or heat. Besides, now I think about it, I find this government a damned bore; they too will not issue visas to anyone who has an Israeli visa on his passport. The hell with them all.

February 12: Here the process of waking was reversed; I left a call for 6.30 a.m. and was awakened by a battering ram on the door at 6 a.m. in the dark. At 7.30, Mr Kabbabé's other son-in-law called on me; he was sorry he could not take me round but the clerk (the everything) of his tourist agency—one of Mr Kabbabé's many interests—would escort me. I spent most of the day and dined with the clerk, Mr Sharir, an Egyptian Copt.

In the morning light, the Blue Nile was pretty between its sandy banks, with palm trees on the far shore and a crowd of white-robed Sudanese waiting for the ferry. Nothing much else is pretty, though the actual joining of the Niles is unusual, the White Nile being mud-coloured, and the waters of the Blue Nile running into it, parallel but not mixing for a long distance.

Mr Sharir and I went sightseeing. We visited the Khalifa's house (the son of the Mahdi), a museum which proves how—in earlier times and certainly in colonial wars—the individual soldier had to be more heroic than nowadays; it is fearsome to see the weapons used, and to imagine the hand-to-hand fighting. The bath in the harem was luscious; I'd have liked to have the sunken pool filled with water and spend the day there. The market is a smaller, dirtier, poorer version of Cairo; strong feeling of the Orient, as in Cairo, and native craftsmen at work in their little shops, fashioning objects out of gold and out of ivory (never see an elephant's tusk without indignation; criminal to kill these great beasts in order to make ugly knicknacks). Mr Sharir says the people are either gloomy from real fasting, or pretending to be gloomy from pretend-fasting.

A boring hot day, followed by dinner with Mr Sharir in a dismal garden restaurant on the Nile; it is the best local-colour place available. Mr Sharir is a novelty. He is small, quite good-looking, brown-skinned and aged thirty-five. He is so bored with life that he does not care if he dies tomorrow. He has no interest except women, and the women are not interesting. He is married; his wife and child live in Cairo, occasionally he goes to see them. He says stoutly that he loves his child, but he is paying lip-service to the role of a father. Obviously the child bores him as much as the mother.

He said he married because there was no other way to get the girl to bed, which was why they all married. After marriage, the girls are not keen on bed (they want marriage), let themselves go, get fat, eat candies all day, and are only interested in their children. So the men continue going to bed, with professionals, and that's a bore too. Here one has the perfect example of justice: the men have kept their women enslaved—the Arabs more than the Christian Copts—kept them stupid and limited and apart, for their male vanity and power; result: the dull women bore the daylights out of the men. Mr Sharir approves of Nasser and says all Egyptians do; not for what he has done in Egypt (nothing much) but because he has made Egypt into a Power—i.e. a nuisance to the world, to be placated.

We passed Gordon's palace, a fine great white house, now the home of the Sudanese dictator and closed to the public. Dictatorship inconveniences almost no one, Mr Sharir points out; you only have to keep your mouth shut and mind your own business, and you are not bothered. It does not occur to Mr Sharir that dictatorship, like the enslaved women, contributes greatly to the boredom of life.

I went to bed at midnight, to be called at 3 a.m. for the plane to Nairobi. This is the end of West Africa, suitably finishing on a note of irritation, discomfort, boredom and exhaustion. Seek and ye shall find, we have been told. I have been seeking for nineteen days and found nothing that I came to find. I am almost afraid to risk hope of East Africa.

It is high time that I learn to be more careful about hope, a reckless emotion for travellers. The sensible approach would be to expect the worst, the very worst; that way you avoid grievous disappointment and who knows, with a tiny bit of luck, you might even have a moderately pleasant surprise, like the difference between hell and purgatory.

There the diary finishes; now I am on my own, with a few fairly useless East African notes and my memory. The prospect is daunting. As near as I can figure, on a straight line basis, I drove some two thousand miles through Kenya, Uganda and Tanganyika and the journey lasted three weeks to a month. Time was not gauged by any previous measurements. Time related only to daylight and the gnawing question: will we get there? Two thousand miles on those roads is equal to ten thousand miles on autobahns, superhighways, the speedy smooth surfaces we are used to. The journey was long, that's sure. When it was over I felt I was Mr Henry Morton Stanley himself.

I spend and waste time like a millionaire; plenty of capital on deposit, I will never run short. And forget with the same lavishness; no need to save old memory since new memories pile up, an unlimited supply of money in the bank, a bank as big as the world. From the day of my arrival in Nairobi to now—writing in temporary furnished quarters in Ta'Xbiex on the island of Malta—I have spent and wasted and piled up and forgotten fifteen years and three months' worth of time and memories. There is no way I can lift out and reconstruct the weeks with Joshua in East Africa. I can trace the journey, remember many events and emotions, and allow myself writer's licence to fill gaps. But I don't want to begin or end each sentence with "as I remember," that unwritten qualifying phrase will be everywhere present.

Having been waked at 3 a.m., after three hours' sleep, a close call for a 4 a.m. plane, I arrived out of breath, slung into my clothes, feeling hollow and sour-mouthed, and waited in the cold dark Khartoum airport until 5.30: engine trouble. Thus far, African travel recalled the dreariest aspects of war. Always up in the middle of the night, always exhausted, always deep in discomfort varying from fierce to nasty, and always preyed on by boredom. The one fine, loved aspect of war was missing: except for two days of C., in Cameroun, I had met no companions of the road. War is full of them, a shifting population of men made extraordinary by circumstance. Nobody to laugh with means the horrors of the journey are undiluted. Very heavy going.

By now, I was a tired lonely ant on this outsize continent. Loneliness caused me to wire ahead to Ker and Downey Ltd, Nairobi, not knowing whether a telegram with no further address would ever reach anyone. I wanted to be met, carried on a cushion, patted on the head, rocked to sleep with lullabies, cared for, cherished, taken in hand. Far below, where the Sudan joined Ethiopia, the scenery was the weirdest and wildest yet; brown-red mountains, gorges, craters, no sign of life, desert in the act of boiling. Was East Africa going to be worse than West Africa? Slowly the earth became green, then greener; Mount Kenya with snow on it, cultivation, big separate trees, not jungle, not bleak twisted thorn. The land seemed livable, the first hint that Africa might be more than an endurance contest.

No other airport had looked like this: small, white, tidy, bordered with flowers. The sky performed the way I had longed for it to do; it went up forever. Soft air, warmed by a high clear sun (farewell to fried eggs) smelled as I hoped Africa would. I was glowing and gushing when I met Mr Whitehead, of Ker and Downey, beyond the Customs barrier; "a shy charming man" (from notes) of whom no picture has stayed in my mind though he was kindness itself.

As a routine courtesy, Mr Whitehead had come to collect a prospective client. I had no idea that Ker and Downey was the grandest safari outfit in Kenya; if I had thought at all, I imagined Ker and Downey to be an East African version of Le Keeng. This misunderstanding percolated dimly through my fatigue while Mr Whitehead was driving me to the New Stanley Hotel. I was given a room on an airshaft with the noise of kitchen pots and pans below but was too broken by Africa to rebel, complain, demand better conditions. I took what I got, aware of being the Unknown American, not entitled to superior quarters and a welcoming bouquet from the manager; I slept.

Nairobi weather is the best you can get, like Cuernavaca, about a mile high in the tropics. A radiant warmth that produces energy and hope instead of dripping sweat and headaches. Everyone looked sunburned, bright, well-dressed, pleased with life. Everyone was going somewhere briskly. Stylish shops and gleaming cars. Jacaranda and flame trees and royal palms and dense dark green trees, perhaps live oak, much favoured by small birds. Narrow garden strips down the middle of clean streets, fountains of bougainvillea, white, purple, crimson, peach, and hibiscus and oleanders. A beguiling little city that felt rich and happy, made to order for white residents and high-class tourists. In the money-spending centre, Europeans crowded the streets, leavened by Asians; Africans were sparse on the ground, squatting beside pavement mats to sell tourist trinkets, hawking newspapers and lottery tickets, begging from polio-gnarled legs, driving taxis, fetching and carrying.

They were very different from their relatives in West Africa, not as cheery and idle, not dressed in eccentric tatters. The social structure was clear at once: Europeans, Asians, Africans ("black" being abusive here); First, Second and Third Class citizens. Perhaps I felt the supremacy of white skin in this British colony with more force because I had just arrived from independent African states where white skin was carefully unassertive. I had no reason to believe these white overlords were not decent and just but I wished the Africans looked less subdued. Always delighted to grab any privileges I can get, I don't like the sense of being privileged by law. I mistrust power for myself and everyone else, especially power bestowed by race, creed or colour. This works both ways; I hadn't been overjoyed by bootlicking where the blacks ruled.

My immediate need was clothes. Shopping for a short while in a new place can be fun; otherwise shopping is a drudgery maintenance job.

Asians ran the shops. Their eagerness to please and their efficiency brought tears to my eyes. I bought everything I needed in no time. Unlike the poor fly-ridden markets of West Africa, the big Nairobi market overflowed with luscious fruits and vegetables, and stalls where one could buy armfuls of tuberoses, agapanthus, iris, roses, cornflowers, chrysanthemums, lilies for a few shillings. I chose a giant bunch of pink carnations to decorate my unlovely little room. The three races jostled in the market, no shortage of Africans here. Suddenly I realized there was no noxious human stench. We all smelled however we did and inoffensive. Yet these Africans certainly didn't have nice bathrooms at home and piles of Lifebuoy soap. Relief from body odour had to be another blessing of the climate.

In a new cotton dress, my hair properly washed, I nerved myself to call on Mr Whitehead and break the news that I didn't want an elegant safari complete with white hunter. Rich people thought it dashing to kill the beautiful animals in comfort and safety; dozens of Africans to manage the camp work like well-trained outdoor butlers and a white hunter to shoot any animal that might endanger the paying customer who hadn't shot straight. Photographic safaris were more sporting because you have to get closer for a good camera shot than for a good rifle shot; but I hadn't used a camera since the Box Brownie of my childhood. It was also possible and pleasant to go on safari in the game parks, camping out, guided and informed by a white hunter who served the same purpose as the scholar–lecturer on culture tours. I wanted none of any of it. I knew exactly what I wanted: hire or buy a secondhand Landrover, pick up a driver to share the work and act as interpreter, and set forth alone to explore East Africa.

There was a road map, put out by the Shell Company of East Africa; if there were roads, why couldn't I drive on them? There was a small booklet, listing inns, rest houses and hotels throughout Kenya, Uganda, and Tanganyika. I didn't mean to camp in the wilds, having neither the experience nor the equipment; I meant to move along marked roads from place to place, stopping in ordinary hostelries. My goal would be the game parks. What's wrong with that? I asked Mr Whitehead.

He looked grave. He hesitated. "Nothing," he said. "In principle. Only it's not a good idea. Not really." This was my first visit, he said, and Africa was different, things didn't work the same out here, he wouldn't like his wife (sister, daughter, I forget which) to make such a trip. Having survived West Africa, I saw no reason to be spooked by lovely tamed East Africa. Mr Whitehead may have thought I was a lemming in human form and though I was of no interest to his company, he couldn't have been more helpful, introducing one of his white hunters with a Landrover to rent. The white hunter said his vehicle had done sixty-five thousand arduous miles and wasn't in what you'd call mint condition. The engine started, it moved; I asked no more. Unfortunately, said Mr Whitehead, he could not loan a driver, all of theirs were occupied on safari.

Various friendly people had swum in and out of my ken (ridiculous phrase) among them the nice Honorary Consul of Israel. Born and bred in Nairobi, he was very much a city man, and very much concerned about my being alone with an African on the distant roads. He offered to find a safe driver. Joshua presented himself in the cocktail lounge of the New Stanley with a chit from the Honorary Consul, guaranteeing that Joshua was "reliable." In local code, this meant that Joshua would not rape and/or rob me. Neither of those possibilities have ever seemed worth fretting over. Instinct, which I regularly ignore, told me that Joshua was not the man for the job.

Joshua was small, cordoba brown in colour, delicate to fragile, neat and clean. We sat on a bench by the wall while Joshua extolled his virtues. He was, first and foremost, "eddicated," that implied higher pay than for an average driver. He had driven a Government Landrover throughout the Emergency (Mau Mau time) and lately had been driving a large American car for a tourist company in the city. I was not enthusiastic about Joshua; there was something finicky in him which I felt would not wear well, and I would have preferred a sturdier type. But I was scratchy with impatience to leave, three whole days in Nairobi were enough. Nairobi was bliss but it wasn't Africa either. I was still searching for the Africa that I had come this weary way to find.

So I hired Joshua, despite the loud alarm bells of instinct, and told him we would leave at eight in the morning. My equipment for the journey was a large thermos filled with cold water, a flashlight, new khaki trousers and shirts, comfortable safari boots, the old straw hat, a fresh stock of paperback thrillers and goofy confidence.

Joshua arrived in black imitation Italian silk pipestem trousers, white shirt, black pointed shoes, black sunglasses in ornate red frames, holding a cardboard suitcase. The lobby of the New Stanley and the Thorn Tree café outside teemed with people going on or returning from safaris, or pretending to do so. The correct outfit was a deep sunburn, well-cut, much-worn, faded starched khaki trousers, long or short, a short-sleeved khaki bush jacket or shirt with ample pockets, old safari boots: new clothes betrayed the tenderfoot tourist. The tone was easy machismo; everyone had been eyeball to eyeball with a lion. African safari servants also wore khaki though rumpled and baggy, not Bwana standard. Departures were impressive and rather theatrical, especially if celebrities were about to venture into the bush. Mr Kirk Douglas and Mr Robert Ruark were leaving glamorously at this time. Joshua looked a comic cut; I looked sheepish. Only the dusty, beat-up, dented, patched Landrover looked right.

I expected Joshua to take the wheel and steer us out of Nairobi to the main Nairobi–Kampala road; gently but firmly, Joshua declined the honour. He could direct me better if I drove. We made the same noise as a tank. If there were any springs in this Landrover I didn't notice them, even on city streets. To change gears I had to push or pull with might and main. Next to walking, the freedom of a car is my favourite way to travel, depending on the car. This heavy ancient vehicle was going to be a beast but between us, turn and turn about, we could rest from the effort.

Slowly we wound uphill past fields and thick forest until we reached the eastern edge of the Rift Valley. Far below, as far as I could see, lay the golden plain ringed by blue mountains. It was true, it was there, and more magical than I had ever pictured it.

Happiness is a good deal better than the absence of pain. To me it feels as if the quality of my blood had changed, something new rich strong is pumping through my veins and exalting my heart, my lungs are filled with sunlit air, the world is too beautiful, I might easily spread my arms and fly. Seized with this happiness, now, I wished as often before that I could carry a tune and sing for joy but I can't and if I started shouting, the only alternative, Joshua would think himself linked to a madwoman. I stopped the Landrover to feast on the dream made visible. Joshua smiled with pleasure over the landscape of his country. That cheered me a lot; scenery gave us a common bond, we would get along as fellow travellers.

"You drive now, Joshua."

"Look at that bad road, Memsaab." The road corkscrewed in tight loops down the side of the escarpment. "Better I watch and tell you."

I drove in second gear, tugging frantically at the wheel on the turns, not daring to raise my eyes for a minute and enjoy the view. I was pretty peeved with Joshua, depriving me of this, but perhaps it was regular form in Africa to have a lookout. The road straightened along the valley floor and I stepped on the gas, only to find that thirty-five miles an hour was our maximum speed. Never mind, I didn't want to hurry. I wanted to see. The road felt almost European compared with West African roads though in fact it was a two-lane macadam surface, liberally flawed. Real cars flashed past us, an old Volkswagen overtook us with a waving hand and a grin, but there was little traffic.

Suddenly, to left and right of the highway, giraffes stood, in the poses that they alone achieve, enormous, sleek, polished dark brown hide marked into uneven rectangles and squares by narrow white lines, and observed the scene through their long-lashed eyes. My cup ran over on the spot. Now I had everything, the plain and the mountains and these perfect animals. "Oh *nice*," Joshua said, and laughed with delight. I didn't then suspect what I later became convinced of: Joshua had never in his life been farther outside Nairobi than the suburbs nor seen any wild animals until he saw those ravishing giraffes. It was all new to him as to me.

We bumped and clanked across the valley, shouting conversation. Joshua was a Kikuyu, the dominant Kenya tribe, reputed to be the most intelligent; he was also a Presbyterian. I don't remember whether he went to a Presbyterian mission school or why he adopted that faith but he had it, earnestly. He could never steal, he explained, because of his religion, nor tell a lie. Having lied his head off about driving a Landrover during the Emergency; like a dope, I had believed that fairy tale.

Joshua was too young, twenty-three now; the Emergency lasted from 1952 to 1960. No African teenager ever drove anything anywhere, and certainly not Joshua starting at the age of thirteen. Transport is as essential as water to Europeans in Africa; they don't entrust their valuable cars lightly to Africans. Joshua was not married and not tempted. African girls were silly, he shouted; the accompanying sniff reached me as a feeling rather than a sound, in the Landrover's general uproar. He wished to get ahead; his ambition was to own a fleet of cars, his own rental agency in Nairobi. A genuine city boy with genuine middle-class dreams.

Three categories of road were marked on the map; thick red for major roads, thinner red for secondary roads, narrow yellow for outright disaster roads and, finally, a red hairline that must have meant a footpath between villages or maybe game tracks. We had turned north at Gilgil onto a secondary road and it was bad. This was the year of the great floods and there was plenty of mud to overcome; mud is for bogging down, dust is for skidding out of control. My aim was Barry's Hotel at Thomson's Falls and it was getting late. I began to worry, as I did every day thereafter, about daylight and distance. Worry is too mild a word. A knot started to form in my stomach around four o'clock and grew knottier and bigger every half hour. The sun set almost exactly at six. I doubted that I could cope with these roads in the dark; I could too easily imagine a breakdown and a long cold black night, waiting for a car to pass in the morning.

There was no traffic at all. Joshua, chilled in his white shirt and cowering as forest closed in both sides of the road, would cry out like a variation on Sister Anne, "How far now, Memsaab, how far?" During the afternoon, Joshua had invented two more excuses for not driving so I knew it was pointless to ask him to drive now that the going was tough. I gritted my teeth like a man and told Joshua to shut up; didn't he have a sweater in his suitcase, well find it and put it on for God's sake, we'll get there when we get there. Which we did.

Our business arrangements had been made in advance. Joshua was to be paid for his services and a food allowance; I would pay for his room wherever we stayed. The amount of money was fixed by Joshua as I wanted a satisfied not disgruntled helper. Someone had briefed me on money dealings: Africans were said to be feckless about money, you must never give them large sums at one time, they will have gambled or drunk up or otherwise lost it all by the next day; you dole out money and never under any circumstances do you loan it. Loans are the beginning of the end. Living on loans, the African feels he is working for nothing, he will not be paid any more nor does he intend to pay back; it becomes a shambles; stick to small regular sums, the only way. Joshua had four days' advance wages in hand.

When we arrived at the hotel, a long verandah fronting a stone building, draped in greenery, I parked the car, told Joshua to bring my suitcase inside and fix himself up. I wanted a drink, several drinks, and a soft comfortable chair. My shoulders felt as if I had been carrying an iron bar on them all the way from Nairobi. I had signed in, said my driver would need a room, and settled by the fire with a large whisky, when Joshua appeared, grasping his own suitcase.

"Memsaab?"

"What's the matter, Joshua?"

"Where shall I go?" It had a biblical ring; Ruth among the alien corn.

I gave Joshua the first of ceaseless lectures, informing him that he spoke Swahili, he was surrounded by his own countrymen, he could use his voice, he could ask anyone who worked in the hotel where drivers' rooms were, he could then ask these same people any other questions which might occur to him. He could not ask me because I did not know, nor was it my business to know, I was extremely tired since I had been driving all day, and I wished to rest in peace. He had no duties except to find his room which should not be too heavy a task, and appear again at nine in the morning but not before. "Buck up, Joshua," I said sharply.

What a lovely Africa this is, I thought, watching rainbows flicker in mist from the plunging river. Giant ferns along the banks glistened with dew. I could taste the air; we were high up, 7,680 feet it said in the hotel lobby. Far off to the east a huge white cone, shining like moonstone, hung in the sky: the snow cap of Mount Kenya. Beside the bridge over the river, an African was carving an elephant; it was identical to the elephants for tourists at Fort Lamy. How did they get the word, from West to East or vice versa, to stylize the shape of elephants? I asked the African where he had learned to carve an elephant this way. He shrugged. It was the moment for Joshua, interpreter.

Joshua was sitting on the verandah steps, looking refreshed and peculiar. He wore his pointed shoes and black city socks, well pulled up, a clean short-sleeved white shirt, the sunglasses and tiny khaki shorts: his safari outfit. I led him to the bridge and told him my question. After a surprisingly long conversation, Joshua reported, "From his fadder." Where then did his father learn? More long talk. "From his fadder," Joshua said.

"You mean you've been talking all that time for him only to say three words? What else did he say, Joshua?"

"That's all, Memsaab. Just his fadder."

"Swahili must be a very funny language if it takes so long to say so little."

"Very funny," Joshua agreed.

Apparently Joshua was not going to be any more active as an interpreter than as a driver. Arguing about Swahili wouldn't get me far so I suggested that Joshua collect some food as I planned to picnic at Lake Nakuru, a National Park, and drive on to Kericho for the night.

While waiting for Joshua, the hotel manager gave me a needed Landrover lesson. I had forgotten to ask how to push, pull, lift, tug the small second gear that puts the Landrover into four-wheel drive. Now I felt equipped for the worst though the gear was brutal but together Joshua and I would surely be able to move it into position.

"You drive this morning, Joshua."

"Better later, Memsaab," Joshua said and nipped smartly into the passenger seat.

The mornings were always easier no matter what the road because the daylight-distance phobia hadn't engulfed me. We made the forty-four miles to Nakuru in two hours, quick work, and I stopped for petrol. Petrol stations were infrequent. Whenever I saw one, I behaved as if I had come on an oasis in the desert and drew in to replenish the tank and check the oil and water and tyre pressure, though we carried two jerry cans of petrol and one of water. Joshua sat and watched while I jumped out to make sure the air gauge was properly read, the oil gauge properly wiped and inserted and inspected, the petrol actually filling the tank.

"Really, Joshua," I said crossly, "You could take care of this."

"Better you, Memsaab. These boys obey you more."

The African Ranger at the gate of Lake Nakuru Park warned me about water-logged side tracks. It would be wiser to leave the Landrover on the main track and walk to the shore. After driving far enough to feel alone in darkest Africa and therefore ecstatic, I parked the Landrover on a reliable piece of stubble-covered ground, got my kit together, sandwiches, thermos of cold tea, *Field Guide to the National Parks*, binoculars and said, "Ready, Joshua?"

Joshua stared at the squashy track and wrinkled his nose. "Very bad mud."

"Are you coming or not?"

"Memsaab, they got lions?"

"No," I said with authority, having read the *Field Guide*, which stated that lions were rare hereabouts.

"I watch the car. Some man could come stealing your clothes." I much preferred to be by myself but thought it would be an awful bind if we had to circle East Africa without getting Joshua's fancy footwear dirty.

The trees here were yellow acacia, fever trees, very tall with bright yellow trunks and branches and small feathery jade green leaves. I squelched along quietly and two tiniest antelopes, not much larger than rabbits, leaped across the track. They were reddish with diminutive horns and butterfly ears and I hoped I could remember them long enough to look them up. The advantages of an experienced African safari driver were all too apparent; such a man would know everything, explain what the animals were doing, and have no anxiety about his shoes. He might even take a turn at the wheel.

Through the trees I saw zebra grazing and held my breath in wonder and delight. I would never be able to go to a zoo again, I would feel too sorry for animals kidnapped from where they belonged. And the poor animals would never again look right. The brief interlude at Waza in Cameroun, giraffes on the Nairobi–Kampala road and this herd of zebra had already shown me the difference between the imprisoned and the free: the shine of their coats. And the movements, the grace of everything they did when living as they were meant to. I was seeing animals for the first time, before I had seen sad copies of the original creation.

At the shore, thousands of flamingoes lifted off and spread in a coral pink streamer against the sky. The sound of flight was like tearing silk. Then the streamer dropped, farther along the lake, and the birds trekked head down, eating; others relaxed on one leg. A field of rosy feathers. Out of three and a half closely printed *Field Guide* pages, giving the names of birds to be seen here, I recognized only egrets and pelicans and herons. Charming names. Bare-Faced Go-Away Bird which emits "a series of deep bleating calls and wild ringing chuckles." What could be better? It was a world of birds and they looked newly made, standing at ease or pecking on the lake bed, taking flight into the brilliant emptiness of the sky as if for pleasure. A short spin round heaven.

A fallen tree trunk was not too wet, just enough to dampen my trouser seat. I settled with binoculars and lunch. On the far side and at the far end of the lake, the land rose in high rocks, studded with candelabra cactus. The water was very blue, marshy by the shore. I ate sandwiches and listened to the silence beneath the steady insect hum of Africa and thought perhaps I was going to have daily attacks of happiness because here it came again, the sensation of being airborne. Canaries flew in shoals through the fever trees, and bigger yellow birds, possibly weavers. Doves sang their sweet mournful song. Those coloured flashes in the leaves might be bee-eaters or sunbirds. So much to see, so much to learn, and no help at hand except the *Field Guide to the National Parks.* At least I could identify the diminutive antelopes as Kirk's dikdik and finished my lunch and weighed the dampness on my bottom against the pleasure of a cigarette here, lit the cigarette and watched a parade of greyish monkeys cavort among the treetops.

If only I knew more, if only I were more capable: I ought to be camping with a tent and walking slowly through the acacia woodland to glimpse the animals before they glimpsed me. Instead I looked at my watch and it was 2.30 and daylight-distance had to be considered. Still I moved quietly on the track, hoping for more visions and again saw the herd of zebra now joined by visiting friends, small antelopes with a black stripe along their tan sides and neat black horns spiralled to a point, and a short black tufted flicking tail. I disturbed them and they ran, bouncing as if the earth was a trampoline. This was all far more beautiful and exciting than anything I had seen in the museums of the civilized world, and music never gave me such joy. At last and for once I had actually found what I was seeking.

The Landrover was turned so that the passenger seat faced the track. Joshua sat therein, with the door open, his knees crossed, one foot swinging languidly outside. He held a miniature teacup and saucer in his left hand and as I stared, transfixed, he lifted the cup, his little finger curled, and sipped daintily. It struck me with the force of revelation: a Kikuyu Presbyterian pansy. Joshua turned and said graciously, "*Jambo*, Memsaab, you have good time?"

"*Jambo*, Joshua, very good." I busied myself looking up the small antelopes in the guide book while Joshua stowed the remains of our picnics and his china ware: Thomson's gazelles. But how could I have guessed, I didn't even know African pansies existed. When you thought of all the clamour about black men lusting for white women and white women lusting for black men due to their massive virility, it was even funnier. What I could absolutely not do was have a fit of giggles.

"Want to drive now, Joshua?"

"I dunno this road, Memsaab."

"Have you ever heard about the blind leading the blind?"

"No, how can that be? If somebody is blind how can he be leading another fellow as well he is blind too?"

"We are going to find out, Joshua, day by day. Get your sweater now, it will be cold later." And thought that before we were through no doubt I would bring him morning tea and tuck him in at night.

The road was never marked correctly on the map, perhaps because no one could draw all those twists and bends in the available space. This was the major road and the surface was quite good though very up hill and down dale with much braking and shifting gears. The scenery was always different, usually glorious, never dull or ugly and most of it has blurred out of shape in my memory. We had to take a turn-off to the left for Kericho and I instructed Joshua to keep his eyes open. Joshua couldn't read a map, not that it made much difference; little to choose from and as time went on I realized the map was more a wistful estimate than a statement of fact. There was really no reason to believe any information, printed or otherwise, but one must have faith in something or founder utterly and I based my faith and my distance calculations on the hotel-inn-resthouse booklet, figuring that it was 66 miles to Kericho from Nakuru but if we missed the turn the next possible stop was Kisumu, 111 miles, and we would never make that before dark.

From another detailed map, which I must have stolen later off an old Africa hand, I see that it had been quite some drive, the road dipping and rising through immense forests with the Mau Escarpment, a 10,000-foot-high range of mountains, on our left and Mount Londiani sticking up 9,874 feet on the right and after the turn-off at Lumbwa, the road dropped down to 6,700 feet at Kericho with a vast spread of thick uninhabited forest to the east. I daresay it was spectacular and that when I wasn't wrestling the Landrover I appreciated it.

Around 5 p.m. Joshua started his Sister Anne act. "Very cold, Memsaab, how far now?" I had told him the distances; whether correct or not, they were the best we had. He knew as well as I did that here, practically on the Equator, the sun set at six; he also knew it got cold in the late afternoon and much colder at night in these high altitudes; he knew as much as I did which wasn't much and by the end of the day I was too tired to feel like playing Nanny. "Oh shut up, Joshua," I said, concentrated on steering.

After a while, he said, "Where we going, Memsaab?"

"Kericho, I told you."

"What is that place?"

"How in God's name should I know? The hotel is called the Tea Hotel so I suppose they grow tea there or maybe just drink it. Think of something cheerful, Joshua, and do *not* ask me how far."

We got in soon after dark, the hotel beaming like a lighthouse to guide us. A bossy Memsaab said she would attend to my boy, and I had time for a quick wash before dinner. I didn't care about dinner and flopped into a chintz chair in the lounge—thinking wearily that it was wonderful how everywhere the English managed chintz and spoke of the lounge—and rang for a drink. The hotel Memsaab, returning, announced that I would be late as if being late for dinner was a felony. To placate her, I explained that I had driven from Thomson's Falls and the

Landrover was old and heavy, and therefore I was in need of whisky. The Memsaab melted and said I was a poor dear but why didn't my boy drive. Out of loyalty to Joshua, I found myself lying; he's not a driver, I explained, he's along to carry luggage and do my washing and be my interpreter because I don't speak Swahili, he's more an indoor boy.

It would be repetitious to describe food; I blamed the absence of eating pleasure everywhere on the Memsaabs who taught the African cooks. The Africans did not eat what they cooked for us, whether by their own choice or for economy reasons. Thick custard sauce on tinned fruit was a special bane, as was thick brown gravy on indecipherable meat. Breakfast was the one satisfactory meal in East Africa though I will never comprehend the theory and practice of cold toast. There were a few other guests in the dining room but aside from murmuring good evening, if glances met, conversation did not occur. Talk at the tables was carried on in whisper voices. The general tone was that of a deadly respectable English provincial hotel. Inside, you hardly knew you were in Africa; outside the night sky told you exactly where you were.

No one else strolled on to the terrace. It was cold but that wasn't why I hastened back to my snug room and drawn curtains. This was not the velvet embracing desert sky at El Geneina; this was infinite space. The idea of no boundaries, no end, is terrifying in the abstract and much worse if you are looking at it. The far-off stars were an icy crust; the darkness beyond the stars was more than I could handle. The machinery that keeps me going is not geared to cope with infinity and eternity as so clearly displayed in that sky. After sunset, the Africans jammed into their round huts and closed everything to keep out the night; if I understood nothing else about them, I understood that.

The morning smell was roses and lilies and stocks. The garden grew everything English only bigger. Rose geraniums and passion flowers and trumpet vines and plumbago covered the walls of the hotel. The lawn was a triumph; in a country where any fool can grow orchids, a smooth lawn is the prize accomplishment. Below this Afro-English enclave, the tea gardens stretched in long neat rows of shining dark green bushes. Beyond the tea gardens, forest, and mountains. I asked the hotel Memsaab, Mrs Simpson, if I might stay on a few days. Travel for pleasure had worn me out. This benign Anglicized Africa was just the ticket for frayed nerves.

Joshua drooped in the passenger seat of the Landrover. When I said I meant to stay here for two or three days he drooped more.

"Isn't your room nice, Joshua?"

"It is all right, Memsaab."

"Do you find what you want to eat?"

"Yes, Memsaab."

"Well, cheer up. You love tea, they should have first-class tea here."

Joshua was bored, no getting around it. I didn't have to arrange my trip to spare Joshua boredom. He ought to have some work to keep him busy and as a matter of fact he ought to do that work every day without being told. I said, "Clean the car, Joshua, inside and out. That's your job, you know. Look at the windshield." It was plastered with smashed insects. "Look at the floor." Hunks of dried mud. "Buck up, Joshua," I said.

In the afternoon, Mrs Simpson sought me out in my shaded deck chair. I put aside the paperback thriller with regret. Mrs Simpson parked on the grass, prepared for a comfortable chat. She began by a bit of probing. It was unusual, she said, for a woman to travel alone. Two unmarried teachers from Nairobi often came here during school holidays but of course they lived in Kenya. Perhaps I was on my way to visit friends? I sketched a noncommittal nod and that seemed to solve me.

"He's a funny one, your boy."

"Oh? Has he done anything wrong?"

"Oh no, he's remarkably tidy and quiet. He's more like a little old maid than an African."

Poor Joshua, I didn't see him giving that high tee-hee laugh or the belly bellow of Africans, nor did I imagine he could join cosily in the non-stop natter which is a universal African occupation. Perhaps he wasn't bored; perhaps he was lonely.

"He looks younger than he is," Mrs Simpson said. "I wouldn't have taken him for thirty-three."

"*Thirty*-three?"

"So he said." To whom was Joshua lying and for what purpose?

"I've lived here twenty-seven years," Mrs Simpson said. "My husband was a tea planter; I took this job five years ago when he died. And I don't know anything about Africans, not their age or what goes on in their heads or why they do what they do or don't do what they should do. The longer you live among them, the less you know. Now our cook, he's been with me the whole time. He makes apple pie at least three times a week. He goes along perfectly for months, then all of a sudden he forgets everything, he cannot make apple pie, I have to start from scratch and teach him again. Then he sulks, as if I were asking him to do something extraordinary and impossible. They never tell us the truth on principle. Every time they want extra leave, it's a death in the family. I have a gardener who's had at least twenty deaths in his family and I only keep him because he's good with roses. But then he forgets too. You have to stand over them every minute, watching, reminding, nagging. It just about drives you up the wall."

"Perhaps because it's different from anything they do for themselves?"

"My dear, they don't do anything for themselves if they can help it. The women do the work on their shambas and that's not much; they grow a few vegetables and keep some chickens. They're bone idle. God help this country when it gets Independence. The whole lot will simply lie down and sleep."

"Will you stay after Independence?"

"Unless they kick us out. I wouldn't want to live anywhere else. I haven't bothered to go home since my husband died; England seemed so small and that awful climate, when we used to go back. I take my leave on the coast now. I haven't set foot outside Kenya for seven years. But imagine what this country would be like if the population was Chinese instead of African. Those clever hardworking Chinese. It would be heaven on earth. Now I must go and make sure they serve tea properly. There's no telling what they'll do. One day they served all the teapots full of hot water, but forgot to put in the tea."

Joshua was mooning about like a displaced person in a refugee camp. I asked if he liked to read. He said he did without enthusiasm, so I turned over yesterday's thriller, upset because Joshua was not enjoying himself.

"Don't you think it's pretty here, Joshua?"

"Yes it is pretty, Memsaab, but I think we go on safari not sit down in one place."

That infuriated me. "It is *my* safari, Joshua, and perhaps I wouldn't be so tired if I didn't have to do all the driving."

"These roads are too bad, Memsaab. If I make an accident then I will have much trouble. You see that Bwana and Memsaab go away this morning; they take one African boy with them but the Bwana is driving."

"Why did you tell Memsaab Simpson that you were thirty-three?"

"When?" Joshua asked with amazed innocence.

"Listen Joshua, I intend to have a good time on this safari and if you aren't having a good time just don't complain about it."

Joshua looked at once hurt and haughty. I left him feeling that our relation had all the earmarks of a marriage made in haste and repented at leisure; but if he couldn't do anything else at least Joshua could change a tyre should the occasion arise and I hadn't learned any Swahili beyond yes no please thank you Jambo.

We started off on friendlier terms the third morning because Joshua was excited by the thriller and wanted to talk.

"What those spy men are after, Memsaab? Diamonds?"

"No." I didn't see how I could explain the fundamental idiocy of spying, real or fictional, and besides couldn't remember the story, being absorbed in the next one. "They're after each other, I think."

"Already two killed," Joshua said, awed. "Very bad job. Those spy men must get much money for such bad jobs."

· · ·

With me and only me staunchly gripping the wheel, we drove to El-
doret, to Tororo across the Uganda border (somewhere, long ancient
crocodiles basked, then slid into the water), to Jinja where the Nile pours
out of Lake Victoria, and on to Kampala. Joshua said at once and with
reason that Nairobi was far better.

"Okay, Joshua, I agree. But I'm going to look at it as soon as I get a
room. Do you want to come along?"

Joshua condescended to accept the invitation. There wasn't much
to see; it was a sloppy unfinished sort of town, more African than
Nairobi. I fell into a temper over the heat. What did they mean by having such a rotten climate? Kampala stood at four thousand feet altitude,
not sea level, and Lake Victoria was near by, the second largest body of
fresh water in the world (cf. the *World Almanac*), and ought to cool the
air. I was indignant to be sweating again.

"Makerere University is here," I informed Joshua. "It's very grand,
it's the university for all of East Africa."

Joshua grunted. We drove past the campus, mock Elizabethan and
ivy-covered, ridiculously like an African version of Bryn Mawr. I was
feeling quite enlivened by this joke when we came to a long line of trees
where suddenly thousands of bats filled the sky, flapping blindly and
squeaking, hanging on the trees like vile bunches of grapes. A bats' sanc-
tuary. Joshua cried out in disgust and clamped his hands over his hair
which was at most a half inch long and offered no room for bats if it is
true that they wish to nest in human hair.

"What place is this?" Joshua cried. "In a city such things! We have
no *dudus* like that in Nairobi!" *Dudu* is Swahili for insect.

"I don't like them either."

"Go on, Memsaab, drive quick before they come to us!"

I had stopped, repelled—bats being an unfavourite form of life—
but fascinated by this strange migration. Why here?

"*Drive quick!*" Joshua ordered, on the verge of panic.

"Listen Joshua, I know when something is dangerous and when it is not," I lied. "So stop acting like a fool."

However, since Joshua seemed not only in a panic but about to cry, I thought it better to move on.

"How long we stay here, Memsaab?"

"We'll leave tomorrow. I have to mail some letters and get some money."

We queued together in the crowded main Post Office; Joshua held a picture postcard carefully twixt thumb and forefinger. I longed to ask who would receive this greeting from afar—did he have a family, a bosom friend—and dared not invade his privacy. Everyone around us smelled like West Africa, that appalling musky stink. I was unprepared for the shock after deodorized Kenya, and shuddered with distaste. Joshua took out his handkerchief and held it openly to his nose.

"Don't do that," I hissed.

Speaking through his handkerchief, Joshua said, "These people are sweating *dirty*. They smell too bad. I don't know these people. In Kenya people are not smelling like this."

"Put your handkerchief away, Joshua. Breathe through your mouth, like me."

In the close heat of this city and in this horrid body odour, which I had happily forgotten, I began to feel sick; Joshua handed me his post-card and some pennies and fled. So my nose was not racist, after all; what a relief. And furthermore I would honourably refrain from reading the address on Joshua's card.

The people in the Post Office looked reasonably well dressed and many were fat, a sure sign of prosperity. They were really black with a purple plum sheen, unlike Joshua, blacker than any Kenya Africans I had seen. The smell could not derive from skin shade; it had to be diet. The European assistant hotel manager said the locals lived on bananas and fish. Hopefully Joshua would disdain the food here as he disdained everything else; it would be too dreadful if Joshua started smelling Ugandan.

· · ·

Plans.

A man in the hotel bar said I ought to go and see old Tom Popper. Old Tom was a card, a character, kept a black harem and spawned dozens of black kiddies, dirt poor, farmed tea more or less, the Memsaabs wanted him deported, he was a disgrace to Britain, letting the side down as far as it would go. On the other hand, old Tom had lived in Africa for forty-five years and there was nothing he didn't know about the country and the blacks (pejorative). Here, draw you a map. Thank you, sounds fascinating . . . The white man gone native is a central figure in Africa fiction and, as Michelin says, *vaut le voyage*.

Alan Moorehead's splendid book, *No Room in the Ark,* tempted me to visit Traveller's Rest, an inn at Kisoro, whence one climbed mountains hoping to sight the rare gorilla, a vanishing species. Alan had done it and made it seem, in writing, highly *vaut le voyage*. And of course Queen Elizabeth Park, for elephants. I studied the map. A *rundfahrt* of southwestern Uganda appeared to be possible, mostly on red lines. I had lost some confidence in red for major roads but curiosity is stronger than scepticism.

I said, "All right, Joshua, I'll get us out of Kampala but then, by God, you drive."

Joshua had a real stunner this time. He regretted that he could not drive in Uganda as his licence was no good here, the tone of voice suggesting that he had anyway driven himself to the bone in Kenya.

"You might have told me in Nairobi."

"I did not know you coming to Uganda, Memsaab. I think it is safari in Kenya."

So it was all my fault. I had tricked this simple creature far from home into an alien land and now I expected him to drive. Joshua was lying. When the three countries were British colonies, they formed a genuine common market: all for one and one acceptable in any other. It passed belief; I was carrying, at sizable expense and some psychological strain, a fellow whose only service was to lift my suitcase in and out of the Landrover, night and morning.

"You know what you are, Joshua?"

"Memsaab?"

"You are a Bare-Faced Go-Away Bird."

Joshua's face closed. It is a special African look. The face and the eyes turn to wood. The face actually looks deaf. They have gone off to some distant place, you cannot reach them. They must have perfected this withdrawal over centuries; it is protection against insult or worse. Joshua obviously thought that I had been swearing at him. Swearing is prelude to the full crazy-mean-European syndrome; in less enlightened times, no doubt swearing led to beating. I steamed with anger; how dared Joshua treat me like Simon Legree when I had in fact been his Nanny.

"And furthermore, Joshua," I said, rather high-pitched, *"Shit."*

The word, so very bad in the mouth of a Memsaab, had no effect. Possibly Joshua didn't know it and I didn't know the Swahili equivalent. We clanked along, always sounding like a tank, in glacial silence.

This was dust country. Sometimes the dust was beige, sometimes brown, sometimes red. Joshua was not a backseat driver, he was a front-seat groaner and gasper. He gasped for peril, when I took a curve faster than I meant to, or skidded in dust, or slammed into a pothole at full force. He groaned for discomfort, heat and dust. I had resolved to ignore this and did, up to a point, at which point I snarled at him, saying that if the passenger was not content he could always get out and walk.

My relation to the Landrover was pretty queer too; the Landrover was my old war buddy, we had come through hell and high water together, without my buddy I was a poor lone orphan, with my buddy beside me I could keep up the pretence that I was a red-blooded he-man. If anything happened to my buddy I might as well shoot myself. But my buddy wasn't in the first flush of youth; I was racked by anxiety about how long my buddy would hold out.

We turned off the thickest red line (major road) onto a track so murderous that I assumed it must be one of the red hairlines on the map. I thought with anguish of the vital underneath parts of the Landrover.

Journey's end was a broken-down unpainted slat house on a hillside covered in tea bushes. Old Tom Popper, looking exactly as he should, greeted me with suspicion. He wore a battered sweat-stained brown felt hat, dirty khaki trousers, faded torn shirt, shoes without laces or socks. He had few teeth, a stubble of reddish beard, a blue drunkard's eye, and no desire for visitors. I ought to have caught on by now; isolated people were doing what they chose and what they chose was to remain isolated.

An offering of whisky ingratiated me enough for a seat in Mr Popper's lamentable living room and a greasy jam jar filled with my whisky and lukewarm water. At first we were alone and Mr Popper answered my questions with an ironical smile and "I coulden say." "I havven an idea." "I wooden know." Slowly, timid as dikdiks, black children toddled in, to be patted by Papa or briefly held on his lap. Old Mr Popper was going strong, the smallest child looked about two years old. I counted ten but couldn't be sure, perhaps the same ones came back for a second peek at the funny European lady. Perhaps a dozen older sons and daughters were out working in the tea garden. There was no sign of a wife or wives, nor any sound offstage to indicate that she or they were on the premises.

I didn't revel in old Mr Popper's teasing tactics and was about to depart in a huff because of the wasted bribe, when old Tom, softened by drink, decided to play fair. "Lady," he said. "I'll tell you the God's truth. I don't know a bloody thing about Africans and never will." He could guess at what they'd do but that was all, and likely as not he guessed wrong; there wasn't a hope in hell of understanding how their brains worked if, in fact, they used brains which he doubted. They used something else, different from whatever we used. "And they don't know a bloody thing about us either."

He knew more about game, wild animals; he reckoned he had a pretty good idea about them from long observation and they were logical, they behaved according to a sensible pattern. But wasn't it lonely, I asked, to live among people who were forever strangers, as all the Europeans seemed to feel; wasn't it also scary? Depends, he said, on the person; he didn't like people anyway and as for scary he always kept a loaded gun handy and a good sharp *panga* and he guessed he could look after himself. When he got to be too old or too sick, he supposed one of them would poison him. He said this cheerily and I dared not ask if he meant his wife/wives and/or children but who else had he in mind? Waiting for ultimate poison in this dilapidated hole might depress anyone but old Tom didn't look the least downcast, hat on head, enjoying the visitor's whisky, relaxed in a Public Works Department chair with springs sagging beneath it.

He warned me against Lake Victoria; I was not to put even a finger in it. It was typical of Africa, 225 miles long and edged all the way by snails which carried bilharzia; bilharzia was a real bugger. That and liver flukes and loa loa. Africans were storehouses of parasites, crawling and creeping with bugs that would kill Europeans. You could hardly blame the poor bastards for being lazy, they were half sick most of the time. Awful place, Africa, not fit for human habitation. But, I said nervously, he had inhabited it for quite a while. That was because he didn't like people. Africa was about the last place where you could keep away from people. This made little sense, in view of his private tribe. I uttered grateful noises, left my whisky, and Mr Popper accompanied me to the front door. Joshua had remained in the Landrover.

"That your safari driver?" Mr Popper asked, taking in Joshua's tiny shorts and pointed shoes and sunglasses. I nodded. Mr Popper gave a great shout of laughter, wished me luck and closed his door.

As we bucked down the dust track from the house, Joshua said, "What is that Bwana, Memsaab?"

"He's a tea planter."

"He has plenty little totos in his house. Kenya bwanas don't have African totos in their house."

A Kikuyu Presbyterian pansy prude.

At Fort Portal—in the hotel grounds? at the entrance to the club?—the famous sign was painted on a board for all to see: "No dogs or natives allowed." I believe that sign is what caused the downfall of the British Empire, though history does not support this view. It is an infuriating sign. It made me as angry as if I were a dog or a native. There was no need to offend Africans with signs; they knew they weren't allowed in and never attempted to enter sacred white precincts so why insist in print.

The pious Victorians thought Uganda a fine field for the Lord's work but less suitable for British settlers. The result was and remained a plethora of missionaries and few white residents. The whites were not landowning farmers, as in upcountry Kenya; they were managers, administrators, professional men. All counted, about ten thousand Europeans among some seven and a half million Africans. So long as they were protected by the British Colonial Service and the rule of law, they were all right, not a shipwrecked handful on a wide black sea.

Independence was due in seven months, it was almost on top of them, and they saw it as danger. The dowdy Memsaabs and the beefy Bwanas on the hotel verandah sounded overwrought, talking too much, too angrily. Between pink gins, they kept saying they'd rather burn down their club than let these black baboons be members. They predicted bad trouble: without Europeans, to oversee and direct, the economy would go to hell; kiss the coffee and cotton exports goodbye; the idea that Ugandans could govern themselves was madness.

All countries have a feel which you sense at once by some emotional osmosis. Uganda felt claustrophobic. It is the smallest of the East African countries, the size of the United Kingdom, nothing by African measure, and landlocked. Where Kenya felt light and spacious, this place felt too lush, too green, the landscape itself closing in; and crowded as indeed it is. Kenya is three times as large and has three times fewer bodies per square mile. (Though at the present moment, African populations are multiplying with the speed of minks which isn't going to do anyone any good.) Forty tribes live in Uganda. As a unified entity, Uganda didn't really exist until the end of the First World War, no time in terms of history. Before that, the tribes were hostile and given to war; they had not become trusting friends fifty years later. Like Joshua, I was not enamoured of Uganda; it made me uneasy.

Joshua was glum and I, as usual, bent over the wheel watching the road. I didn't see, I felt a change, and thought some kind of violent African storm was building up miles off to the west. The dusty flapping canvas roof of the Landrover limited our view. That distant black wall looked bad, rain like never before, and I had not noticed any side curtains for the Landrover even if we could figure out how to put them up. The black wall stayed oddly in place. I stopped the car to get out and diagnose the situation.

The black wall rose, from flat scrubland, straight into the sky; either a trick of light or a fact, a single perpendicular mountain that stretched along the horizon. And had no summit; the side of this mountain or range of mountains soared out of sight. Stupid, of course I couldn't see the top, it was covered in cloud. Above us and all around, the sky was clear blue. I stared harder; not cloud, snow.

"Joshua, binoculars, quick!"

Yes, snow, a snow field as long as the mountain.

"My God, what is it?" It was too strange, too unexpected, it wasn't like any mountains I had seen anywhere, beautiful and unreal, a dark dream of mountains. As I watched, cloud drifted down, lower and lower, leaving only a black rim along the sky.

The *Field Guide* and the map told me what I had been seeing: the Ruwenzori, the Mountains of the Moon. No wonder it looked like nothing else.

"Africa is too big, Joshua. Everything in Africa is too big. People were never meant to live here. It should have been left to the animals. They came first. It's their place."

"Memsaab?"

"See that over there, that black thing against the sky?"

"Yes, Memsaab."

"Gorillas live there." And right for gorillas. According to those who know, like Leakey, Ardrey and others, our species evolved from the ape here, in Africa, in this zone of Africa. I think it was an evolutionary intrusion; this wasn't our territory, it belonged to the animals. I wasn't sure any more that the Africans belonged here; they'd been around since the very beginning and they hadn't had much effect on the place.

A mile inside the Queen Elizabeth Park, the road sign said: "Elephants have right of way." How to take that? As a joke or a suggestion that tourists were crazy enough to dispute passage with elephants? Joshua spotted them. Africans have eyesight like built-in binoculars, I don't know why.

"Look, Memsaab! *Tembo!*" Off to the right, in single file, a herd of elephants plodded slowly towards the lake. The soil was red, the elephants were dark red from their daily dusting and rolling. I watched them through binoculars with reverence. They inspire that emotion if you can watch them in safety. The lion is supposed to be king of the beasts but I have never seen any lions that were a patch on elephants. These stately animals followed their leader and turned to cross the track.

"*Tembo* coming!" Joshua whispered. "Go away, Memsaab!"

"They're not coming here. Be quiet." I was relying on accepted doctrine: you are safe in a car, protected by the petrol smell, and if you don't tangle with elephants they won't tangle with you. The enormous bodies moved over the earth without a sound, padding down the dry lion grass and thorn bushes. There were about twenty of them, including babies and young ones, led by the matriarch. They disappeared into the trees at the left, giant ghosts.

"How wonderful," I said.

"They got much *tembo* here, Memsaab?"

"Yes."

"Lions?"

"I hope so." The *Field Guide* said there were lions in the Kigezi parkland, wherever it was, which had developed a propensity for climbing trees; I looked forward to that.

"You going to the hotel, Memsaab?"

"Yes. I'll get a room and then drive around, for an hour or so."

"I stay in driver's room."

"Why Joshua, don't you want to see the animals? That's the whole point of the safari."

"Better I stay in driver's room."

Mweya Lodge was built on a bluff above Lake Edward, an attractive stone building with the usual wealth of flowering vines and comfortable rooms, but shabbily kept like everywhere else in Uganda. Joshua deposited my suitcase and scuttled off in search of a room far removed from ambient animals. When I announced my plan of sightseeing, the manager said it wouldn't be a good idea alone, as I might get lost on the tracks and why not go out on the launch in the Kazinga channel, plenty to see and the best hour for it. There was plenty to see, especially the inside of the mouths of yawning hippos and elephants drinking and spraying themselves with evening shower-baths and monkeys performing acrobatics and all the birds whose names I didn't know.

I was eating dinner at my solitary table when a handsome youngish man, grey-haired, wearing a red bandana around his neck and an aura of film star, spoke to me. Would I like to come out with him and his friends tomorrow? A scene for a movie had just been made here, a famous movie if I could remember the name. In this scene elephants stampeded and the daring Game Warden or whoever the hero was, drove through the dangerous milling mass for some unclear noble purpose. The star's double, the stuntman who actually played the scene, was the chap in the red bandana, a white hunter.

He said that the movie stars shivered with fear all through the filmmaking, they were scared to death of the animals. In the course of this trumped-up stampede, an elephant had been hurt and he had to find it tomorrow so that he could shoot it and put it out of its misery. I said indignantly that I didn't think any movie was worth killing an elephant for and he looked at me with amusement. It was a silly thing to say to a man whose business was shooting animals.

His friends turned out to be a dark-haired girl, giving off waves of adoration. We three sat in the front seat of a Landrover and as we drove into the bush, searching for elephant, the white hunter told stories of derring-do, close escapes and the like, in which he modestly figured as the man who saved the day. I disliked him before we found the elephants, after which I detested him. He had explained the formation of herds, the females with young separate from the male herds and the old males who go off on their own and eventually die from hunger because their teeth are worn down to uselessness. We came on a herd of females and their young in a field at the edge of forest. The white hunter drove round them quickly and said, "Sally's not here."

"You know them all?"

"Every one," he said. "Sally's a mean old lady, I'll have to track her on foot. Want some fun?"

Before I could say no, he started to race close to the elephants, banging on the horn, and the elephants reacted, the "aunties" gathering to protect the young and the babies, the other females flapping their ears and raising their trunks, ready to charge. I was of course speechless with fear, having no wish to die so that this show-off could impress his girl. The elephants were trumpeting now and he went on circling them until a big female charged, stopping short as we sped past.

"Bluffing," said the white hunter. "This is nothing to what we had before, we must have had a hundred of them in a fine old tizzy."

As far as I could see we had an adequate stampede going right now and I hated it and objected to it. What point was there in frightening these splendid beasts; surely harassment would only drive them farther away from man and cars so that we tourists would never have a chance to see them, or else they would get the idea that cars were hostile and begin to charge innocent drivers. The white hunter was laughing happily, his adoring girl was open-mouthed in admiration for his nerve, I was sweating with dismay and outrage, and then an elephant charged and did not stop and our hero stepped hard on the gas and drove off, saying, "Not bluffing that time." So now I knew, lucky me, what a medium-size elephant stampede was like. Doomed to see elephants in the company of lunatics. All I wanted was to watch them with love and respect, at a reasonable distance.

"Enjoy it?" he asked the girl pressed to his side.

"Oh it was too thrilling, Richard," she breathed.

"You, Memsaab?"

"No," I said stonily. "I don't even enjoy baiting people."

We parted with frozen politeness at the Lodge. I hired an African Park Ranger to serve as guide and drove quietly with him, seeing buffalo and more elephant and lions at a very reasonable distance, lolling under but not climbing a tree, and baboons and monkeys and I found this resembled museum visiting in that you cannot look at too much for too long, fatigue and blindness set in. The first sight of those silent elephants had been the best, the empty silent land around them, the surprise. I was ready to leave in the morning and sent word to Joshua that he could emerge.

Perhaps we were between Rukungiri and Lwasamaire and perhaps not. The map was dotted by place names in small print but I had seen none of the places, nothing at all for at least two hours. Nobody to blame except myself. I thought a yellow road was a short cut and would get us to Kisoro faster than a thin red road. The surface of the road is a type well known in Africa, ridged or corrugated mud like a washboard. There is no good way to drive such a road but the least painful is at speed, trying to hit the top of the ridges and avoid the valleys. We could not drive at speed, even our pitiful speed, due to the twists and bends in this abominable road. Every foot of the way jolted the spine up into the back of the head while also jarring the teeth. I had passed from daylight–distance intestinal knots to despair. Wooded hills rose on both sides, a stream ran below us. The road led nowhere and nobody lived on it and I did not know where we were and in a few more hours, in darkness, we and the car would shake to pieces. The thing about Africa is that you cannot give up and take the easier way out because there is no easier or other way. It must be very good for building character. You have to go on, the alternative being suicide.

"We'll never make it, Joshua."

"Make, Memsaab?"

Keeping the wheel steady took all my strength and talking sounded like bad hiccoughs. Above the rattling roaring noises of the Landrover I heard something else. Something human. Thank God they had people here. Joshua could ask where this road went, if anywhere. We came on them from behind. They filled the road. They were a screaming crowd. I tried a tentative honk on the horn, then less tentative. They made room for us to pass. Every face was twisted in fury, every mouth open, shouting. They carried placards and jumped up and down, as if bitten by vicious insects. I was not inclined to stop among these enraged people to ask road directions. Joshua could see better from his side.

"What do the signs say, Joshua?"

Leaning out of the car, he reported, "Down with Poppie. Down gravy umage."

"What in hell are you saying?"

The man couldn't do anything, anything, he couldn't even read. Having passed the shrieking throng, I drew up, motor running, and got the binoculars. I was careful not to stick my head far out of the Landrover, just enough to check those placards. Hand-painted, they said "Down with the Pope," "Down with Graven Images." Mrs Simpson and Mr Popper had not exaggerated the puzzling quality of Africans. In the middle of nowhere, on a washboard road between desolate hills and primeval forest, a crowd of Africans was yelling against the Pope.

Less than a mile farther, we ran head-on into another crowd of howling Africans. The scenery was the same, trees, hills, stream; the whole insane lot might have sprung from the ground: head-on I could see for myself. A dripping Bleeding Heart, simpering pink-and-white portrait of the Virgin, a single placard saying "Heretics" in big red letters. This gang also blocked the road and again, close to hysterical laughter, I honked the horn and they made way. They hardly saw us; they were so busy screaming, shouting, waving their fists and glaring forward to the enemy. They too did not recommend themselves as people to chat with. Better lost than torn limb from limb.

Presumably when they met, Protestants and Catholics on this narrow road, holy war would break out. Ugandan Africans were the most literate of East Africans thanks to missionary teachers. I thought they could all have lived full happy lives without learning to spell "graven images" and "heretics." They were rich enough in tribal hatreds, they didn't need theological furore as well. The road continued to be back, neck, and teeth breaking and we were still nowhere but at least clear of religious fanatics.

"Crazy people," Joshua said. "Smell bad. Act bad. Bad country."

He was as alarmed as I was; he seemed to have grown paler; he sat hunched and miserable, clutching the roof support to keep from bouncing out of the Landrover.

"You believe in God, don't you Joshua?"

"Yes, Memsaab. God in church. Those crazy people making that noise about God?"

"I guess so. Never mind. But since you believe in God, then pray."

"What for, Memsaab?"

"That we get there."

"Where?"

"Anywhere. It doesn't matter. Anywhere will do."

I don't know how or when we reached Traveller's Rest in Kisoro, not that night certainly and I think I took a day off in Kabale to ease my bones. Kisoro is singularly dim to me: a small bearded genial man, aged between fifty and seventy, the owner of this outpost of civilization; a wood dining room with kerosene lamps and innumerable insects buzzing about and seeking death against hot glass; soft steady rain on endless forest. I could hardly climb in and out of the Landrover, no question of climbing these matted mountains on the chance of seeing a gorilla. I would settle for Alan Moorehead's fine description of the climb and the giant coal black primates.

On the other hand, I had to walk somewhere before I lost the use of my legs. Since the end of January I had walked only the terrifying moments in Waza game park; I got more exercise any day in Hyde Park than in all of Africa. It was morning, cool at this altitude, and the dirt road cut through a tall bamboo forest. Bamboo is always lovely and lovelier here because it was familiar, friendly, creaking in the breeze, very different from the ominous thick trees we had left behind. I stopped the car and got out.

"I'm going to walk for an hour, Joshua."

"Where, Memsaab?"

"Just down the road. If I'm not back in an hour you can drive on to meet me. There aren't any police around here to catch you."

"What shall I do, Memsaab?" He looked scared and bereft. I might have been abandoning him in the centre of the Sahara.

"Wait in the car and read your book." Joshua was still working away at the thriller. I had explained that Istanbul was like Nairobi only bigger and that St Sophia, where the spies spent much time dodging around behind pillars, was like the Nairobi cathedral.

Mute, Joshua fixed me with accusing eyes.

"It's perfectly safe here. Nobody will bother you. *Buck up,* Joshua."

Out of sight of the Landrover, I felt suddenly relieved of great burdens. Relieved of noise and the strain of driving and worry about the roads and the health of the car and relieved of Joshua. I was free. I had an hour to breathe the mountain air and listen to the trees. I skipped foolishly, light-headed with pleasure. It was the first attack of happiness in Uganda.

"You gone more than one hour," Joshua said angrily, holding out his wrist-watch. "A snake was on this road."

"What of it? They can't climb." Like hell they can't. "If you were frightened, why didn't you drive to meet me?"

Joshua tossed his head, the gesture of an offended damsel, and withdrew into sulking silence.

I was struck by my second revelation about Joshua; I was willing to bet he couldn't drive at all, never had, didn't own a licence. He was just a sharp city boy who wanted a job and took a chance on a dumb European tourist. The thought made me tremble with anger. Miserable little cheat, I'd force him to show me his licence; I'd rub his nose in it; I'd wring his neck. I lit a cigarette to calm myself and was swept by weary resignation. If I was right, Joshua would lie about his licence, he'd lost it in Kabale or something; if I was wrong he'd just be more shirty and tedious. We had a long way to go, almost too long to think of and we were going it together; peace is preferable to war. Joshua stared out his side of the car, pointedly snubbing me. There was a limit to what I'd take.

"Listen, Joshua, I will damn well not put up with bad temper from you. You're getting a free ride through Africa—a *paid* free ride—and you better be thankful. Pull yourself together right now, you hear me, and stop sulking or I swear I'll kick you out and you can walk home."

He looked at once pathetic and cowed, the helpless African bullied by the cruel European. Patience, everyone had said from west to east, patience is what you need most in Africa.

Madame Dupré lived on an island in the middle of a torrent. The island was just large enough for her house and a small encircling garden. A flimsy swaying footbridge connected the island to the riverbank. Madame Dupré had two guest-rooms and took in travellers if she liked their looks. I don't remember where this island was, somewhere between Kabale and Mbarara, nor remember how I heard of it. Finding it was a feat. I tiptoed down the steep descent of the bridge and presented myself to Madame Dupré who noted my dusty bedraggled weariness and accepted me. The Landrover and Joshua were to stay on the riverbank where Madame Dupré's servants lived. Perhaps Madame Dupré rolled up her drawbridge at night.

She was a bird-size Frenchwoman about sixty years old, with pale wrinkled skin, no makeup, grey-streaked brown hair wobbed on top of her head, brilliant malicious eyes, and the sort of old black crochet shawl worn by Paris concierges. Her sitting room was walled in books from floor to ceiling, as were the short passages between bedrooms. The sitting room had much charm, a round table covered by a tasselled cloth under a hanging lamp, comfortable chairs in faded blue cotton brocade slips, long curtains of the same material, a good walnut writing table; a very French room. Madame Dupré led me down the hall to my bedroom where I spouted Gallic effusions to express my delight. A big brass bed with a white lace bedspread, a dressing table with a pink satin flounce, frilly white curtains, roses on the carpet, more books, and no hateful mosquito net, screens on the low windows. Madame Dupré hurried out and back, bearing a vase of flowers for the dressing-table. There was plenty of time for a bath and drinks before dinner. She dined at the civilized hour of eight-thirty.

If I had been travelling as a reporter I would have asked all the questions that swarmed to be asked and risked any rebuke; as a lady of leisure I felt I had no excuse to pry at barriers of reserve. Barriers of reserve were everywhere; these isolated people might have been hiding from the cops, concealing dread secrets; personal conversation was taboo. So I learned nothing about anyone including Madame Dupré, not where she came from in France, nor why or how she happened to live on this astounding island. Over an aperitif of gin and grapefruit juice, Madame Dupré did inform me that she had lived here for twelve years and, darkly, there were those who only waited their chance to seize the island from her. I couldn't imagine who. Jungle forest lined both sides of the rushing river. Her bridge lay at the end of a rough dirt track which branched off from a rough dirt road. The nearest towns were not metropolises and she wasn't near them anyway. You would have to be immune to claustrophobia or crazy for it to live here.

Madame Dupré said that we were going to have *un souper très léger* as she had not expected company. Delectable cold fish with superb mayonnaise, a casserole of tenderest meat and onions in a sauce flavoured with red wine, perfect green salad, warm banana cake crusted with brown sugar and a soupçon of rum. We spoke French because Madame said she was glad of the opportunity and this allowed me a full range of praising adjectives, from *exquis* to *fantastique*. As I gobbled the glorious food, Madame talked slightingly of her cook, *un imbécile* like all Africans but he knew she would give him *des coups bien durs* if he permitted himself serious stupidities. The serving boy passed the casserole on the wrong side. Madame said to him chattily, *"Imbécile.* Idiot. Black monkey. That is not the way, go around."

He grinned cheerfully and circled my chair. I was as surprised by this as by the wonder of the meal.

We took coffee, marvellous coffee, in the sitting room. We talked about Africans, the staple topic of conversation for all Europeans. Madame said that, after Independence, she expected to have her throat cut. I thought she must be joking, saw she was not, and asked why with some horror. To rob the house, she explained. It will be easy for them. Do you mean your servants? Oh no, they will disappear as soon as there is trouble. Other Africans from the bush, from the villages. I will shoot a few but they will kill me in the end. Of course it might be that the one who coveted her island would arrange to have her killed quickly.

Pagaille would be total after Independence. *Ils vont se tuer et se manger, tout tranquillement, comme les sauvages qu'ils sont. Chère Madame,* the fool missionaries believe they have made Christians of these black apes; they are too stupid, the missionaries. Then you hate the Africans, you fear them? But no, they are like bad children; if you discipline them strongly, they behave; if not, they will do anything they like. And first of all, they will drink; after that, catastrophe.

Since they were all so convinced that disaster was inevitable, come October and Independence, why didn't they leave? It was mad: Mr Popper waiting to be poisoned, Madame Dupré waiting to have her throat cut, the owner of Traveller's Rest waiting for what—rabid gorillas? I wouldn't have started living in Uganda, I agreed heartily with Sir James Hayes Sadler, the Commissioner around 1900 who decided that this land should belong to Africans, it was not desirable or sensible for European settlement. But I would most definitely pick up and run now, if years of living here had given me no confidence in the local Africans. When I suggested departure to Madame she said, "This is my home. I shall not leave it of my own will." Then we talked about books, a happier subject.

In the night, I heard snuffling and scuffling noises outside my windows. There are always night noises in Africa and my system had been to think about something else. This was too loud and too permanent. I got my flashlight and looked out through the windowscreen on to the huge back of a hippo, in touching distance; the said hippo was eating up the flower beds along the house wall. As their tremendous mouths, jaws, teeth can cut a man in half, munching flowers seemed rather sweet. I didn't think saying "Shoo!" would do much good and went back to sleep. In the morning, when I told Madame of this invasion, she said, *"Ils sont détestables, ces bêtes,"* as if talking about rabbits in the lettuce patch. Yes, the river was full of them. She tried putting up a fence but they trampled it down; she tried putting pepper on the flowers but *ces bêtes* seemed to like that even better; she simply didn't know what to do about hippos in her garden.

I thought then that the British in Fort Portal and Madame Dupré were half cracked. Though Independence in West Africa was inefficient, in no way impressive and in many ways ludicrous, it wasn't gruesome, it wasn't deadly. After the whingding for President Tubman, I suspected that Independence would mean much hanky-panky for the benefit of the rulers. Corruption is a lousy way to run a country but not a new technique invented by Africans. Since I am devoted to my own freedom, I didn't think it just to deny other people theirs; and a basic freedom must be to be bossed by your own kind, not by foreigners.

I was all wrong about Uganda, the Fort Portal people and Madame Dupré were right. They foresaw ruin, they did not foresee anything as barbarously evil as Amin. Independence has been an affliction in Uganda. Above all for the unfortunate Ugandans who expected Independence to bring dignity, prosperity, the good life. The British in Fort Portal surely got away safe but I fear for Madame Dupré.

It will take a long time but some day Africans will sort out their own rulers; no one else can do that. They'd do it quicker if the rest of us kept hands off. Cold War rivalry in Africa, which amounts to competitive bribery of African rulers, hasn't helped the mass of ordinary Africans. On the contrary.

It was a long long trail a-winding: to Mbarara, to Masaka, along Lake Victoria looking blue and attractive despite the bilharzia snails, to Kampala, back to Jinja and back into Kenya where Joshua brightened immediately. He brightened too soon. My plan was to drive south from Kisumu and enter the Serengeti from the Lake Victoria end. The roads were marked on the map, so why not? Because nobody does if they can avoid it, because it is a hellish way to go. Past Kisii, the dust road branched or seemed to; it didn't deserve a red line but then maybe we were not on the red line road. I could make no sense of the map. We sat at this ill-defined crossroads in the heat. Two Africans appeared, as they do, like djinns out of a bottle.

"Ask them, Joshua."

"I say!" Joshua called, kingly, from the passenger seat.

The Africans stood where they were and stared.

"*Joshua*, get out and go over to them and ask them in *Swahili*, for God's sake. Which road goes to Musoma?"

Joshua returned, rather cross from demeaning himself. "They say Yes."

"What do you mean, Yes?"

"They say Yes this road, Yes that road."

"It's impossible, the roads are going in different directions."

Joshua shrugged. "No good to ask those fellows. Country fellows. Not eddikated. They say Yes so Memsaab is not angry."

I decided to take the right branch as Lake Victoria had to be somewhere there. It was getting late and we ought to be hurrying but perhaps we were hurrying the wrong way. I had a good-sized knot in my stomach when we came to the river. There were faint blue lines on the map to indicate rivers and had been many before but nothing to warn of this flood. It shouldn't have been a flood; in an ordinary season it would have been a shallow rivulet, easy to ford. The unusual rains produced this wide swift flowing stream. We had to ford it anyway; we couldn't get back to Kisii before dark.

"Joshua, take off your shoes and socks and find a long stick and wade in and measure the water. I don't think it's too deep to cross, it just looks bad because of the current."

"I do not swim, Memsaab."

"Of course not, if you had to swim it would be over your head and the Landrover couldn't make it. If it's over your knees, I'm not sure we can do it. Go on, get going."

"Memsaab, we wait here, soon some country fellows come along, they can step in this water."

"What country fellows? We haven't seen anybody for an hour. *Joshua, it's five o'clock. Get going.*"

He found a good strong stick in the brush beside the road. He walked to the edge of the river and took off his right shoe. Then he stood like a flamingo on one leg and turned a face of woe and fear and said, "I will be drownded."

I got out, cursing, grabbed the stick and waded in, shoes and all, since I do not have African feet which can walk on anything. The streambed was littered with stones and small rocks and I used the stick for a cane in the current, as much as for a measuring rod. More than halfway across, the water had not covered my knees so we would chance it. Joshua was back in the passenger seat, huddled away from me. I drove very slowly, thinking of all the innards of a motor, Runic sayings about water in the carburettor, water in the spark plugs, how did I know. I held my breath, hoped I was not making waves, hoped we wouldn't stall in the middle, hoped. When we lumbered out on to dry land I stopped the motor and leaned on the wheel. We had crossed over Jordan but where were we?

"You are too wet, Memsaab," Joshua said timidly.

"Well, you're not so that's all right. I think we'll be spending the night in the Landrover."

"Here in this car?" Joshua asked, appalled.

"Not necessarily here but somewhere like here."

We might as well drive on while daylight lasted. We came to a village with kerosene lamps already lit in the shacks by the road.

"Go and talk to them, Joshua. Ask where we are. Ask if there's a government resthouse anywhere that we can stay. Ask if there's food to buy. Ask anything you can think of."

I was too tired and uncomfortable to care. We could park in this village where we were unlikely to be besieged by lions or hyenas. Numbly I watched Joshua, engaged in a marathon talk fest. It must be Joshua; I couldn't believe that Swahili was a language requiring ten words for a single word in any other tongue.

"There is!" Joshua announced, beaming.

"There is what?"

"What you say. Resthouse for govermint. Here, up this road. Here is a man with key. You can buy tins, Memsaab, nice sardines. Also one candle for you, one for me. You give me money, I will buy."

The key man walked ahead; Joshua brought back his loot and we followed to a one-room wood house which would have been fine if I were fully equipped for safari travel. An iron cot with a mattress, a table, a chair, a washstand with bowl and pitcher, all okay but no bedding, no towels, no kerosene for the lamp. Count your blessings, I told myself gloomily, it was far better than sitting up in the Landrover, wet to the knees. Joshua and the key man, a grizzled old boy wearing an antique postman's cap, stood around muttering.

"What now, Joshua, for heaven's sake?"

His eyes modestly lowered, Joshua said, "The terlit is the little place back there."

In the candlelight I changed to dry clothes and unpacked my two sweaters. Sardines by themselves are filling if dispiriting. I had whisky and boiled, bacteria-free water in my thermos, and the thermos cup. I could make a hump, to imitate a pillow, by putting my wet boots and rolled wet trousers under the mattress. I could, thank God, drink and, God willing, get drunk. I could not read.

And so realized that thrillers had saved my sanity. Every night, unnerved by Africa, I escaped into the dream world of cops and robbers; an underground atomic rocket factory in Albania discovered and dismantled by a fearless secret agent; the skilful kidnap from his electronically guarded jungle hideaway of a German super war criminal. I left Africa and moved to Finland and Turkey and Brazil and Egypt in the company of colossally brave and inventive men, bent on important insanity. I had not touched *War and Peace* or Jane Austen. Who would have the energy to cope with a real complex Russia or the wit to enjoy eighteenth-century English provincial society, after a day's driving on African roads? It was a sombre night on that mattress, drinking whisky from a thermos cup and watching insects cluster around the candle, with no therapeutic thriller to dispel Africa. Drinking oneself to sleep is folly; the morning hangover awaits with sharpened claws.

Musoma had nothing in its favour except a hot bath and after bitter argument since it was past regular hours, breakfast. Before the town sank from morning apathy into motionless afternoon torpor, we needed to buy food. Better get enough for four days, I told Joshua. The hotel-inn-resthouse booklet guaranteed six fully furnished rondavels at Seronera in the centre of the Serengeti Park, bedding, towels, crockery, cooking utensils, but no victuals. My appetite and imagination failed as I walked from one airless little shop to another, collecting tins of soup and cornbeef and vegetables, crackers, cheese, tea, condensed milk, cereal. Lack of foresight must be the foundation of African contentment and though Joshua wasn't by any means a happy-go-lucky gather-ye-rosebuds-while-ye-may type, he couldn't think four days ahead. He got a small sack of *posho,* tea and sugar, counting on the Memsaab to stave off starvation.

It was hot. The locals splashed in bilharzia water at the edge of Lake

Victoria, cheerfully absorbing the malign worms. As Joshua was a cleanliness addict, like me, I gave him a medical scare and retired to my room. A boring day wasn't the worst fate; I had a bed with pillows and a tranquillizing thriller. The map suggested sixty miles to the western Park entrance; after that, the map had no ideas to offer. I wanted to drive peacefully into the promised land, not haunted by daylight–distance dread.

The Serengeti, that lyrical name, was my highest hope of the journey. The Queen Elizabeth Park had been disappointing, too small and too tourist haven. But the Serengeti was several hundred square miles larger than Connecticut, larger than Northern Ireland, with only six small round huts in all this space as a concession to man. It had to be the golden dream plain, ringed by blue mountains, where a multitude of beautiful wild animals roamed free.

Joshua never vexed me by showing up late. "This is Tanganyika, Joshua. How about driving here?" That was a friendly tease and accepted in the same spirit; grinning, Joshua babbled about his Kenya licence. We clanked off in the cool dawn, both amiable, and less than two hours later, without hesitation, I took the wrong road. Due to this error, the next eight hours nearly finished all three of us, the Landrover and Joshua and me. For a while, the road was merely frightful but that was not new. I kept looking for a Park gate or a Park sign and was puzzled by scrawny maize patches and a few crumbling mud huts off the road. Surely we had gone far enough to reach some sort of decent surface, befitting a famous game park. After three hours on this narrow rutted and holed track, I knew I had made a mistake but to turn back meant another night in merry Musoma.

The colour of the road was changing and I didn't like what I saw though I had never seen it before. Dust had become black spongy mud. This sinister stuff is called black cotton and combines the qualities of quicksand and chewing gum. Experience has taught everyone that the only way to handle it is to go around or go away. Having no experience,

I went on though very disturbed. I could feel the Landrover wheels churning and slowing. At this point, Joshua began to slap himself and say *"Ai, Ai!"*

Wildly anxious about the road, I said, "What's the matter with you, stop it, shut up!"

Joshua was now beating at himself as if putting out a fire, and moaning.

"Joshua, stop it!"

"Dudus!" Joshua shouted. The wheels were sinking, the man was an idiot, what did insects matter when we were about to founder in mysterious black muck? Then the first one bit me. I wore long trousers and had rolled down my sleeves in the morning chill, but Joshua was half naked. The first one bit my neck, like a bee sting, and I swatted at it but was still concentrated on this alarming mud. Then they came in like dive-bombers, biting my neck and hands and face and even zooming up my pants to sting my legs. Joshua was now screaming with pain and with cause. Lean long black and brown flies swarmed around us. I was terrified by this attack and helpless and stopped the car, the worst possible response since we were now sitting targets. Maddened bees can sting people to death, I remembered dimly; bees were slowpokes compared to the speed of these flies.

I shouted "Christ!" at the top of my lungs while Joshua screamed on a steady high note and both of us beat wildly at the buzzing air. These were tsetse flies, a hellish curse of Africa; because of them vast areas of the continent remain empty. Neither man nor cattle can live where they live. As an added attraction, they are also the carriers of sleeping sickness. Joshua was crying salt tears, still screaming, and I felt that I was sweating blood but there was nothing to do except go on and going on, if possible at all, required the four-wheel drive.

"Help me, Joshua!" I bellowed, tugging at the small second gear. He was past hearing. I hit him on the arm and pointed to the gear. "Pull it, pull it, for God's sake, we have to get out of here! *Both hands!"*

He stared at me with vacant insane eyes; I grabbed his hands and fastened them on the gear knob, under my hands, and pulled as hard as I could. The intention got through to him, we pulled together, the gear shifted into position, I stepped on the gas and the Landrover moved sluggishly but it moved. So did the tsetse flies, easily keeping pace. Joshua had lost the strength to scream, he keened in a low wail, while I took the Lord's name in vain shrilly, knowing that I would lose my mind if these things didn't stop biting.

As suddenly as it had started it stopped; we were clear of the black mud and the murder flies. I drove on a few miles, to make sure of safety, and stopped. We were both soaked in sweat, Joshua's eyes were red and glaring, probably mine were too but I couldn't see them. We sat, collapsed and stunned in the Landrover. I recovered enough to give us water from the thermos and lit a cigarette with unsteady hands.

"If we see these *dudus* again," Joshua said in a small voice. "I will die."

"Look, there aren't any marks on us." We should have been quilted in red lumps, like bee stings; the bites didn't even itch.

"Memsaab, what is this bad bad place you take me to?"

"I don't know."

Joshua glanced at me with a strange expression, part hopeless, part hate. He had stupidly given credit where credit was neither due nor wanted: the Memsaab, that cardboard tower of strength, knew what she was doing and where she was going. So far, Joshua had been a lot better off than I was; he had me to lean on. A dose of delayed but realistic doubt might be a good thing. Joshua had made a man of me and I resented the role. He could be his own man now and see how he liked it.

The road was no better but seemed lovely because it was honest dirt colour. We jolted and rattled and swayed and came to an enchanted place. In a semicircle of golden plain with blue hills behind, a frieze of giraffes was outlined against the sky. Around them, zebras and badly constructed bearded beasts grazed; antelopes, of different sizes and with differing delightful horns, nibbled and frolicked; a herd of buffalo stood with raised heads, looking enormously powerful but not dangerous so far off. I couldn't count them, there were several hundred animals at home with each other, the very picture of Eden.

Joshua begged, "Don't stop, Memsaab." I ignored him, and watched through binoculars, trying to fill my memory with them all, one perfect sight to save from the journey. While Joshua nagged, I studied the *Field Guide;* since I didn't know where we were or if we would ever reach Seronera, I might as well enjoy and educate myself. The gnu, the lesser kudu, impala and more Thomson's gazelles, if I'd got it right, and mongooses or mongeese whichever it was, small dark creatures scurrying among the various hooves. The giraffes began to walk towards the hills, their necks waving like fantastic asparagus; the antelopes leapt and ran, their movements beautiful beyond description; cumbrously the buffalo headed our way. Joshua pulled at my sleeve; it was time to go. I wasn't about to tell Joshua that buffaloes scared me too.

We drove from grass plain into small forest and past outcroppings of volcanic rock. Terror in his voice, Joshua said, "Lions." Exactly like Ali, I said, "Where?" Nearer Joshua but in general too near, a lion and three lionesses were draped on and beneath a rock pile. Close enough to look into their mad fixed yellow eyes. Joshua shivered as with fever. Equally frightened, I heard myself say, "They're quite tame, Joshua. They're used to people, tourists always drive around here." I wished they did and were. But this was years before the great travel boom hit East Africa, years before zebra-striped minibuses toured the land bearing loads of women in halter tops and men in flowered shirts who really thought the lions were tame, posed for their cameras. Lion was the Serengeti speciality, lion abounded, I hoped fervently that we never found ourselves so near them again.

Before it would have tensed my nerves; now I took this short river crossing calmly. All I had to do was keep the Landrover on a ledge of rock. The drop was a mere four feet, just sufficient to do us in. Joshua said to himself, "Bad place. Everything bad." Then, sharing his anxiety, he said, "Four o'clock and one quarter, Memsaab." As if I didn't know, as if I didn't have a knot the size of a pumpkin in my stomach.

"We'll be there soon," spoken firmly. And if not, we would put up the side curtains, at sunset, and cower inside while lions circled round and both of us turned to jelly from fear.

Joshua saw the rondavels first; the knot which was almost choking me dissolved. A caretaker African unlocked the door of a pleasant little house and took Joshua away with him. Wherever Joshua went, I knew he would stay in it, closing windows and door and praying for the night to end. I showered, and lay limp on the bed until revived enough to get out the whisky and cook a delicious meal, cornbeef and vegetables and soup all heated together in one agreeable mess. The caretaker African, flashlight in hand, knocked at the door.

"Fire ready, Memsaab."

What fire? It was part of the local hospitality, a bonfire beyond the rondavels where the happy visitors could sit on tree trunks beneath the stars and swap news about the animals they'd seen that day. There were no other visitors. Sitting alone, I listened to hyenas laugh though I cannot think why that sound is called laughing and saw, or imagined I saw which amounted to the same thing, dark shapes moving outside the firelight. I told myself that this was a rare and wonderful experience, no barriers separated me from Africa. Rare, yes; wonderful, no.

The Park Warden lived a few miles away but I didn't know that; African Rangers lived another few miles away. As far as I knew, the caretaker African and Joshua were safe together somewhere, while I had those terrifying shadows and the loud hyenas to keep me company. I longed with all my heart for a white hunter, any white hunter except the chap with a red bandana, an Africa expert who would hold my hand and say there there, this is fun, this is great, this is Africa, this isn't simply hair-raising hell.

Joshua actually smiled when we reached the Lake Manyara Hotel. It had been a long but harmless day, some ten hours on the road crossing the great Serengeti plain and winding up through green hills upon which zebra grazed like sheep to Ngorongoro, where I looked at the vertical descent into the crater and decided it was more than the Landrover and I could manage. After that the road snaked in the usual style down to the western wall of the Rift Valley. The Lake Manyara Hotel was civilization, a restful shelter to us both. Built on top of the Rift wall, it was a charming stylish resort hotel, set in a garden, with plenty of normal people wearing summer clothes and drinking around the swimming pool. Real cars parked in front of the hotel. I think Joshua felt he was almost back in blessed Nairobi.

Joshua stopped smiling promptly at seven-thirty in the morning when we entered Lake Manyara Park. This is a small beautiful and mystifying park. On paper, it appeared straightforward; the park is a long narrow strip, 120 square miles, between the cliffside of the Rift and Lake Manyara. Thirty miles of well-maintained motor track, said the *Field Guide*, suitable for saloon cars, with numerous circuit tracks for viewing the abundant game and myriad birds. A cinch, I thought, until I got lost.

The *Field Guide* also noted that lions climbed trees here to escape the torment of tsetse flies. If lions felt that way about tsetse flies, Joshua and I had been justified in going off our rockers. I hesitated to risk another onslaught, but the *Field Guide* was too appetizing—giant fig and mahogany trees, acacia woodland—and game parks were the goal of the journey and I had skipped Ngorongoro. Tsetse flies attacked us in burning hot midday; we ought to be safe during the fresh early morning hours.

A large troop of baboons crossed the track. They do not appeal, with their raw red bottoms and mean faces and convincing teeth. Jabbering at us, and all too capable of leaping on to our laps, they were dislikeable except for babies clinging underneath their mums' tums. Joshua saw immediately a sleepy lion stretched along a branch almost overhead. He shrank into his seat and into silence. I turned on a circuit road and passed buffalo wallowing happily in a mud bath and farther on, in an open field by the lake shore, giraffes eating the tops of acacia thorn trees while new varieties of the antelope family meandered around. A single rhino, the first to come our way, stood in the middle of the field looking ugly and bad-tempered. It was marvellous, it was what I had come to see, I was delighted with this mini-park which bestowed its gifts so easily.

Then it was not so easy. A thick branch, thick as a tree trunk, had fallen on to the track. We could not drive over it or around it through the dense bush. "Get out and move it, Joshua."

He said "No," quietly and finally.

I was bent over pulling the heavy branch when Joshua shouted "Memsaab! Memsaab!" and waved his arm like a frenzied semaphore. The rhino was galloping slowly towards us. With the strength of panic I moved the branch far enough to let us through, leapt into the Landrover and roared off, the rhino galloping purposefully behind. This seemed uncalled-for hostility and I was ready to depart. All tracks looked the same. I went round and round, hoping to meet one of the saloon cars for which this park was suitable, but again we were alone. In eerie silence, five elephants emerged from the trees; I stood on the brakes ten yards short of them. In eerie silence they moved across the track into more trees.

Joshua said, "I *hate* this place. I *hate* animals. Memsaab, you take me home now. *Now,* Memsaab."

"*Buck up,* Joshua! Do you think I'm doing this for a joke? I can't find the way out!"

The Landrover began to make parlous sounds, from below, as if a vital part was breaking off. I didn't know what I could do but had to do something such as look under the car. Joshua was no more likely to set foot outside the Landrover than put his head in a hippo's mouth. I steeled myself to wriggle beneath the car. A long dead branch had caught in the works, where it banged against the oil pan. I pulled it off and jumped back in the Landrover, dust-covered, panting.

"You take me home," Joshua said threateningly.

"You shut up," I said just as threateningly.

Round and round. Salvation appeared in the form of a maroon sedan. Bleating like Joshua, I cried, "Where is the gate?"

"Been lost, have you?" said a stout unruffled gent; his friends laughed merrily. "You're on top of it. About a hundred yards straight ahead."

I felt an abject fool. We had spent only two hours in that maze but they embittered Joshua and can't have had a salubrious effect on my nervous system. Joshua shut up for good. Smiles were a thing of the past, gone with the tsetse flies; now he refused to speak. To my surprise, Kilimanjaro lifted across the plain, the tremendous pyramid slopes of the sides, the long snow field hanging in the sky. It is one of the wonders of the world. In joy, I forgot the hazards of the early morning and Joshua's sourness.

"Look, Joshua! It's Mount Kilimanjaro! Isn't it beautiful?"

Joshua neither looked nor replied. In Arusha, I stopped for beer and a sandwich and petrol and the sound of voices. The scenery between Arusha and Namanga was the most magnificent of the whole journey, waves of smooth mountains. Kilimanjaro showed itself again, obliquely, the snow pink in afternoon light. All spoiled by Joshua, hunched in frigid silence. Damn Joshua to hell. He was no bloody use, he'd been cargo the entire time, and still he had the insolence to act put upon. I wished to God I could get rid of him, I was sick of him, it scarcely helped when I was scared out of my wits to have to cope with his chronic fears. He was good for nothing except occasional conversation and now not even good for that. I was enraged by his face, set in sullen disapproval.

We crossed the Tanganyika–Kenya frontier without a word to each other. Joshua didn't relent on his native soil; he had made up his mind to suffer. At the Namanga River Hotel, we parted to go to our quarters in unbroken silence. The hotel was an attractive rustic caravanserai just off the road, a central high-roofed wooden building with rooms tacked to either side and all buried in a pretty welter of flowers. I couldn't appreciate it, I was so infuriated by Joshua that I muttered aloud a litany of grievances, while showering and brushing my dust-caked hair. The massed tensions of the journey burst like a bomb on poor Joshua. I had a bad case of African dementia.

At the bar, a couple of sane serene people talked about the weather.

The man hoped it wouldn't rain in the night, the unpaved road had been sticky enough on the way in. "Oh well, it's only a hundred miles to Nairobi," his wife said. "Someone will give us a hand if we need it."

There might be an unwritten law against talking to strangers in East Africa but I was desperate. "Excuse me," I said, "if you're going to Nairobi tomorrow and have room, could you possibly give my boy a lift. He hasn't been feeling well and I want to stay on here a few days." Far from telling me to peddle my peanuts, they showed me their blue saloon car in the parking lot, said they were leaving at eight o'clock and would be glad to oblige. I refrained from kissing them.

The next step was to locate Joshua. A waiter winkled him out and Joshua appeared, wearing the same odious expression.

"Some people here are going back to Nairobi tomorrow, Joshua. I said you weren't feeling well and they'll give you a lift home."

The hateful shut-in look evaporated in a beaming smile.

"*Thank you*, Memsaab!" It was the first time those words had passed his lips and I thawed slightly.

"Well anyway, we made it, Joshua."

We had indeed, no minor miracle. Neither of us fell sick, we'd had no accidents, not so much as a single puncture, and I drove every foot of the way. Now, thank heaven, I would have one day free of Joshua and his annoying psyche, a lovely light-hearted day in the Amboseli Park, another night in this pleasing hotel, and an easy run to Nairobi. I led Joshua to the car park and pointed out the blue saloon car. He stroked the fender and said, "Oh *nice*." Of course; it was a proper city car.

We shook hands in the morning, Joshua having forgiven me, wished each other luck and I waved them off, delighted to see the last of Joshua. Over breakfast, I ruminated on the strange fact that I had travelled longer with Joshua than with anyone else in my life except U.C. in China and my mother on a journey, which was the opposite of a horror journey, in Mexico. What did Joshua and I know about each other after so much time? I knew that Joshua was a hundred-percent city boy, with very weak nerves. I still didn't know if he could drive. He knew that when I was tired I was as lovable as a rattlesnake, and I had been increasingly tired every day. Not what you'd call a true meeting of minds. The hell with it. It was over and the next time I chose to circumnavigate the globe I would be more careful in selecting my companion. For a start, I would ask him to drive round the block.

Oh what a beautiful morning, oh what a beautiful day, I sang silently and with satisfaction. I hadn't a care, I wasn't in a hurry and I felt disinfected. As if Joshua's perpetual fears had been contagious and gradually sickened me, like catching spiritual bilharzia. Impatience leading swiftly to boredom is my vice, not panic. Alone, at ease in my skin, Africa was dandy. I would watch the animals in peace and I would have hours to contemplate Mount Kilimanjaro, a clear view as soon as I got past this low scrub country to the Amboseli plain. I had barely glimpsed that wonder mountain on yesterday's unpleasant drive, just enough to know it had a mystical meaning for me, all the power and beauty and strangeness of Africa. I chugged along, confident that I could manage whatever happened next.

What happened next was a rushing stream, a creek really, narrow, shallow, dotted by sizable rocks. The trouble was the banks, far too steep, making a sharp V with water at the bottom. The Landrover would go nose down all right, but how would it go nose up. This was a baby canyon and needed a baby bridge across its top. Still, others passed this way so it must be a possible operation. Sitting here didn't solve the problem; taking it fairly fast in second gear might be the best method. The Landrover sped down, the front wheels landed past the middle of the stream, the rear wheels stayed on the rear bank, and in this inclined position stopped dead. I shifted to first gear and heard a grinding noise. No movement. In vain I tried to pull the four-wheel gear; either it had jammed or I had run out of muscle.

A mammoth bore if ever I saw one, but no cause for alarm. Someone would come along and help me shove the four-wheel gear or push me or tow me. The place was shady and cool, insects were minimal and not carnivorous; though I didn't have a view of anything, waiting for aid wouldn't kill me. Patience. No one came along. Since it had not rained any day on our long journey, I had forgotten the floods. I had also forgotten a newspaper story, casually noticed in Nairobi, about excessive floods in the Amboseli and airlifting stranded rhinos out of the water. The details of that improbable job made no impression and only now, as the solitary hours passed, I began to think that perhaps others knew more than I did and were giving Amboseli a miss. Perhaps the unusual rains accounted for this baby canyon, an earlier torrent having cut away the ground. I ate my picnic lunch.

With nothing else to do, I read the *Field Guide to the National Parks.* Under different circumstances, there were certainly remarkable things to see here such as the spectacled elephant shrew, the lesser leaf-nosed bat, the silver-backed jackal, the zorilla, the white-tailed mongoose, the aardwolf, the red duiker, the gerenuk, Coke's hartebeest, the African dormouse not to mention giraffes, lions, leopards, rhinos, elephants, hyenas, zebras, and a nice selection of antelopes. As a welcome if brief distraction, some monkeys nipped through the trees, either black-faced vervet or Sykes, according to the list of local mammals. Even more birds frequented Lake Amboseli than Lake Nakuru, four pages' worth, but I was probably twenty miles inside the park and the lake, where the birds flocked, would be farther ahead. I read about the parks I had not seen; I read and read and the afternoon wore on.

It was four o'clock, time for the regulation knot in the stomach but I was through with anxiety, I had had enough to last a lifetime. The hotel expected me back that night, my suitcase was there, my room reserved. When I failed to return, they would send out a search party, that is if they assumed I had gone into the Amboseli, otherwise it would hardly be practical to search Africa for one lost woman. Of course they would know I had gone where others sensibly did not go, even a nutcase wouldn't take a picnic to drive back into Tanganyika and there was no other road.

Five o'clock. I wished I hadn't left the whisky at the Namanga River Hotel. The *Field Guide* no longer held my interest. All right, it had to happen sooner or later; before dark, I would find and put up the damned side curtains. The menace hereabouts might be bats, of which twelve different varieties inhabited the Park. No rational animals, with three lakes to drink from, would walk miles to drink at this miserable little stream.

It hadn't occurred to me to step into the stream, clamber up the bank, and at least stretch my legs. I had taken a turn recumbent on the back seat; I had lain across the two front seats with my legs hanging out. I was beyond any kind of feeling, stoically numb, when I heard a car. Another Landrover stopped on the far side of the bank and a man got out. He was the perfect safari type, deeply sunburned, wearing clean starched khaki shorts, short-sleeved bush jacket, long khaki socks and old boots. He could have been the Park Warden or a white hunter or simply an old Africa hand.

He said in a tone of mixed wonder and irritation, "What are you doing there?"

"Sitting."

"Why?"

"Because I can't move. Why else?"

"Is your car busted?"

"I don't know. I can't get the four-wheel drive gear shifted."

"Well, I'll be damned," he said and slithered down the bank into the water. I shuffled over to the passenger seat. He shifted the four-wheel drive as easily as if flicking an ant. He put the Landrover into reverse, which produced a horrendous grinding noise but no motion.

He muttered something in which the word "women" was discernible. He got down on his knees, careless of his lovely clean clothes, and looked under the car.

"Didn't you think of moving rocks out of the way before you took a nose dive into this?" he asked crossly. Obviously I had not. "You're stuck on a whopping big rock, you've busted your axle." Maybe axle, I'm not certain of that; I know it was a vital organ.

He shouted in Swahili and an African I hadn't seen jumped out of his

Landrover with a long spanner. Between them, both wet and far from joyous, they dislodged the rock and any other obstructions. Again in the driver's seat, he reversed my Landrover up the bank and turned it. "You'll have to stay in four-wheel drive, it'll get you to Nairobi and you'll have a shocking repair bill."

I thanked him profusely but he wasn't charmed by me.

"If you don't know your way around, it's not the best idea to go mooching off by yourself," he said and waded back to his own car. He had enough room on the track to pass me. He navigated the canyon deftly in four-wheel drive and rattled by. Slowly, slowly, sounding like two tanks, I ground my way back to the hotel.

Starting at daylight, I ground through eighty-seven miles of thick mud, slightly faster than walking, the unpaved stretch between Namanga and Nairobi. I stopped frequently, to let the motor recuperate from heatstroke. I poured water into the radiator. I used the emergency petrol cans. Any moment, I expected the four-wheel drive to give up the ghost. From Athi River to Nairobi the road was paved and felt like velvet. When I parked the Landrover outside the New Stanley Hotel, I bore no resemblance, living or dead, to the proud sunburned well-pressed citizens who returned triumphant from their chaperoned safaris.

Quite apart from African politics, cause enough for sorrow, I feel a special sorrow for Africa which doesn't affect white statesmen or Africans, high or low. The beautiful wild animals. They have no value except as Chartres and the Prado have value and they will not be saved. No powers will think their continued existence is of prime importance.

The elephants in Kenya have been decimated so that their ivory can enrich a Top African Person. No one knows what has become of the elephants in Uganda but where people are murdered so readily why spare money-bearing beasts. The last rhino has already been shot in Amboseli because rhino horn, ground to powder, is worth a fortune as an alleged aphrodisiac. The giraffe, sweet and strange as the unicorn, is easily killed to make a thin bracelet from the hairs of its tail. You can see signs of the dead animals in curio shops anywhere, everywhere, just look around you. If you are as rich as an Arab, you can buy elephant tusks mounted in silver at Harrod's.

The superb wild four-footed creatures of Africa haven't a hope. We will preserve sad jailed animals in zoos, for our children. I know this will happen, and it is unbearable to think of the loss. We are really a terrible species; the greediest predators.

"I'm afraid it's going to cost you a packet," Mr Whitehead said and listed the damage to hidden parts of the Landrover. I said I was terribly sorry to cause this trouble and please have it fixed before the white hunter came back and the price didn't matter. Nothing mattered. My hair was washed, my nice Nairobi dress was clean, I had slept twelve hours, but I did not feel renewed. One of the kind helpful people I met during the first Nairobi days sauntered in, greeted Mr Whitehead, and took a thoughtful look at me.

"You've been through the wars, haven't you?" he said. "You better go to the coast and rest up before you go home. They'd have to take you off the plane in a stretcher."

Go to the coast? Where was the coast? I didn't know anything about the coast. The idea of more African travel was blood-curdling. He insisted, he'd have the tickets sent to my room, a friend of his would meet the plane tomorrow morning in Mombasa, the Nyali Beach Hotel would put roses in my cheeks. I obeyed like a zombie, grateful to be taken in charge, grateful to let someone else think and plan for me. Like a zombie, I stepped from the plane into a hot green world, was whisked off in an air-conditioned Mercedes by a large friendly man, followed my suitcase to an air-conditioned room and fell into bed. When I woke in the late afternoon, weariness and strain had been slept away.

The Nyali Beach Hotel was then a spacious Edwardian building with dark-panelled public rooms and wood ceiling fans. The bedrooms were done up in the depressing navy blue rep curtains and brown varnished furniture so popular in Africa. I had been given the first redecorated room, a modern luxury nest of imitation white leather and pale wood and the air-conditioner which I quickly turned off, opening the windows to look at the sea and breathe the soft air. This was the only hotel on miles of wide white sand beach and now, past the high season, it was nearly empty. I dumped out my suitcase to find the bathing suit and ran down long steps through gardens scented by frangipani and camellias to the Indian Ocean and into the clear silky water.

Wine connoisseurs, those crushing bores, go on and on about the different subtle flavours of wine. I am a connoisseur of swimming water and able to bore anyone in great detail. Only the best of the Caribbean—around St Martin and Virgin Gorda—could rival the Indian Ocean here. Swimming had never been more deliriously pleasing; my body was returned to me after endless imprisonment in cars.

Africans walk in Africa if they have to or if it is their lifestyle, the nomadic cattle-herding tribes. Europeans do not, the distances are forbidding. They exercise in European style, tennis, golf, polo, swimming pools. I can't hit any ball in any direction and swimming pools are a necessity for health, but the spirit does not soar while ploughing dutifully back and forth. At last, the intimidating size of Africa could be used: a beach that stretched out of sight, an ocean to myself.

Released from the tyranny of time–distance, I walked on the hard sand at the water's edge and watched the sunset colours, pale green streaked with banners of mauve and pink, watched the sky turn into translucent sapphire, *l'heure bleue,* and the first stars. I walked back to the hotel in the sudden equatorial dark. There was no terror in the blazingly brilliant night, the air felt like satin on my skin. Happiness swept me at gale force. This place was different from anywhere else in Africa. It was easeful.

Bright and early, I donned mask and snorkel, breast-stroked and floated, gazing at underwater wonders finer than any I had seen before. Brain coral, mushroom-shaped, as big as round dining tables, waving forests of fern coral, purple and rose, tall white antler coral, and thousands, tens of thousands of reef fish. There must be an ecological reason for their colours and design but to my uninformed eye they look like the creation at play, fantasies invented for the delight of invention. Time passed unnoticed, one hour, three hours, I was buoyed by the water and enchanted. Thirst finally drove me ashore. Already, climbing through the gardens to my room, I felt heat. A backward look in the bathroom mirror showed my skin painted bright red from neck to heels.

Burns are graded by degree; I don't know what degree I had achieved, but I was burned rigid. Lying flat on my stomach, I swallowed aspirin for fever and Vitamin A as recommended by the English housekeeper, and from time to time a little African maid doused my flaming body with vinegar. I was in pain and I despaired of myself. Some mechanism, which I imagined in the shape of a hand-brake doubtless due to my recent relation with cars, had been left out. Adults were equipped with this mechanism; it restrained them from folly. They used it unconsciously; without thought, they avoided excess and imbecility. I was an incurable fool. I didn't have enough common sense to fill a teacup. I would grow old but never grow wise.

"Cheer up, dear," said the visiting English housekeeper. "You aren't the first to get in this fix. Foreigners don't realize how strong this sun is."

"But through water?" I asked, struggling not to whine with self-pity.

"Yes indeed, as you've found out. It's best to wear a T-shirt if you mean to stay in for any time. And wear a hat when you walk on the beach. You really haven't got the colouring for this climate. But never mind, the blisters are coming up nicely, you'll peel in a day or so and be right as rain."

I'll never be right as rain, I thought, sunk in gloom, I'll always find some new way to be idiotic. And meanwhile I was losing precious days and my neck muscles hurt from lifting my head enough to read and if I tried to drown my sorrows in drink, probably I would catch fire.

But I did recover, though I had doubted it, and swam with a T-shirt and wore a hat to walk on the flawless beach in the cool of the morning and in the late afternoon. When the sun was straight overhead, I lay in my pleasant room and read Jane Austen who had come into her own here. There was not a speck of litter or a pellet of oil on the beautiful beach, no pollution in the perfect water. Only fifteen years ago, I would have been scandalized by either; now both are readily available everywhere, even there.

I climbed the steps into the airplane with reluctance. I had fallen in love with the land and the sky, the fauna and flora, the weather of East Africa. This adoration of the natural world did not extend to mankind in Africa or its differing ways of life. Like a lover, I wanted to know all of the beloved, in every mood and aspect; I wanted to live with Africa. Anywhere else would be passionless, a dull substitute. Ten months later, I returned to that coast and established my ninth permanent residence. The task was as grim as it always is but I endured the daily turmoil with unusual hope. Once the house was fixed I would put my feet up, except for gardening, and rest in happiness. I believed I had found final heart's desire.

The love affair with Africa was long, obsessed and unrequited, lasting off and on for thirteen years. Africa remained out of reach except for moments of union, when walking on the long empty beach at sunrise or sunset, when watching the night sky. Or later, when I had built my two-room tenth permanent residence high in the Rift Valley and could look at four horizons, drunk on space and drunk on silence. Or always, driving alone on the backroads, when Africa offered me as a gift its surprises, the beautiful straying animals, the shape of the mountains, wild flowers.

Moments were not enough; we live all day; we cannot lapse into coma between moments. I needed a job related to Africa, like botany or zoology or geology or farming. Writing was hopeless. I felt both puny and pretentious, trying to write in the grandeur of that natural world where everything was older than time and I was the briefest object in the landscape.

Then too, not understanding Africans bothered me though I didn't expect to be the genius exception, the one "European" or Asian for that matter, able to penetrate the mysteries of the African soul. I was harassed by uncertainty; not understanding meant misunderstanding. Africans are outwardly (the only way I knew them) the best-humoured people I have lived with. They laugh easily almost constantly about anything, but their jokes were not mine. The barrier between us was what I had noted so long ago in China.

I would have been blissful in Africa and at home and still there if only I could have been Mowgli or Tarzan or a giraffe.

The infatuation is not yet dead. Retracing that first journey with Joshua, the place names still excite me and I yearn to see the places I missed. But Africa has changed, politics and the tourist boom spoiled much of what I loved, and perhaps I have only grown wise enough to know when to give up.

A month after I got home to London, where I spent my time mourning for Africa, a letter arrived from Joshua. It was written in purple ink on green notepaper with a daisy stamped at the top right-hand corner. Joshua must have bought this fine paper especially for the occasion. He said that he would never forget our safari, he had never been so happy in his life, and I was his mother and father.

China, 1941

Five

ONE LOOK AT
MOTHER RUSSIA

I knew this was going to be a horror journey before it began, which puts the whole thing in a class by itself. I couldn't get out of it; it was a moral obligation; I had to go to Russia where I most ardently never wanted to go, not even on the childhood streetcars. Forewarned is not forearmed.

Though Russians write with poetic tenderness about their landscape, I had my own idea; I was sure Russia would look like the Middle West, too flat and too much of it. The climate repelled; the cold, the snow, the frozen rivers. I didn't believe in a Russian summer. Obviously that dappled sunlight through birch trees, those butterflies were a figment of literary imagination. Summer in England is largely imaginary; Russia had to be ten times worse. I was quite content to know the Russia of their great writers and the impetuous broody characters in their books.

Modern Russia is a universal obsession; millions of Russia-watchers were welcome to it. Improving the quality of life inside the democracies seems to me of far greater strategic value than counting Soviet tanks and surmising on Soviet threats. I could not exist in any dictatorship and detest the kind of people who are outraged only by Communist dictatorships. When I thought of Russia, which was by no means often, I pitied the citizens of the Soviet Union, who haven't had a square deal in their recorded history, and my ardent desire never to go there grew more ardent.

How then did I get into this fix? By chance, through a book in Harrod's Lending Library. It was a fat book and not fiction, two strikes against it as I read for pleasure and fiction is my pleasure. But I had never read anything written by a Russian woman so I took the fat book home and began it with lukewarm curiosity. And was electrified and read it straight through, pausing for food and sleep. Nothing before had shown me exactly how it was to live, day by hunted and haunted day, in the terror of a dictatorship. There was so much to admire in this book that I didn't know where to start. The woman's courage? The power of her memory? The fast clean prose that said without effort what she intended to say?

Ever since I was fourteen years old and wrote Carl Sandburg the glad news that I thought he was a fine poet, I have sent a letter of praise and thanks to anyone who writes anything that gives me the excitement of new understanding. This is no more than common politeness; we say thank you without meaning it, why not say thank you when really grateful. I couldn't write to the Russian woman but I could write to the translator, addressing the letter in care of the publisher. The translation was a work of art itself. I could thank him for his share in this noble book and ask him, if he had any contact, to tell the author of my reverence, awe, etc. Presumably he forwarded my letter.

Time passed during which naturally I forgot that thank you letter and was open-mouthed with astonishment to receive one morning a letter from Moscow. Four lines on a piece of coarse yellow paper from the author herself. "Dear Mistress Martha Gellhorn. Thank you very much for your kind letter. Your letter was the best I read about my work." The envelope was exotic; cheap paper, the airmail insignia being a stylized stork flying through stylized clouds, bearing a large stylized rose. The big stamp was a beautiful Renoir portrait of a beautiful redhead. No return address. I had not thought of Russia having an ordinary postal service with mail going in and out. I was as surprised as if the letter had arrived by stork.

A second letter followed, with a return address, and thus we became pen pals. I have twenty-eight letters; the stamps are fabulous. If one judged a country by its stamps, the U.S.S.R. would be the pinnacle of culture. My letters were long because much of the time I was alone on a mountainside in the Rift Valley and instead of talking to people I talked to the typewriter. Hers are usually one page written by hand, written around the edges. I have just re-read them and see why I felt obligated. This extraordinary woman, then aged seventy-two, believed she had a short time to live. She could never come to see me but I was free to go and see her. I could not refuse unless I was a cold-hearted monster. That was a little over five years ago and I am happy to say she is still alive.

Meantime we wrote. She asked what I did in my African hermit's eyrie; I described the charms of pioneer-woman life, adding that I snuggled down at night with thrillers. She didn't understand the word and I was not about to endanger her by sending a package of those skillful tales, wherein eighty percent of the baddies are KGB. Her addiction was detective stories, which I had outgrown. I sent her all the best: Margery Allingham, Ngaio Marsh, Nicholas Blake, Edmund Crispin, the wonderfully stylish English writers. She didn't care for them. She wanted Ed McBain and Mickey Spillane, that type. I was hard put to lower my standards and find the tough stuff she liked. She was also eager to try pornography but there I failed her completely. I didn't know what to get or where to get it; I am blind to the lure of pornography, even the statutory sex bits in thrillers bore me, and anyway I saw no point in upsetting the Soviet postal censor. I sent her photographs of animals in Africa. She was thrilled by an enlarged out-of-focus shot of that great frieze of giraffes in the Serengeti, still there year after year. She had a pal, a twelve-year-old boy, who collected and trafficked in stamps; I sent stamps.

Some things in her letters were funny; more were sharp. She was occasionally so opinionated that I, who suffer from the same failing, was narked by her nerve. Faulkner isn't the *only* good modern novelist in

English, for God's sake. Faulkner and perhaps Djois. Balls. And why did I have to declare myself pro-Tolstoy or pro-Dostoyevsky, opposed and exclusive positions she said were taken by all Russians. She was pro-Dostoyevsky. Then *War and Peace* and *Anna Karenina* were for inferior readers? Balls again. There were changing references to her health in every letter; she was too tired to get up, she could hardly walk, she had an ulcer which was active only in spring and autumn, a weak heart, could I find something for diabetes. She was ready to die but feared a stroke. To stay alive though gaga was the worst fate. She had earned her ailments; for thirty years, after her husband died in a prison transit camp, she lived alone, teaching in provincial schools, hiding her true identity, a life of unremitting physical and emotional misery.

When at last I decided I had to go, we got down to cases: what I should actually bring. I left for Moscow on 3 July 1972, bearing the biggest suitcase I own, loaded to bursting with the following: six of Yehudi Menuhin's records, three jars of orange marmalade, six blocks of good writing paper and envelopes, a dozen Biros, fourteen pairs of Nylon stockings, three bottles of pills, a Dutch medicine (incredible efforts by my doctor and me to find it) for her seasonal ulcer, winter dresses and sweaters (mine) for her friends to use or sell, a cashmere shawl for her, Arpège eau de toilette by Lanvin, twelve paperback detective stories, and a large manila envelope from her publisher, stuffed with clippings, reviews of her book which had become internationally famous. She was now considered one of the great modern Russian writers but the news hadn't reached her.

To choose clothes for myself, I had been checking the Moscow weather report in *The Times*. The Moscow I have known for so long in print is always buried under snow. The temperature was alleged to be 89, 90, 93, 91 Fahrenheit. Clearly a typographical error; they got Moscow mixed up with Malta. My share of that huge suitcase was a second pair of heavy tan jeans, two T-shirts and a sweater. For the plane I wore jeans, T-shirt and sandals. Whatever my worries might be, I wouldn't have to worry about being well dressed in Moscow.

You do not simply send Intourist a cheque for one week's bed and breakfast between such and such a date; your travel agent applies for a visa. This took so long that my proposed departure had to be cancelled and gave me the wild hope that I would be turned down and spared the journey. Like hundreds of others, I sign every petition that comes my way, protesting maltreatment of Russian dissidents and Russian Jews. I couldn't seriously expect that my name had been noted among so many but toyed with the dream of disbarment. No, it was just the regular Soviet method for making travel agreeable and easy. After the delay, I learned that Intourist will not tell you where you are staying in Moscow; you are assigned a hotel at the Moscow airport.

I was nervous about my suitcase, much more than nervous, shivering and quaking. Even in a normal country, a customs officer might find the contents of that suitcase peculiar for a tourist's one-week visit in midsummer but in a normal country you would explain that you were bringing presents to a friend. If questioned, that was the last thing I could do; I thought of my fingernails torn out while I refused to divulge the reason for three jars of orange marmalade and Yehudi Menuhin's records. An American friend in London had an American friend working in Moscow; he offered to ask his friend to meet me and see me through the airport.

The arrival hall in Moscow airport was loud chaos. I couldn't figure out where to find my suitcase and stood there like a country bumpkin who had never before travelled. A tall dark handsome stranger came up and kissed me on the cheek. Chatting as to an old friend or relative, he guided me past the Customs who did not so much as glance at my nerve-racking luggage. The tall dark handsome stranger probably thought it took all kinds to make a world, including an inordinately jumpy and fulsomely grateful middle-aged lady. He could hardly understand my state of mind since he didn't know of my crazy cargo. He had to hurry off on his own business but directed me to a group of sour women, behind a counter, who were doling out hotels to baffled travellers. The travellers milled and questioned and were treated with scorn, the first taste of the prevailing manner. I asked if I could change money. No. *Nyet*. I should change money at my hotel and the taxi was outside.

The taxi was very old, an old limousine, slumping to one side. The driver looked sour, too. Though we couldn't exchange a word, a smile wouldn't have come amiss. He drove as if this were the Monte Carlo Rally, at breakneck speed on an almost empty road. The scenery was dull, flat and meagre, Midwest at its lowest ebb. I saw some birch trees. As we know, Russian literature is alive with birch trees. These weren't as good as birch trees in Wisconsin and there weren't many.

After a very long drive, the taxi turned off the road in the middle of nowhere and I found myself dumped at what might have been a motel in any other country, a new structure, sardine tin with rooms, set in a small copse of pine trees surrounded by empty land. Inside at a desk, another sour woman. "But where is Moscow?" I said. It seemed that we were on the road to Minsk. I said furiously that I had not come to Russia to be anywhere near Minsk. I had paid to go to and be in Moscow. This was no skin off her nose; she didn't bother to answer.

"You must go to your room," said she. At least I could wash my sweaty face before resuming the battle. The room was like a fifth-rate motel, small, with the sort of bentwood furniture that was mass-produced right after the war, called utility furniture in England. Since I couldn't even see Moscow from the fourth floor, I hurried downstairs (lift not working) and began to sound like all of the Three Sisters. *"I want to go to Moscow!"* It was either to die laughing or die of a seizure. I had seven days, including day of departure and arrival, and I hadn't made this pilgrimage to sit in a miserable pine wood.

First, how about changing money. *Nyet*. BUT THEY SAID I SHOULD CHANGE MY MONEY HERE! Shouting. *Nyet*. Two other apoplectic travellers appeared, a big fat Texan and a small Asian, of indeterminate nationality. The Texan was splendid. Red in the face, he announced that this was the goddamndest lousiest place he ever saw, who wanted to be stuck off here, what the hell kind of stinking country was this. The Asian, though less articulate, was no less displeased. He waved his camera at the lobby, nothing in it except bare walls, bare floor and the reception counter; he waved his camera at the outdoors, skimpy pine trees. NO GOOD PICKSHA! he said in a high indignant voice, NO GOOD PICKSHA!

I was still screaming about money. They joined in, being also short of cash. The sour woman deigned to break her contemptuous silence by saying we could take a taxi to Moscow. HOW? we bellowed in unison. No sign of life or cars here, just us and her. What did a taxi cost? It amounted to twenty dollars. The bloody-minded receptionist condescended to change some dollar bills for me. She made a fifty percent profit on the deal, private enterprise. The three of us, pooling our roubles, could scrape together enough for the taxi. Then we had to cajole and finally threaten her into telephoning for a taxi; telephoning for taxis was not her job. How in God's name, I said, with passion, did she expect *us* to telephone? What language did she suggest that we use? "Didja evah see such a bitch in yuh whole life?" the Texan asked. Then we waited for the taxi; then we drove the tedious miles to Moscow.

At the Hotel Metropole, after intense argument, I convinced the woman whose job was to change money that she should actually change some money. I was in such a temper that I was hardly coherent. Now I had to find another taxi and since night had descended that was no mean trick. Mrs M.'s address was written in Russian on a little slip of paper (I was prepared to eat it in the best tradition); this I showed to the taxi driver. We set off again. Moscow is an enormous sprawl, scarcely lit. It must be the all-time opposite of a swinging town. The driver had no idea where Mrs M.'s street was and there were few people to ask. Those he asked gave different answers; we followed all the different directions. I couldn't believe that this particular sleazy cement building, among so many sleazy cement buildings, was really journey's end. Fourteen roubles poorer; the official artificial exchange rate makes the rouble very expensive. This horror journey, already off to a good start, was going to have certain classical features such as the high price of hardship.

The entrance hall was as wide as the wooden interior stairs, and covered in worn soiled linoleum. I rang the doorbell on the ground floor. The door was opened on a chain. She peered out, undid the chain and was revealed as small, square, old, with thin grey hair untidily pinned up, a loose Mother Hubbard type garment, and an expression of wondering surprise. She let me into her hallway, not large enough for two people to stand side by side, and said, smiling, "*Marta.* They said you were not coming today." Who, "they"? Tomtoms do not beat only in Africa. It is logical that rumour, accurate and inaccurate, must be the means of communication where you can never find out any facts for sure. Imagine a capital city *without a telephone directory!* Doesn't that beat all in mad secretiveness?

A friend was with her; I think Mrs M. was rarely alone, except to sleep. The friend was in her mid sixties I guessed, tall, still handsome, with natural poise, presence, and fluent English. She wore the sort of faded cotton dress that black cleaning women wear to work in the U.S. I had brought some of my freight in a duty-free plastic bag, having planned to unload bit by bit every day to avoid suspicion, those unseen watching eyes. The goodies gave us a topic of conversation. Mrs M. handed over several pairs of stockings to her friend who was radiant as if receiving pearls not Peter Jones lower-grade hosiery. Mrs M. said in her soft voice that she had never had any scent, which made me feel tearful. I put some Arpège on her wrists. "It is *better* than French," she said. "It is French," I said, and wished I could learn to keep my mouth shut. Mrs M. was so delighted by the Menuhin records that she couldn't speak; she just held them.

It was late. Mrs M. was tired and I had to cope with the problem of getting back to that charming caravanserai on the road to Minsk. Mrs M.'s friend helped me to find a taxi. This driver had never heard of my distant hotel and was not enthusiastic about heading for Minsk if in fact he knew where Minsk was. Money works wonders in the Soviet Union as elsewhere, perhaps more than elsewhere. It took two hours to return to my nasty little room. I would have been overjoyed to leave Moscow on the next plane.

In order to flummox the KGB, I scattered basic notes on the journey inside my engagement diary and wrote in such a scrawl that I can scarcely read them. But I decipher this comment on the first day: "the *happy* unhelpfulness." That was the immediate and enduring impression: the people appointed by the government to assist foreign travellers took positive satisfaction in saying *Nyet*. Po-faced and rigid, they did their best to make everything as maddening as the law decreed.

I was wretched enough to be in Russia at all but to be a commuter was past bearing. I had to get a room inside Moscow and turned to the airport saviour, having no right to turn to him but knowing no one else and desperate. He wangled a room in the Hotel Ukraina. By ten o'clock I had moved to my new luxury quarters; the switchboard of the Hotel Ukraina denied to the last day that I was in residence because officially I must still be in the pine woods, as assigned.

The Hotel Ukraina is high Stalin-Gothic. If I hadn't been dripping sweat, close to heatstroke, and unceasingly enraged by the sheer stupidity of life in the capital of the Soviet Union, I would have found it funny. Alas, I took an almost total leave of absence from laughter for seven days. This hotel, Moscow four star, has three cathedral spires with a red star in lights on the highest spire. The front is covered with an acne of stone ornamentation. It is a skyscraper, twenty-nine floors high, one thousand rooms, but there are only four lifts, two to each side in the entrance lobby, and of these only one was working, hand operated and always by a blonde whose posture and face were the very picture of hate-filled bitterness. You queued to get to your room. People fought like tigers for a place in the lift. Then were stuck together in the stifling heat of the airless box, as it slowly rose. After waiting half an hour, I would willingly have climbed to my room but there were no stairs.

On one's room floor, where the corridors met, sat the floor wardress, like the Medusa. Her job was to give you your key and collect it when you left the floor. This is convenient for searching rooms. I wondered if the police, alerted by that grim woman, broke in on illicit couples. Or whether the grim woman nipped love in the bud before a couple could reach a room. In fact, I never saw any travellers who looked cheerful enough for a sexual bash. They all looked as if they too were counting the days, yearning for release from coaches and lectures by Intourist guides.

My room, aside from being as hot as everywhere else, was merely dingy with grey plush, in want of a good clean. The window was opposite one of the foreigners' ghettos where my new American friend and his wife lived. This ghetto was a row of yellow brick apartment houses, with a guardhouse and soldiers at the gate into the compound and barbed wire strung about. Short of shooting them, there could be no clearer warning to Russians to keep away from foreigners. The main streets in Moscow can only have been built for six tanks in line abreast. You could cross through long tunnels at specified points or run like hell; the traffic was scant but always practising for the Monte Carlo Rally. There may be many crooked old cobbled streets of small wood houses and assorted nooks and crannies of picturesque charm. I saw only the tourist high points and the outskirts and, believe me, it's Depression City.

Since my residence problem was settled my remaining problem was hunger, having eaten nothing after plastic lunch on the plane the day before. Dinner was lost due to finding Mrs M., breakfast was lost due to telephoning to escape from the pine woods. Moscow is not a town where you can stroll to a Hamburger Heaven or a Wimpey's or a sandwich shop or a drugstore and get a quick snack; nothing of the sort exists. The only food recommended by everyone and available on the street is ice cream but owing to the heat ice cream had disappeared. *Nyet.*

This was July the fourth and on July the fourth American Embassies give receptions and my new friends had offered to take me along so all I had to do was survive another hour or so and decide which unsuitable winter piece of give-away clothing I would wear. I raced across the tremendous street and argued past the ghetto guards. The entrance to these superior apartments looked like a scruffy service entrance anywhere else. In marked contrast, my new friends, tall man tiny wife, looked lovely and elegant, as did their American car, now transformed into a symbol of untold riches. After less than twenty-four Moscow hours, my standards of value were somersaulting.

I don't own a car because I don't need one. I regard the getting and keeping (and the upkeeping) of possessions as a waste of life. No one can be wholly free but one can be freer, and the easiest trap to open is the possessions trap. I have the things I require and neither covet nor collect from choice. Or rather I only covet airfares and would not say no to a season pass on all airlines. Now I saw that fewer and simpler needs is an idea that comes from living in an Affluent Society, up to its ears if not half-drowned in excess things.

Plunged into the Squalor Society, I thought it just dandy that people in our part of the world earn enough to shop like lunatics for any things they fancy. And dandy too that there was so much nonsense to buy, so much low-price ornamentation, plenty of pleasing junk. The jolly Spaniard who favours me with six hours a week of her valuable time to clean my flat had been consulting me lately about silver-gilt candlesticks. I thought she had lost her marbles; why on earth did she want silver-gilt candlesticks? How times change. I was delighted that she could treat herself to silver-gilt candlesticks and feed and clothe and spoil two schoolchildren and buy a long evening dress for a wedding, on her wages and the government disability pension of her husband.

These profound thoughts occupied me until we reached the American Embassy Residence, a rather French medium-sized mansion built in 1914 by a Moscow merchant. It was the first pretty building I had seen. Edward parked the car. At once a man in uniform began to bark and bawl.

"What's that about?" I asked, bristling at the tone.

"He wants me to park somewhere else." Edward twisted the wheel to move. We were all sweating gently in the front seat.

"Why?"

"He doesn't have to have a reason why."

I would get an ulcer in this country in a week and not only in spring and autumn either.

The house was sparsely and nicely furnished, cool pale colours, dark polished wood, an oasis of civilization. I intended to throw myself on the mercy of the ambassadress, Mrs Beam. Mrs Beam didn't give me time to apologize for gate-crashing before she spoke of our meeting twelve years ago in Warsaw as if it had been yesterday. The altogether enviable courteous diplomatic memory. This emboldened me to describe my gnawing hunger. Mrs Beam led me to the garden where a crowd stood under trees, holding glasses and making polite party sounds.

The sun was high and hot overhead at noon, not the best time for drinking but the Kremlin protocol people had stated that, on this one day in the whole year, no single Russian guest would be able to come at the scheduled hour in the late afternoon. Hence the inconvenient noon hour. If foreigners are prone to ulcers, obviously they cannot live in Moscow. Mrs Beam stationed me by a door into the house, saying that all the trays had to pass this way. There I made a hearty lunch off canapés and little sausages and nuts, not forgetting the drink. When I felt restored, I looked around to see what I could see.

The guests were chiefly Russians since there are few Americans in Moscow. Men in uniform, men in lamentable suits, a couple of Orthodox priests strolling by themselves. Apart in a summer-house, four diminutive men in skull caps stood silently in a row. I didn't know about anybody else here but I knew about them, an oppressed minority, and bounced over, shook hands all round and told them that Israel was a great country, one of the finest in the world. They recoiled as they spoke no English and I was twice their size, a towering blonde, smiling and chattering. I got the impression that I was spreading dismay and alarm instead of goodwill so thought I might as well eat some more but came across Mr Beam and asked who was the man with a laughing lively face and an ill-fitting electric blue suit. He looked different from other people; he didn't look careful. Rostropovich. Oh, good, then I'll go and congratulate him on helping Solzhenitsyn. Mr Beam felt that it would be better to wait for a less public occasion.

Back to the hotel to get into nice hot jeans and collect the day's offerings for Mrs M. I had heard that everyone connected with foreign tourists was obliged to report to the KGB and taxi drivers, whose beat was the tourist hotels, were regular police informers. It is not my imagination that you feel you are living inside a spy thriller in Moscow; it is only that I am used to reading not living this atmosphere and it fussed me badly while resident foreigners' nerves are better adjusted. With a big bottle of airport whisky, the manila envelope of clippings and orange marmalade, I walked in the Saharan sun searching for a safe non-reporting taxi. Again the driver could not find Mrs M.'s street in the outskirts far beyond the University. By day her building looked worse, a scabby cement box, five or six storeys high, one in a huge congeries of identical cement boxes, a recent housing development already in a marked state of disintegration. Not a tree, not a flower, scrub grass and wasteland.

I rang the doorbell twice; that was the rule. One ring meant a stranger, she opened the door on the chain while guests inside got ready to leave through the windows. By day the flat looked worse too. A door in the microscopic hall led into a room never entered but glimpsed as windowless and repellent, the bathroom. Mrs M. had written me that having a bathroom made her "almost happy." The kitchen–sitting room was about eight feet wide by twelve feet long, furnished with an old cooker and fridge, a small sink, a kitchen cabinet, a high-backed carved dark wood bench, a round table and metal folding chairs. The bedroom was also twelve feet long but only wide enough for a less than single bed and small bedside table. Bookshelves were nailed high on the wall in a corner, a chest of drawers and a small round table filled the end by the window.

Except for the cooker and round table in the kitchen, every surface was covered with a flotsam of books, papers, objects, clothes, food, and to top it all there were glass jars of dead dry colourless flowers. Mrs M. owned this cheerless dwelling, for you can buy property in the Soviet Union, just like us capitalists. It was her first privacy, her first separate home in thirty years. Not that she ever had an assured home since the

Revolution; her life with her husband was happily pillar to post until it became tragic pillar to post.

Outside in gay mad Moscow, the temperature wavered between ninety and ninety-four degrees Fahrenheit; inside Mrs M.'s flat it was much hotter.

There were always visitors, whatever the hour. Sometimes they stayed all day, sometimes for a short call like three hours. The talk never slackened. Mrs M. chain-smoked and coughed. The long choking cough of emphysema. You felt that shreds of lung were going to be coughed up. Then she lit another cigarette. She is much loved. The telephone rang constantly, brief chats, everyone making sure she was all right. No names were spoken over the phone, recognition by voice. The same people see each other, year in and year out. Friendship cells, the small human answer to the huge hostile bureaucracy of the state.

Mrs M.'s friends were of course the intelligentsia, scientists, writers, translators, professors. Manners maketh man, not clothes; the men dressed in rough work clothes, the women not much better. In the Soviet Union power brings wealth, not like us where wealth brings power. Nobody here was a Party member, none had any power. By our standards they were painfully poor except in spirit. They were not "activists," they were liberals, which simply meant they thought for themselves but that is not tolerated by the Kremlin. What seemed to me the mildest criticism, jokes, dissenting views, are unsafe except in a trusted circle.

Up to the age of sixty everyone must have a job; four months unemployment classifies the unemployed as a "parasite," which is a felony. If you are intelligentsia thrown out of work, you are deeply out of luck; you can't get a job as unskilled labour because the unskilled labourers don't want you around. The obvious suspicion is that jobless intelligentsia must have dangerous ideas or why did they lose their jobs. This system is special hell for Jews who are dismissed from their work immediately upon applying to emigrate to Israel and are then in limbo, doubly unwanted as Jews due to endemic anti-Semitism and as traitors.

What more disloyal than to wish to leave this Eden where all is well and all men are equal?

Mrs M.'s kitchen in that tiny tenement flat was a salon. Her entourage had read her book in Samizdat and revered it but she was also the widow of a great man. Fame and position do not depend on interior decoration and real estate. Russians take literature far more seriously than we do, the proof being that Stalin thought it advisable to kill so many writers, while his successors send writers to concentration camps or insane asylums or deport them. Total censorship also shows how the state fears the independent power of words. The makers of the words are honoured. Mrs M. had the important rewards and didn't mind the appalling conditions in her tenement, nor did her friends. I was the only one who minded.

At three-thirty in the afternoon, T-shirt wet against my back, I showed up with the airport whisky. Mrs M. sketched introductions to six visitors. I can't remember names in English let alone name and patronymic in Russian. My name was easy: Marta. I was accepted as if I had been coming to the flat for years like the rest of them. Mrs M. distributed cups as she had no glasses and poured the nicely warmed whisky which they all drank neat, saying it was better than vodka. I shuddered and said I would wait.

Private talks were held in the bedroom. Mrs M. and I withdrew so I could give her the manila envelope. I don't know if she used spectacles to read; I never saw her wearing them. She spread the clippings on top of the mess on the bedroom table, seeing her photograph and her husband's because there had been new translations of his poetry and I think a biography. She could see the size of the reviews but I doubt if she understood what that meant in terms of success in our papers and magazines; she could see the quantity. She touched all this with her fingertips and smiled uncertainly and said, "I did not know, I did not know. Is it true?"

We returned to the kitchen–sitting room. Small helpings of greasy fried mushrooms were passed. It was four-thirty. I wondered if this meal could be tea, the mushrooms a special Russian twist, but mushrooms were the beginning and the end. To keep me partially in contact a mish-mash of German, French, and English served. Mrs M. heard all the conversations and would turn from one person to join in another conversation. Everyone talked at once; a mystery, how anyone heard anything.

At 5.30, without warning, small helpings of fried aubergines appeared. I had been listening to a partly translated fierce argument about mushrooms. Mrs M. said, "Do you believe in Paradise, Marta?"

I thought the subject was mushrooms. I said, "Well no, I'm afraid I don't."

"Lena is absolutely sure she will meet her mother in Paradise," said Mrs M.

"*Sa mère est morte il y a neuf jours,*" said a young man beside me, whom I saw every day, a surrogate son or grandson I suppose.

Lena, the subject of this talk, spoke only Russian but did not speak at all. She was nice-looking, fair, young. Mrs M. had introduced her lovingly as "my adopted daughter."

Mrs M. said, "What is that name you said about my cough?"

"Emphysema."

Mrs M. talked rapidly across the table to a man of about forty; he had a big unruly head of black hair, a two-day beard, heavy hot workman's clothes: her doctor. "No," Mrs M. said with assurance. "In Russia we do not have this disease." Then she coughed until I thought she would choke. Her doctor was finishing his share of aubergines and arguing loudly, above the horrendous noise of Mrs M.'s cough, with the surrogate son.

More visitors arrived; more folding chairs were opened. As I felt I might faint from heat, I moved to the bedroom where I met again the lady of last night. She had been telephoning. She said she had known Mrs M. for fifty years and "I do not like this new religiosity. It is all due to Lena. No, Lena is not a girl; she is forty and has been married three times." She greeted in Russian a woman who must just have come. "Sit down, sit down, you don't look well."

Indeed the newcomer didn't; she was white as chalk and breathed shallowly. This lady was recovering from her third severe heart attack. She was in a dangerous state of tension because her son had applied to emigrate to Israel and was now threatened by conscription into the army, a common form of punishment and imprisonment for Jews. Her telephone had been cut off for months and a KGB agent, stationed in the hall, escorted visitors to her flat.

"Why?"

The tall lady said, "So no one will go to visit her and she will be more alone."

You want to scream. And feel suffocated. What in God's name did the Soviet government have to fear from an ailing elderly lady or from her son, a youngish ordinary Jew?

The tall lady said without emphasis, "My friend's husband was killed in Stalin's purge of the doctors."

The white-faced lady smiled a sad ironic smile and said, "Her husband was an ambassador. He was killed in Stalin's purge of the diplomats."

Stalin widows. Three in one small flat. There must be millions of them in the Soviet Union. It is not a safe category either: guilt by association with the dead.

I returned to the kitchen–sitting room. Small helpings of fried potatoes and mushrooms were being passed. The whisky was finished. It was seven o'clock. The surrogate son said, *"Tout est beaucoup pire depuis Nixon."*

"Yes," Mrs M. said, with her alert ear, "for the Nixon visit many Jews were arrested and many telephones cut off; it is much worse. He asks [pointing at a new face] if you like strawberries."

Strawberries were put on a plate in the middle of the table. I wasn't quick enough; I got two.

Mrs M. said, "They are talking of . . . ," a name I didn't catch. She laughed and coughed. "Marta, when seven or eight people made the demonstration in Red Square about Czechoslovakia, one and half are Russians, the rest are Jews." She repeated this in Russian, I assume, and they all laughed gaily.

A man began to explain something partly in German, partly in English. Mrs M. took over. "He says if you are Jew criminal or feeble-minded or tuberculosis or cancer or unskilled or very old, they will let you go to Israel. Most from Georgia. But if young or professional Jew, no."

Small helpings of tomatoes and cucumbers were passed. It was eight-thirty. Ten people sat around the table. Apparently visitors brought contributions of food and as it was brought it was eaten. Mrs M. laughed very hard, coughing more. "It is about . . . ," again the name I didn't catch. "She is a poetess. She was the only woman in Red Square. They let her alone for a year and then put her in a mental asylum for three years. She has come back. She said the doctors treated her well, something not previously known, you understand. But I think that she is pretty crazy all the same, always running after men."

I wanted to ask if running after men was cause for being sentenced to a loony bin here, and also what was the sanity status of Russian men who ran after women but I don't know how I could have asked anything unless I banged the table for silence.

"*Sa fille avait deux ans et maintenant elle a cinq ans et elle a des crises de nerfs de peur que sa mère va repartir,*" said the surrogate son.

"Yes, that is true," said Mrs M. "That is sad. Nobody should have children."

A man said something and they all went off into peals of laughter.

Since college, when first I started reading them, I thought the great Russian writers *invented* this kind of dialogue, where all speak, few if any listen, and *non sequitur* piles joyfully or gloomily upon *non sequitur*. There is no other dialogue in literature like it; I gave the Russian writers credit for inventing something totally new in the world, like Edison and

Marconi. Invent, my foot. They were reporting. Russians talk this way. Everyone around Mrs M.'s table was straight from Chekhov and Dostoyevsky. I went off into my own peals of laughter. Six hours of real-life Russian dialogue had left me feeling light-headed not to say unhinged.

"Why do you laugh, Marta?" Mrs M. asked and departed to answer the telephone.

A man said, "You know how to fix telephone so is safe? No? Come, I show."

Mrs M. had finished the usual quick chat. The man pushed the dial all the way round and locked it in place with a pencil. I have never been able to do it since so cannot have seen right.

"That way they do not hear what you are saying."

Did the KGB really spend its time recording such dotty innocuous conversation all over Moscow? If the KGB had personnel enough to harass a poor sick harmless woman, they had time and personnel for anything.

"Also a cushion over is good," said Mrs M.

It was near to the closing hour, ten o'clock. After about twelve hours of this non-stop sociability, Mrs M. retired at ten. People began to drift off in pairs or alone, making no noise; as if this guiltless gathering had to be disguised, as I am sure it did. They knew their country.

"Yuri will find a taxi for you," Mrs M. said, sending me out with the surrogate son. "I will see you tomorrow?"

Oh yes, every day, it was why I had come to hateful Moscow. In the taxi I told myself how fortunate I was, how privileged, to move directly from the airport (via the Minsk hotel, screaming, arguing, two taxis) into real Russian life, not an official masquerade for foreigners. It is an experience, I thought with the deepest gloom, to remember.

From the first day, I knew what was best in Mrs M., best for my taste. Her eyes, pale blue, tired, sad but still with a look of innocence in them. The touching innocence or vulnerability came and went; enough to know it could be there. And her laughter. She *enjoyed* herself. Despite the past and the present and the always doubtful future, she was ready to take pleasure in life. She loved having a good time, it was fun for her to be surrounded by friends in that ugly hot hovel. Laughter had not been crushed out of her. That was her greatest triumph, her very own victory.

I went sightseeing entirely as a cover story for the KGB. If questioned— *What were you doing in Moscow?*—I had to be able to say "Looking at the wonders and beauties of your glorious city." In this spirit, as fast as possible, in the course of the week, I ran through the Kremlin, Red Square, the Pushkin Museum, the entrance to the University, and GUM. Unbelievably, I haven't the faintest notion what Red Square looks like, not a shadow of a picture in my mind. Not much better about the Kremlin: there was a church with scaffolding outside and dutiful schoolchildren inside and ikons everywhere. I saw very little in the Pushkin Museum to forget. The University is also Stalin-Gothic. I seem to remember there were trees in a small park outside the Kremlin and somewhere near the University; in general I think that Moscow was barren stone. And no birds sing.

GUM was different. I went to GUM to buy something heavy to weigh down my suitcase for the homeward journey; I was as terrified in advance of the empty suitcase as I had been of the packed suitcase. GUM, the great department store of the U.S.S.R., is a hybrid born of Macy's basement and an oriental bazaar, and you'd have to be Russian not to see it as a big black joke. Elbowing, shoving, and pushing with the other citizens, I found a counter selling curtain material. A weary saleswoman, besieged by shoppers, got the idea that I wanted four metres of some fairly odious thick yellow cotton brocade. I took a chit to the cashier and back to the sales counter and so spent one boiling hot hour on a single purchase. Even so, a suitcase with a pair of jeans, two T-shirts, a sweater, four metres of curtain material, and a lot of scrunched-up newspaper was not going to be easy to explain.

I had paid the State for breakfast and meant to collect. The hotel diningroom was enormous and all the tables had dirty cloths. After twenty minutes a thin pale tired young waiter, also dirty, strolled over and said, "*Thé? Café?*" "*Thé* please." After twenty-five minutes he returned with a small glass like a medicine measure of watery fruit juice, a tin teapot with lukewarm brownish water in it, a small yellow cowpat, cold, scrambled eggs made from powdered eggs, and stale bread. Many people never touch breakfast and feel fine. I feel murderous without breakfast but I couldn't handle this mess and never tried again. I just felt more murderous than I already felt.

After no lunch, back to Mrs M.'s with ulcer pills, detective stories, and sweaters. In the bedroom, she and Yuri were listening to a Menuhin record with lighted faces. They stood by the table in the attitudes of worship, close to the gramophone.

"Why don't you sit on the bed?" said I, always seeking the *douceur de vivre* angle than which nothing could have been more futile. Neither heard so I sat on the bed. And noticed a half-empty bottle of Chanel Five in the dense disorder of the bedside table. Mrs M. probably thought "scent," the word I'd used, was different from perfume. Or she wanted to give me pleasure as the bearer of a unique gift. Or she had survived only by stealth and guile and was so conditioned by the long endurance contest that she couldn't be straightforward. I mused on this puzzle again when she put the ulcer pills in the kitchen cabinet where already there was a small collection of the same jars. Her life in this hell country—*ce pays maudit de Dieu,* as one of her friends remarked—had made Mrs M. complicated in ways I would never understand, though a five-year-old Russian kindergarten child might also be beyond my comprehension.

Lena arrived to be greeted with special warmth; then an influx of friends.

"How did you ever write your books, Mrs M.?"

"I lay upon the bed and typed with one hand. The typewriter on the bedside table. Ten hours each day."

She had written two fat books, the second not then published.

"I meant with so many interruptions."

"There are no interruptions. I do not hear if I am writing. I write very easily."

Now that we were all sweating around the kitchen table, Mrs M. began a tease that curled my hair for days. She said, "I will emigrate."

"What?"

"But I wish to take Lena with me; I cannot go without Lena and she is not Jew. I say she must marry a Jew then we can go."

"Go where?" Oh Lord, I thought, not London.

"I think London."

"Mrs M., it's not a bit like Moscow. I mean we don't drop in on each other, we telephone and make engagements. We don't visit very long either or ring up all day. I think you'd find it boring, rather cold and sad, not what you're used to."

"I must take my furniture," Mrs M. said dreamily.

"What?"

"This is a very old bench. It has been many generations in my family."

I didn't believe it for a minute but refrained from saying that she could buy its cousin if not twin in any of the junk antique shops on the King's Road beyond World's End. I saw my future, running errands and keeping company. Already to my relief, I knew I had not come to attend a deathbed but feared I had come to be appointed her private American Express. Daily, she changed her plans. Perhaps Paris for the food and intellectual life. Perhaps Rome would be better for the climate. This tease kept her friends wrought up too, some saying you must not go, you will die of loneliness, some saying she would get good medical treatment abroad. As a worry, the emigration gambit was a great success. She never meant a word of it as I soon guessed. She could no more live outside Russia than I could live in it. Russia is the home of the heart, despite everything. Anywhere else is exile.

Mrs M. said, "I must go to London to be near Anthony Bloom. He is a saint." Father Anthony is the Archbishop of the Russian Orthodox Church in England.

I said irritably, "Since when did you get so religious?"

"Since I have seen Anthony Bloom. Also my grandfather and my father converted." I didn't believe that for a minute either.

Yuri whispered, *"Elle croit dans le paradis parce qu'elle veut voir son mari là-haut."* I felt guilty yet unconvinced. I suspected her Christianity, about which she protested too much. But if her new or old Christian beliefs gave her hope of finding that long-lost man, what difference did it make how she talked.

Mrs M. said, "Solzhenitsyn writes very bad style. He is crazy too." I didn't know that they were now talking about Solzhenitsyn but was thoroughly irked and said he was the finest Russian novelist of this century which was also rot because I know nothing of modern Russian literature and the minimum about pre-modern Russian literature. Jealousy is a universal human vice, by no means limited to writers. Mrs M.'s jealousy was not for herself but for her husband; he was to be the only great Russian writer of this century. I was getting hotter, hungrier and crosser every minute.

"Yakir has a complex to be a martyr," Mrs M. said. These remarks were thrown up like driftwood from waves of Russian talk. As if suddenly Mrs M. remembered me and, assuming I had heard and understood all before, gave me the benefit of her conclusion. Yakir had been arrested; I knew nothing beyond that he was a central figure in the *Chronicle of Current Events,* a secret publication of dissent. I wasn't clear as to who he was or what the publication was but it seemed enough that the man had dared something and was now in grave trouble.

In America then, we had our own dissent against the Vietnam war. We despised and loathed the policy of our government and were united in a single aim: stop the killing. Anyone who stood up to be counted was a brother. I could not imagine speaking ill of the motives of another dissenting citizen. Not that I would be so firm and fierce if my every word was a passport to Siberia. And yet I was outdone; what did it matter how or why Yakir or Solzhenitsyn or anyone dissented? The whole point was that dissent itself was defiance of fear and an affirmation of the dignity of man.

"What is your opinion of life in Moscow, Marta?"

"I think it is hell."

That made her laugh and cough; it made them all laugh. "You do not know," Mrs M. said. "It is paradise now compared to before. Paradise. It has not been so good since 1917. I am a coward, not a fighter. I would like to write a book about how life is today but I am afraid to do it here. I must emigrate to write such a book. I can earn my life as a newspaper-woman, I am a very good newspaperwoman."

How could she know, I wondered, since she had never been one.

"Intellectuals are very few in this country," Mrs M. said. "They do not matter for anything. If the people have bread that is all they care about. They have bread now, they are content."

They sure didn't look it. I never saw such a glum people. You might think laughter was forbidden by decree of the Politburo and anyone caught smiling got a twenty-rouble fine or twenty days in jail.

"Sinyavsky is becoming a very good writer," Mrs M. said, as if she was making up her mind about bestowing the Nobel Prize. She was intolerable today with her tease and her pronunciamentos. "Now he is out of the camps at home, he is writing two books at once. I hope they do not learn he is writing again. Masha is wonderful, his wife, you know Marta, she is my friend. But they are afraid to see a foreigner now. Masha earned her life and for her child all the five years and nine months Sinyavsky is in the camps, by making pins and rings from silver."

Lena exclaimed. Mrs M. turned up the palms of her hands. Her hands are very small and fragile. The palms were lipstick red.

"What is it?" I asked, alarmed.

"I do not know. It has not happened before." She stared at her hands, alarmed too.

Across the table a man was talking and people were actually listening. When he stopped, Mrs M. laughed so hard she cried. "It is a *very* funny joke about Khrushchev." She had forgotten her hands.

To my relief and joy, I was dining with my American friends. Their flat was high-class housing for the effete foreign bourgeoisie. Palatial compared to Mrs M.'s residence, otherwise very modest: a small living room–dining room, small kitchen and bath, three little bedrooms for them and their three children who were spending the summer in the U.S. They had imported simple Swedish furniture and light-coloured material for curtains and upholstery; the walls were white; it was clean, even cool. Ice in the drinks made me "almost happy."

They said that their two women servants were sweet and very fond of the children but naturally KGB informers who reported all they heard and saw. The telephone was of course tapped and a bug or bugs planted on the premises. How could they stand it? It would drive me barking mad. Oh no, everyone got used to the rules of the local game; life in Moscow was fascinating, the climate was much better in the winter; the little foreign world was fun and full of friends; unofficial Russians were delightful; one was never bored. But if everything you say is taken down and can be used against you or someone else, doesn't that make conversation about as bland as cream soup? Well, it made you cautious.

After dinner, we went on an underground sightseeing tour. The Moscow subway stations resemble vast subterranean Turkish baths, with a touch of old-time Roxy movie palaces. Giant murals in mosaic and brilliant paint; statuary in niches, many-coloured marble, pillars and arches. It is the most sumptuous public transport system in the world. Stupefying. Why this opulence below ground when above ground all amenity is lacking? On the other hand, for once I approved the Soviet system; there was not a speck of litter in the subway carriages or stations; not a cigarette butt, not a shred of paper. Perhaps the penalty for dropping litter is the firing squad and if so, maybe it's not a bad idea, might be worth copying.

Muscovites lined the bench opposite. Riding on subways does not bring out the sparkle in people anywhere but these citizens looked the same on the streets. They cannot all have been dressed in grey, brown, black, but that was the impression. Dull clothes on heavy bodies topped by tired expressionless faces. In this blazing summer, skin was still pale concrete colour. A diet of bread and potatoes? They certainly didn't look like any people in Western Europe, being built to last rather than for beauty, and well suited to this heavy drab town. I take pleasure everywhere from life on the streets, from faces, from the wild variety of clothes, from unpredictable public behaviour but here, above or below ground, what you got was the blues.

Across from me a small man, smaller and thinner than the general run, green-white rather than pale concrete in colour, was drowning in the depths of drunkenness. Poor little man. His head lolled onto a shoulder to the right, was brushed off like a fly, then lolled to the left, again brushed off. If someone didn't let him rest a while, I despaired of his future. Why shouldn't he be dead drunk? I'd be glad to be dead drunk myself except it was too hot to drink. No wonder alcoholism is a prime problem in Russia.

All focusing eyes in this part of the carriage were fixed on me. Surely pants and a T-shirt were not unknown in Moscow?

"What are they staring at?" I asked my hostess.

"Your toenails."

"Do you mean to say this is the first time they've ever seen degenerate Western painted toenails?"

"Looks like it."

I wanted to amuse Mrs M., do something different, have a party; I also hoped to get a square meal. I called in a taxi to take her to lunch and found that Lena was coming too. "She will not speak," Mrs M. said apologetically. Dressed up, Mrs M. had shed ten years. She wore a black patterned bandana tight around her head, an embroidered white nylon blouse, a straight grubby mustard-coloured skirt and mustard-coloured corduroy shoes. I had been meaning to ask her why Russian women were so bowlegged, eight out of ten I reckoned, but observed in time that Mrs M. without her enveloping Mother Hubbard house garment had legs so bowed that they formed a V from hip to ankle. She looked more stylish than anyone I had seen but her body was typical: a heavy solid torso, hips as wide as shoulders, set like a rock on short muscular legs. I had thought this was a peasant's shape but Mrs M. had no peasant blood or heritage.

We drove the long distance to the centre of town. Suddenly Mrs M. shivered; I felt her whole body shake. We were passing a huge yellowish edifice. "The KGB," Mrs M. whispered. I had no time to study it; it looked like an old-fashioned apartment block. She said it had been a hotel (in fact, it had been the office of the All-Russian Insurance Company, heavy irony) and was no longer used as a prison, only for interrogation and headquarters. The sight of the Lubyanka and the attendant memories cast a black pall over our party.

Having vetoed Lena's choice, the Hotel Russiya, in appearance a state hospital, the biggest hotel in the world and doubtless the worst, we fetched up at the Armenian Restaurant. For couleur locale, it was a failure, being simply a hot crowded room.

"Oh Lord," I said, "send us a waiter. Mrs M., if one ever comes, please get something cold to drink right away."

After a long thirsty half hour, a waiter joined us. There was nothing cold to drink, and no ice. We had to drink something or perish; red wine was available. The menu was a large leather-bound book, its pages spotted with grease and gravy stains. Mrs M. talked; the waiter said *Nyet*.

"Mrs M., why not ask him what they do have and we can order from that?"

"I did so ask him. He says No, I must read through the menu."

"*Why?*"

Mrs M. shrugged. Her eyes looked bewildered and almost frightened. She sought wordless help from Lena who was blank and useless. Of course she brought that stupid companion along because she was nervous of going alone to an unfamiliar place. I was useless too, since I didn't know how to handle the situation; anywhere else one would have left in a fury and found another restaurant where the service was acceptable but where did you go in Moscow and I sensed that any sort of scene would be unwise. I should never have pried her away from the safety of her burrow and dragged her out into the oven heat to be bullied by a waiter. Another brute who didn't have to have a reason why. How I hated this city where you had to take whatever the bastards dished out, in silence.

We smoked like chimneys, she suppressing her cough so as not to make a noticeable noise, me trying miserably to make conversation. In the end we got what was really on the menu, little hard meat balls in a thick brown gravy and red cabbage, both barely warm. I was ready to cry or scream with frustration; how could we force down this rotten food with nothing, not even tap water, to drink. There was no question of reminding the waiter of our order. With dessert, small but welcome portions of ice cream, we were graciously given the bottle of red wine. The red wine was iced.

The wine relaxed Mrs M. and made me slightly tipsy. This was the only time I would see her alone, Lena was no more than an extra chair, and I wanted to hear about her life. Her life was her marriage, nearly nineteen years together and thirty-four years staying alive for the sole purpose of resurrecting her husband from an unmarked unknown grave. In our savage epoch, this is not a unique chronology; she was in a vast company of women with such truncated lives. The difference was in the quality of this particular man and woman, their talent and the intensity of their union.

"You adored him," I said.

"No, I answered to his love." She pronounced answered as antsword and looked suddenly very gay.

She talked on: he was a coward who did brave things; sometimes he was afraid of nothing. He was always right, always; she was never bored with him. He did not want her to learn to cook or to clean a house; he wanted her to be at his side. She could never be alone, nor could she have her own friends. Either he stole her friends for himself or threw them out. Her memory of "happy times" was memory of their laughter. She said, "He kept his gaiety to the last day."

"How did it begin?"

"We met in Kiev in 1919 and went to bed the first night."

"Love at first sight," I said like a dummy; I never discovered how to talk with Mrs M.

"I would not call it love." She glanced at me and I saw her then as a girl, a reckless mischievous sexy girl, not beautiful, she can't ever have been that, but dark and small and slender and filled with the joy and excitement of living. What fun they would have had, the poet with his glowing romantic eyes and the gaiety that never left him and the girl bride. They didn't seem to have been troubled by mundane matters like money, they earned and borrowed, roamed about, nesting wherever they found themselves, believed in poetry and music and painting and friends, hated politics but were not blind to its cruelty.

In the thirties, Stalin's reign of terror must have been like the black plague scourging the country. The poet read aloud to a few friends, as was the custom, a new poem in which four lines branded Stalin as a murderer. One of the friends was a Judas. The four lines doomed the poet. Did Stalin himself, ruling a nation of over two hundred million people, actually learn of those four lines heard only once in private, and himself order the obscene slow destruction of this man, the loss of employment, the refusal of publication, the eradication of his published work and finally his arrest and death? Or did the machine of Stalinism, geared to crush the smallest dissent, simply mesh and roll over his life? Hitler wouldn't have needed four lines of poetry as a reason for murder since the poet was a Jew.

"It can't ever be so bad again," I said.

"What?"

"The world. We'll never have a Hitler and a Stalin again, not even a Mussolini."

"Oh Marta," Mrs M. said and laughed and coughed.

John Shaw, the *Time* magazine correspondent, gave me lunch in his flat in the foreigners' ghetto and took me to the Dollar Store. This is a minisupermarket, where foreigners can buy all the good food the heart desires, except fresh vegetables, for foreign currency, and Soviet VIPs can do the same with vouchers. I stocked up on delicacies and more whisky; we would eat well at Mrs M.'s tonight for a change.

By now I had learned the transport trick. You wait for a private car; there are not many and there is no traffic problem in Moscow. You step out from the kerb and raise one finger (one rouble), two fingers (two roubles), or if me and frantic, three fingers. The car slows and stops. You run to it and show your little piece of paper with the address in Russian. If the driver is going your way, he opens the door; if not, he shakes his head and drives on. Private enterprise. It worked much better than the taxis; the private drivers knew where they were going.

I had a big haul of food and winter clothing but it was a bad day. Mrs M. returned from the telephone looking white and shaken and spoke in Russian. Then, "They have arrested Medvedev." Dr Medvedev had been refused permission to attend an international conference on geriatric medicine at Kiev; he went anyway as geriatrics is his speciality and was arrested. "In a telephone kiosk," Mrs M. said. The tomtom spread this news before any reporters heard it; spread the news and the fear. Mrs M. didn't know Medvedev but any arrest is as if the old plague had broken out again; all are in danger.

Because of this news, the atmosphere in that stifling kitchen changed. They were tense; they talked politics in their disjointed way. I don't think they knew much more about Russia than what they heard in swirling rumours or saw in their own constricted lives. And knew still less of the outside world; foreign books are few and printed in very limited editions, the press is official propaganda not news, the radio was jammed. Somehow Vietnam came up and led to a parting of the ways. I had been in South Vietnam and that war had obsessed and tormented me for six years by then, and paralysed my life; nothing seemed worthwhile except ending this evil. They sat around the table and gave me the Nixon party line and I erupted like a volcano.

I told them they were inhuman, they could not imagine or feel any suffering except their own. They were as immoral as their government if they believed that ends justified means. We were destroying a country and a whole innocent peasant population while proclaiming that we were saving them from Communism. Had they any idea how children looked and sounded when half flayed by napalm? Could they picture an old woman screaming with a piece of white phosphorus burning in her thigh? We had uprooted and made into refugees millions of helpless people by unopposed bombing of their villages. We were hated in Vietnam and rightly; we had prevented free elections and were no better than the Nazis and Fascists helping Franco win the Spanish Civil War. This war was the greatest disgrace in American history and a denial of every moral value America was meant to stand for. It was ruining the Americans themselves in Vietnam and darkening our own land. South Vietnam was a corrupt police state and finally their talk made me sick and I was revolted to listen to it.

Well, I tell you. Since I hadn't got a word in edgewise until that moment, they stared at me with shocked surprise, an infuriated stranger in their midst. Yuri tried to calm me while Mrs M. maddened me by making categorical statements.

"If North Vietnam wins, they will shoot three million people."

"Why? On what grounds do you say that?"

"Here they shot three million people."

"Fortunately, everywhere is not Russia." As I remember, in 1975 Vice-President Rockefeller predicted a million executions which didn't happen either. "Why would they kill their own people? The real collabos are a very small group and they will escape; they have plenty of money outside Vietnam."

"The Chinese will take Vietnam when the North Vietnamese win."

"Why? The Vietnamese have been enemies of China since God knows when. That's why they want Soviet aid, to keep their independence from China."

"The Chinese are terrible. Do you know they cut off the hands of the Chinese pianist who won the Tchaikovsky prize here? They executed a Chinese student who was accused of stealing ten roubles."

Unless she had seen the handless pianist or the execution, or knew someone who swore to being an eyewitness, she could not know this was truth. It was certainly the Soviet party line.

"Oh, for God's sake, Mrs M., talk about something else."

A visitor, a new face to me, said, "Marta, do you not think the Spanish are better off with Franco than the Russians?"

A dirty blow. I had hated Franco all my adult life, yet Spain was better off. I could have said I thought anywhere in the western hemisphere was better off than Russia. And not only now. I could have said that Russians seemed to have a peculiar historical genius for oppressing and being oppressed. That it seemed to me they had always lived in a permanent quarantine, isolated from the changing outside world, and the quarantine itself had sickened the nation, as a life sentence in jail must deform the prisoner. That more than half of Spain had been defeated and oppressed thereafter by Franco but I didn't believe Spaniards could be oppressed forever; they were not Russians. And said none of this because Russians are patriots and adore Mother Russia and they would have been outraged at the suggestion that the horrible wrongness of the Soviet system was also due to something wrong in Russians and Russia. I could hardly say that Spaniards had to be better off simply because they lived in Spain.

So I said, "In spite of Franco, don't you see? I think a capitalist dictatorship works better than a communist dictatorship because people are natural capitalists. Everyone wants to own something for himself and for his family; people naturally want to earn and save and give their children a better life than they had. But all dictatorships are abominable. Some more abominable than others. You will not get me to approve of Franco just because your dictatorship is worse."

After that, at least we could eat the goodies I had brought and I wouldn't have minded a drop of soothing whisky. But no, everything was put away in the kitchen cupboard. It was unfair; we ate other people's contributions. I felt a flicker of that slit-eyed complex which besets the rich; I was being used. And went away hungry and angry and stood with three fingers raised until I got a ride back to the cathedral spires. The pri-

vate enterprise owner-driver dropped me far up the street, beyond the
hotel, where he ran no risk of being spotted with a foreign passenger.
Those unseen, watching eyes.

At seven-thirty in the morning, my American friends picked me up to go
to the peasants' market, already crowded and the liveliest place I had
seen. The peasants arrived at dawn with their produce in a suitcase or a
sack. They rented a foot of counter space and a weighing machine, displayed their scant wares, set their own prices and kept the money. Legal
private enterprise. Mrs M. had told me that without the small vegetable
gardens of the peasants the country would starve; certainly this doll-size
commerce provided vegetables for Moscow.

People queued for six carrots. Lettuce was sold by the leaf. People
bought one flower from one vase of flowers and walked off, holding it
with extreme care and a look of rapture. The young American wife asked
advice of her husband on the subject of radishes. Nothing was cheap.

Honest to God, after fifty-five years this was all the Kremlin could
manage in the way of supplying fresh food to the capital. What availeth
the conquest of space if you can't organize adequate grocery stores on the
ground? Isn't it arguable that the Kremlin is more terrified of us than we
have any right to be of them? Flawed as it is, our system produces a lot
of butter as well as an oversupply of guns.

An American breakfast was like manna from heaven and I returned
to my room. I was worn out by the heat and lay upon my bed, too limp
to move, and brooded through the day. I was thinking about Poland
where I spent three weeks twelve years ago, collecting material for an article about the postwar generation, those who had been small children
under Nazism and grown to university age under communism. I wanted
to see how this experience shaped minds and personalities. And found,
contrary to logic, that personalities were of the greatest charm and gaiety and minds beautifully free, inquiring, thinking their own thoughts.

The Polish police state was in good working order; you could hear
the telephone tap, an echo, a gentle whirring; my room was searched, all

that kind of thing. The landscape of Poland is leaden and flat; the weather in early winter was cold rain and cold wind; poverty wrapped the country like a shroud. Warsaw still looked bombed and burned out, blackened façades, hollow buildings. War had wrecked their country and their lives. Peacetime Soviet policy was to keep Poland poor and tightly controlled. None of that mattered because of the Poles.

They are an unusually handsome people, the young quite dazzling. There was nothing heavy and patient about them. I remembered them all as quick and expressive, recklessly open. Travel was forbidden, as in Russia, but they knew about the world outside Poland, they did not seem cut off, they were Europeans, in no way alien. I arrived without any introductions and the same day began to collect funny companions of the road. It was far from prudent to welcome a strange foreign journalist into their homes and lives. I expected to be interested, I hadn't expected to rollick through the weeks, laughing at their jokes, and loving everybody. I was bewitched by Krakow, unkempt and neglected since 1939, and so happy there that I returned a few years later just to see them all, and I am still in touch.

They knew that the régime, imposed and maintained by the Kremlin, was immovable short of war and no one wanted war ever again. They could only hope for gradual reforms. Meantime they poked fun at their rulers. It was a national sport. In a student nightclub the kids did a striptease of a Socialist Realist statue of Stalin, brassière, panties and all, to the uproarious delight of the audience and the city when news of the joke spread. The trial of those concerned was also a great pleasure. Agnostics flocked to Sunday Mass to swell the crowd outside the church doors. The older generation kissed hands everywhere, helping a lady on to a streetcar, in the corridors of the law courts, in grocery shops, at every chance encounter on the street. Manners were of a special old-world courtliness and everyone was carefully called "Pan," "Pani," Monsieur, Madame, never Comrade. They abhorred the Nazis but talked with a curious condescension of Russians, their dull clumsy masters. They dreamed of Scandinavian Socialism as the ideal form of government.

Poles were no more free than Russians but they had kept a private freedom and with what panache, what bravado and style.

There was nothing like that in Mother Russia. This city was out of the world, literally. Out of any world I knew, not part of Europe, altogether alien. Either the octopus state had squeezed the life from these people or else they were hiding behind those joyless faces, mistrusting each other, never knowing who informed. The Poles, the Hungarians, even the regimented East Germans, even the slow Czechs had rebelled against the insane oppression of Stalinism; why not the Russians? Russians had suffered more and longer than any others exposed to such government. Was the country simply too big, revolt impossible because it could not be planned and coordinated? Or were these strong heavy people unable to imagine any other government except rule by force? They endured their tsars from first to last, then endured plebeian tsars. They needed another revolution to break the age-old Russian pattern of prisoners and jailers but that was their problem.

I pitied the prisoners and admired with awe those who had the iron courage to dissent. But oh me oh my, a very little of this country went a very long way. The worst hardship of any horror journey is boredom. Never having been in prison I cannot say what it is actually like to be stir-crazy, but I thought it must be boredom to the degree of pain and I was so afflicted here and now. Malaria would seem exciting compared to this, and preferable. Summoning up Mr Ma's tigers always made me laugh and steadied my sense of proportion. Mr Ma's tigers were no help here. I felt that my brain, my skin, my bones, my soul were turning concrete grey, the very colour of Moscow.

So I rose in the afternoon and used a toothbrush glass to give myself a shower in the grimy bathtub and set off for Mrs M.'s flat with the last of the loot, stationery and Biros and remaining winter clothes. It was my duty and there were only two more days.

At noon an Establishment figure was to call for me and take me to lunch in the country. I had met him a few days earlier at an eerie little dinner party given by a journalist. Alex was a slim Italianate young man, *fils à papa*, papa being a very big shot in the régime. This sample of second-generation privilege seemed naïve and harmless and I was curious about the life of the upper class. At noon, I was in the hotel lobby, ready to leave. At twelve forty-five, I queued for the lift to return to my room where I waited with increasing anger for a telephone call. At one-thirty, I decided I would have to descend again, cross the street and beg a crust from John Shaw or my Americans. In the lobby I saw Alex, flustered but cheerful. He rushed up and said, "I am sorry to be a little late. It took more time to arrange the camera."

"You are an hour and a half late," I said, in the manner of Edith Wharton displeased. "What camera?"

"The TV camera, there by the door. You can talk for fifteen minutes or so about American writers, for the cultural programme."

I turned on him like a striking cobra. "How *dare* you come here an hour and a half late with a TV camera? Who gave you permission to do such a thing? What makes you think I would dream of talking for your TV about anything at all? I consider this the damnedest insolence I have ever seen."

"Please, do not be so angry! I will send them away if you wish."

"You will certainly send them away at once and the only reason I don't send you away is that I can't get lunch without you."

In this mood of happy camaraderie, we drove off in his little Russian Fiat. He was cowed and apologetic and I was haughty. We crossed a brown river where people were bathing and sunning on the banks; the first agreeable sight thus far.

"We will go to my *dacha*."

Visions of caviare and iced vodka cheered me immensely. I would be glad to lap up some of their concealed luxury. In a clearing among undistinguished trees, the *dacha* was a small stone house, half built. We clambered over the usual debris and Alex called a name. "She is upstairs."

The house might have charm when finished but in its present state didn't look as if it would provide caviare and iced vodka. On the second floor, in a room where evidently they camped, Alex introduced his fiancée, Vera. His divorce was not quite complete. I was impressed by the Russian talent for squalor. There would have been no period in my life, irrespective of finances, when I would have wished to weekend in a room like that. The young woman had long brown hair, a friendly eager face, and the best body I had seen which meant it was normal for her age, not overweight or bowlegged. She spoke only Russian.

"Alex, what about food?" I said, trying to keep a snarl out of my voice.

"Yes, yes, we are going now to the restaurant."

The countryside was flat with mediocre trees, featureless Middle West. The restaurant, possibly the Moscow version of Pré Catalan, faced a thick shady wood. The building was a modern box with plate glass windows, from floor to ceiling, a wide terrace covered by tables, and an imposing collection of parked private cars. Every table was occupied.

Alex said, "We will look at the Yusupov Museum and then there will be a table."

It was now three forty-five, less hot than in Moscow but plenty hot, and I thought this young man a flop. First a TV camera, then his useless dacha and now no reserved table. The Yusupov Museum was once a country house of Prince Yusupov, very pretty in the Palladian style. Visitors put on large felt slippers over their shoes so as not to mar the parquet. People were shuffling through the rooms in respectful silence, admiring a few pieces of furniture, some paintings, some china in showcases.

"Do you like it?" Alex asked. "It is a very beautiful palace."

"It's a nice house," I said. "But you can't expect me to get terribly excited. There are hundreds of Palladian houses in Italy and some in Ireland and England. Not museums. People live in them." Heat and hunger do not stimulate good nature or even good manners.

There was still no free table on the restaurant terrace; we could sit inside. Sun came through the sealed plate glass windows like a laser beam. This chic joint for the Moscow élite was served by three tired sweating

disaffected waiters. Alex made unavailing signs and signals. Time passed.
It was now five-fifteen. As a lunch hour, it left much to be desired.

When the waiter grudgingly addressed us, he informed Alex that
there was nothing cold to drink; for food, the spécialité du jour was
goulash. "He says in half an hour."

"Alex, tell me, what do the poor do here when they want to have a
lovely Sunday outing?"

"What do you mean?"

"I mean I've seen the pleasures of the rich and I'm going to have a fit
if I stay here another minute. Haven't you got some food in your flat in
Moscow?"

Alex drove like the Monte Carlo Rally, too; perhaps moving at speed
in their cars was the only sensation of freedom in this blighted land.
Speaking for them both, Alex said how much they admired American
writers. Why did so few visit Russia? I pointed out that a country where
native writers are killed or incarcerated isn't apt to tempt foreign writers.
Hemingway was their hero; Alex talked about him the way kids used to
rave about baseball kings and movie stars when I was young. Previously
Jack London was the Russians' favourite. They couldn't understand why
Hemingway had never come here where he was so loved.

"If he had been Russian, you would have killed him. You killed
Babel, and he's your Hemingway."

After an unhappy silence, Alex said, "I am not on the side of the
killers."

"What is it about this country? Why does your government perse-
cute writers?"

"*Idiotisme.*"

"Cheer up, when you come to power you can change all that."

"People like me will never come to power. This country is run by
provincial engineers. They choose and train others like them."

"Alex, to tell you the truth, I have lost all interest in this country. I am
interested in nothing except food and strong drink."

They talked in Russian. "I am afraid there will not be anything to drink. Vera says she has nothing and this week there is a new law against alcoholism. Vodka isn't sold on Saturday or Sunday to prevent the workers from spending their week's money and getting drunk."

The last small comfort left to the downtrodden masses. In Poland there would have been instant riots. I was beginning to feel that obedience was a sin. It didn't occur to Alex that there would be any trouble from the deprived working class or that there was anything to think about, such as: why do they all get dead drunk, might it not be an indication that life was scarcely roses.

At six o'clock we climbed wearily to Vera's apartment on the top floor of a building and larger than Mrs M.'s but so poor, so bleak, so graceless. I got a cheese sandwich.

"One thing about Russia," I said. "It teaches you to count your blessings."

"I do not know that expression: 'count your blessings.' "

"Well no, why should you?"

Mrs M. and I were dining out. The parents of the twelve-year-old stamp merchant had invited us to a farewell celebration. In the taxi I told Mrs M. the Babel repartee. She said, "Babel was so afraid of dying that he went every day to the KGB chief and to Gorky. But the KGB chief was executed and Gorky never helped anyone." Babel had fought bravely in the Civil War; his writing is beautiful and not the work of a coward; being hunted by the KGB terrifies everyone. Had it not terrified her and her husband? Her book described their scurrying search for aid and safety. She wasn't the only one in this part of the world who had led a frightful life; and besides Babel was dead.

I followed her up the badly lit dirty stairs, thinking unfriendly thoughts. Who said suffering ennobles? Probably someone who had never suffered. There is no reason for suffering to ennoble; above all, it tires and hardens. Mrs M. had had the wrong sort of suffering; long, grinding, sad, lonely; thirty years of fear and no one to trust and talk to. She had pretty well lost the quality of compassion along the way.

Ahead of me, Mrs M. panted like an animal in distress. She could hardly breathe even when not climbing stairs, the heat was torture for her. She leaned against the doorpost, trying to get back her breath before seeing her friends. She looked so old—and seventy-two isn't a great age in our world—and small and exhausted that my own compassion, which had been drying up, flowed again.

This flat was much pleasanter than Mrs M.'s, one big room walled from floor to ceiling with books, a big table covered with books and papers, a daybed, a few chairs. Another room unseen. The parents, the boy (now at a holiday camp) and the grandmother lived here. Grandmothers are essential as nannies and housewives in the Russian family where both parents work from necessity. Baba Nadia was seventy and looked a healthy pink-cheeked happy eighty. That night she was leaving for the country to take care of Solzhenitsyn and his child while Solzhenitsyn's wife had her second baby. "Nadia says Solzhenitsyn is a good man," Mrs M. reported. That made Solzhenitsyn all right; recommended by a member of her own circle.

We ate from plates on our laps, balancing on the daybed. The other guests were young Yuri and a woman who spoke good English and wanted to talk about religion. She was a Believer. It would have been a better party without me though I wasn't much in the way, only as politeness required occasional translation. They were very jolly; a dinner party is a rare occasion; they chattered, giggled, argued. Suddenly I wanted to say: "In London the bus conductors, whether men or women, white or black or brown, call you 'ducks' and 'love.' Sometimes an inspector gets on to check the tickets. Last week an inspector gave back my ticket and said, 'Thank you, my blossom.' " I felt a great need to tell them this vital information but they wouldn't have understood.

Mrs M. said, "Marta, are you afraid?"

"Is that what you're talking about? Fear?"

"We do not have to talk of it. We feel it always. And you?"

"No. I feel angry. Every minute about everything." But that was half the truth. I felt fear too, you breathed it like nerve gas in the air. An irrational fear that I wouldn't get out of this claustrophobic prison-land. A nagging fear for all of them. And a specific fear about the hour of reckoning with my suitcase. I was bitterly angry that I was driven to feel fear, I was humiliated by it, it was an insult to my self-respect. If I hated six days of this emotion with such passion, how did they handle lifetimes of what must end as self-hate.

They made sweet speeches and presented me with gifts as mementoes of my visit to Moscow. I knew I wouldn't dare to pack this tray, this box, this vase; how could I explain them if my suitcase was inspected. And truly I did not wish for souvenirs of Moscow though touched by their generosity, and grieved that they had spent any of their money on me.

Mrs M. had been talking with our hostess and coughing and suddenly she stood up, bent almost double, with her hand clamped against her side. I thought: this is it, the heart attack, or whatever happens when the lungs collapse. I was on my feet too, saying "What's the matter? What's wrong? Shouldn't she lie down?" They were all babbling and strangely merry. When Mrs M. could breathe and stand up straight she explained that she had got a stitch in her side from laughing.

All I had to do was deposit the farewell gifts with my American friends and rush out to Mrs M.'s for a last quick visit. I tried not to look as joyful as I felt. Mrs M. had visitors, of course, a smiling dark-haired woman and her beautiful husband, a giant with a blond beard and cornflower eyes, and their attractive fair-haired son, a student at the University. The parents were also Believers. The man showed me the small wooden cross he wore around his neck under his shirt; his wife had a hidden silver cross. "We all do so," the wife said. Like the talisman of a secret society. Mrs M. said to the boy, "Tell Marta what the young think."

I guessed that he was bored by this family call, embarrassed, longing to get away from the old folks. He said, "Nobody believes what they tell us but nobody fights. Everyone wants to live without trouble and have as good a material life as possible. For that, it is better to be in the Party but they are not serious."

Now I had kissed Mrs M. and was off. Pick up my suitcase; taxi to the airport; home in London tonight. It was extraordinary, I thought, none of them had asked me one question about life where I came from, not a single inquiry of any kind. Yet apart from Mrs M., who had been abroad before the First World War, and the Ambassador's widow, and Alex who had made a trip to South America, none had been outside Russia. I kept trying to remember something I had read about a species of fish that was born, lived, spawned, died in the dark waters of a cave; and all were blind.

There was a final scene at the hotel. I started to carry my suitcase from my room. A manservant and two stalwart maids were chatting in the hall. The man took the suitcase. I assumed he would carry it downstairs. I waited by the lift but nothing happened, walked back down the corridor and saw my suitcase. Picked it up. Was told by the floor wardress that I could not carry it. WHY? Because she must telephone downstairs for a porter to come up and collect it. WHY? It is the rule. *Do it, do it, do it,* I jabbered. And let me get out of this vile country before I blow my top.

My American friend was busy and could not escort me through Customs. He delegated the job to an amiable Englishman who was puzzled by my trembly condition. I was rehearsing my speech about the suitcase: I own only one suitcase and could not afford to come here *and* buy a smaller suitcase, but I couldn't resist this beautiful yellow brocade, we have nothing as fine in the West. Again we sailed past Customs without a glance. Again the sun pierced like a laser beam in the glass-walled exit hall. There was nothing to see, eat, or buy and a delay in departure which caused me to smoke twelve cigarettes, bite two fingernails and age considerably.

When the flight was called, I was first aboard the British Airways plane. A cool correctly smiling English stewardess stood by the door. I said, "I'm so glad to see you, you'll never know how glad I am to see you." In her line of work, of course, she was used to meeting queer characters. I overcame a desire to kiss the carpet which was technically British soil and sank back into air conditioning and iced drinks, served with a smile, and read avidly the little booklet that lists all the junky things you can buy on our splendid capitalist airplanes.

My last notes say: "Main sensation is pure Big Brother fear. The fear (based on facts and fed by everyone's imagination) serves the régime— keeps the people silent and in line. If the rulers ever released the people from fear, it could be a great nation." But then, released from fear, the people might string up the rulers on the nearest lampposts.

Usually, I am not elated to come home, to any of my homes. Home is where the chores begin. This time I was in ecstasy. Oh, what a beautiful clean bare cool place I live in, I told myself, I will never again complain of anything. I will count my blessings every morning and every night. And I will count everyone else's blessings too. In the inspired words of E. M. Forster, *Two Cheers for Democracy.*

It was harder and harder to keep up the pen-pallery with Mrs M. since I realized that she cared about nothing except her own past and her present circle and Russia. How wearying she must have found my long discursive letters from Africa, too tedious to read. Besides she now had many foreign admirers and visitors and didn't need me. She also found pen-pallery an increasing strain. I am sure I was a disappointment, not an acolyte, and my horror of everything in Moscow must have wounded her for after all it is her home and she loves the city. The best service I could render was intermittent packages of detective stories.

In one of her last letters, Mrs M. wrote, "Everyone who leaves here is gone forever." I knew three travellers who would never return: the big fat Texan, the small Asian of indeterminate nationality, and me.

With her mother, Edna Fischel Gellhorn
in Cuba, around 1940

Six

WHAT BORES WHOM?

In 1971, I made my fifth journey through Israel; purpose of journey, a book that never jelled. Tired of being serious and taking notes, I went to Eilath to swim. Outside Eilath, on the bare hills and *wadis* by the Red Sea, the travelling young of the world congregated, the new-style travellers, the hippies, the young who roam as a way of life, a vocation. I was very interested, hoping for "insights" into travel, and spent much time in a discarded water tank which housed seven of them, and in shacks made of cardboard and tin scraps, and beside campfires, listening.

I was convinced that they smoked hash, a commodity traded by Bedouins, because they were bored nearly to death, and didn't know it. Hash soothed the gnawing ennui and induced giggling or dreaminess. They talked of little else. Like their bourgeois elders, who swap names of restaurants, they told each other where the hash was good. It is impossible to escape a painful amount of dull conversation in this life but for sheer one-track dullness those kids took the cookie.

They had been everywhere. Their Mecca was India and ashrams and the pure soul-state of the spiritual East. Some had actually made the journey, a tough one without money through Iran and Afghanistan; they deserved respect for guts and grit. I do not intend to go that road (God willing) and asked about the terrain; the name, Khyber Pass, singing its predictable siren song to me. Great, gee it's great, they murmured. Three words sufficed for the experience of travel: great, beautiful, heavy.

Why, why, I kept asking, bribing them to talk with groceries and Mount Carmel wine. Why did they travel? I wasn't prying, I only wanted to understand. Yes, I can see why you ran away from Long Island and lovely Copenhagen and Tokyo—who wouldn't run from Tokyo?—if your parents were heavy. But after you have fled your homes, what do you find? *What is it?* As their basic rule is live and let live, they were patient with me and my questions.

Only two young Israelis lived in this settlement, taking a holiday from life. And I met only two foreign Jews, Americans. It was a Gentile drop-out transient camp including the Japanese. The Japanese kept to themselves, kept their hillside startlingly neat, kept fit by fierce exercises. They grew their hair long, smoked hash with bright-eyed wonder—the joy of crime—and were in a state of beaming happiness like kids let out of reform school. Which is what they were, all scheduled to cut their hair sadly and return to careers in the Tokyo rat race.

Books were either nonexistent or a hidden vice. No one expressed any interest in man-made beauty; art and architecture were for old squares. They littered the landscape (superb landscape) while condemning Israelis for doing the same. People who foul landscapes do not take their sustenance from the natural world. I decided that what they found were companions of the road but their code forbade them much conversation apart from long-winded stories about how stoned somebody was. Either they despised words or hadn't yet dominated their use. Did they communicate like birds who manage all right with a limited range of notes?

Alone with me on the beach or sitting in a *wadi,* they were less chary of speech. In their view, they were travelling to find themselves, rather as if oneself were a missing cufflink or earring that had rolled under the bed. They admired those among them who meditated in the lotus position for a fixed period of time each day. Like I mean he's really into meditation. The meditators were closer to finding themselves. I couldn't imagine any of them ten years hence, having never known such shapeless people.

I asked about their parents; nobody came here from stately homes and filthy riches. A few disliked their parents but most pitied the poor slobs who spent their lives working to make money, for what? Well, to rear these children and give them all the little luxuries like food, clothing, shelter and as much education as they would take. Money orders from home were welcome but accepted as due; the old man worked, he could afford the cash. Work was a four-letter word meaning slavery. They were not going to be slaves of the system.

I can now hear young voices telling me to knock it off, the kids were putting me on. (Did Margaret Mead ever suspect that the Samoans were putting her on?) True, someone who smokes nicotine not hash in such company is like a teetotaller in a saloon. I explained that I had tried pot once, before they were born or anyway lapping up baby food, and once was enough. For twelve hours I lay like a stone statue on a tomb, unable to move or sleep, while a few flies circled round, as loud large and terrifying as bombers. They said probably the vibes were bad. I said the vibes were first-rate, the trouble was me, I was allergic to pot and besides Mount Carmel wine did for me what joints did for them.

They thought I was crazy to smoke cigarettes, didn't I know cigarettes gave you lung cancer? I said I was living dangerously, like them. In fact, apart from their hash and sex intake, they were living like a Boy Scout's dream of camping, but much rougher than Boy Scouts' well-equipped excursions. I think they hardly noticed me, being half sloshed most of the time. In the water tank, daylight filtered through a small square hole in the roof; I was also hardly seen. When a hump of blankets started to hump energetically, I wondered whether the blankets were due to my presence but, after further study, decided that this was daytime style for copulation.

They had no cliques or sets. Even if they thought someone heavy or otherwise a nuisance, they never shut anyone out. Children learn and

adults perfect the social tricks for making a fellow being feel unwelcome.
They did not practise this sort of unkindness. They were generous; whoever had anything spread it around. These are the good manners of the
heart and altogether praiseworthy. I couldn't tell whether a diet of hash
explained a general lack of intelligence.

The girls surprised and amused me by confirming that the secret of
success with boys is the same for hippy chicks as for debutantes, has always been the same for all girls: appreciative listening, tender care of
male vanity, keeping your place in the background. How to be popular
in a water tank. Poor little girls. Physically less resistant than the boys,
they were often wrapped in a lonely blanket, coughing their heads off,
shivering with fever, weak from diarrhoea. If attached to one man, they
seemed like Arab women, permanently bringing up the rear. If unat-
tached, they still did the cooking and washed the pots and plates under
a distant spigot.

Like birds, they had all winged their way south to the slum they created at the tip of Israel, remarking that it was a pretty good place in the
winter, as warm as you'd find. They knew nothing about Israel and
didn't approve of it; the fuzz was heavy. At least they knew something of
the cops wherever they'd been, which is one way to learn about a country. At the end of a week, they began to make me nervous; I was afraid I
might grow up to be like them.

Thinking of those kids at Eilath has given me a new slant on horror
journeys. They are entirely subjective. Well of course. If I had spent any
time analysing travel, instead of just moving about the world with the
vigour of a Mexican jumping bean, I'd have seen that long ago. You de-
fine your own horror journey, according to your taste. My definition of
what makes a journey wholly or partially horrible is boredom. Add discomfort, fatigue, strain in large amounts to get the purest-quality horror,
but the kernel is boredom. I offer that as a universal test of travel; boredom, called by any other name, is why you yearn for the first available
transport out. But what bores whom?

The young hippies had not been condemned to an indefinite sentence of aimless hardship travel. They believed they were living; the rest of us were merely existing. At their age, I travelled around Europe with a knapsack too but would have thought their doped and dirty communal drifting a horror journey then, as I did now. At the opposite extreme, people enjoy grand culture tours with an attendant charming scholar lecturer to inform and instruct. They are guided round the antiquities of Greece, the Coptic churches of Ethiopia, the mosques of Persia, and other splendours. The companions of the road are civilized and couriers spare them the trying aspects of travel. I would die of it.

As also I would die of a cruise which is super delight to vast numbers of travellers. It bores me even to think of such a trip, not that I mind luxury and lashings of delicious food and starting to drink at 11 a.m. with a glass of champagne to steady the stomach. But how about the organized jollity, the awful intimacy of tablemates, the endless walking round and round because you can't walk anywhere else, the claustrophobia? One of the highly extolled features of a cruise is restfulness. If you really want the top in rest cures, take a three months' cruise on the *QE2*, the penthouse staterooms at one hundred thousand pounds would be best but you can relax in some sort of hutch for a mere five thousand pounds.

The longest time I ever passed upon the waves was eighteen days in 1944, crossing the Atlantic on a dynamite ship. The ship was manned by Norwegians, forty-five of them, the Captain and the First Mate had a working command of English, talk was basic. The deck cargo was small amphibious personnel carriers, which left hardly any space to stretch the legs. The hold was filled with high explosives. There were no lifeboats. I was the only passenger. Smoking was forbidden though by special permission of the Captain I could smoke in my cabin with a big bowlful of water as ashtray. The food was terrible and we had nothing to drink.

Though we didn't know it, this enormous convoy was part of the enormous final build-up for D-Day, eleven days after we reached Liverpool. It was freezing cold and the diversions were icebergs, a morning of splendidly snafu manoeuvres, evasive action against submarines, the air rent by curses, and gunnery practice, nice and noisy. Fog shrouded us most of the way. The Captain was worried about day and night fog, his cargo and the risk of collision with Liberty ships which he regarded as more dangerous than submarines, saying angrily, "They try to handle them like a taxi." I didn't understand enough to be worried about anything and thought it a pleasant interesting trip though not a barrel of fun, rather lacking in excitement. I kept skimpy notes, the last one is: "The voyage has been a fine rest cure."

I wouldn't willingly spend eighteen days afloat ever again but if the choice was between a cruise ship and a dynamite ship I'd have no trouble in choosing.

And then there's Bali, a name of guaranteed glamour, known to all. Before the Second World War, I had heard of incomparable Bali from aristocrats of travel—those who could pay for the expensive journey— and plenty of picture books proved the beauty of tiny deadpan temple dancers with fingernails like quills, handsome native houses of woven mats and carved wood, a landscape of exotic elegance. Oddly enough I had no interest in seeing Bali, very odd considering my interest in seeing almost anywhere. I'm not sure why; perhaps I imagined it as a museum island, boringly exquisite, filled with poor beautiful people being stared at by rich beautiful people. But Bali was a transcendent experience for me too, in rare circumstances: the Japanese surrender.

This momentous occasion took place in March 1946. The reason for the delay, so long after the Japanese defeat, was that no one had time to get around to Bali. A single warship was assigned to handle the peculiar D-Day. For two nights we waited on deck, crammed with troops, in heat, dirt, thirst, everyone asking aloud and bitterly what we were waiting for. Then the great day dawned and we swarmed down nets into landing craft. The welcoming committee of Japanese officers could be seen on the black sand beach and in order not to lose face we were supposed to make a ceremonial approach, all landing craft in line abreast. There followed a scene of glorious confusion; landing craft scurried like maddened water beetles, if two got in line, the others strayed. The troops became increasingly browned-off as well as seasick. We were pitched about inside these uncomfy steel jobs while the impassive Japanese watched, no doubt wondering how our side won the war.

Finally someone in command, outdone by this display of anti-seamanship, bellowed to get ashore and the hell with it, so we straggled in to land. Whereupon Japanese officers surrendered swords as if giving away fountain pens. A Japanese photographer from Domei sprang around clicking his camera as though this were a fashionable first night. I laughed myself into uncontrollable hiccoughs, further stimulated by seeing the neat composed Japanese officers drive ahead in fine cars which we followed in ratty old trucks. When the troops caught sight of bare Balinese breasts, they cheered. Breasts were covered at once throughout the island.

My notes on that week are as meaningless as if written in Sanskrit. Place names, people names, problems, politics, Balinese festivities, descriptions of scenery, kampongs, conditions under Japanese rule. All I remember is laughter, joy in life.

I think I had the best of Bali, better than the stylish pre-War travellers and much better than the hordes who now invade the island which has become a hippy haven as well as providing high-class international beach resorts. Rumour says that the gentle Balinese are as skilful at gouging tourists as everyone else in the mysterious East. It sounds like an Oriental Capri, and worth avoiding.

Yes indeed, what bores whom? The threshold of boredom must be like the threshold of pain, different in all of us.

With Gregory Hemingway in Idaho, 1941

Seven

NON-CONCLUSION

Amateur travel always used to be a pastime for the privileged; now it is a pastime for everyone. Perhaps the greatest social change since the Second World War is the way citizens of the free nations travel as never before in history. We have become a vast floating population and an industry; we are essential to many national economies not that we are therefore treated with loving gratitude, more as if we were gold-bearing locusts. People of all categories and ages travel with assurance. The grocer and his family are off to the Canary Islands to sunbathe and swim; the hairdresser is going to Seville for the bullfights; elderly ladies in drip-dry cottons have left their gardens for a coach tour to look at tulips in Holland; football fans in yelling hordes follow their teams from country to country; Icelandic housewives charter a plane to shop at Marks and Spencer where they find Arab housewives in *yashmaks* similarly engaged; Americans overload their own National Parks and resorts, fly by millions to Europe, inundate Mexico. Are we having the time of our lives?

I have seen many people who looked as if they were on their own kind of horror journey. Men with lightless eyes carrying parcels for voracious wives; how cheap these leather wallets are in Florence, this pottery in

Oaxaca, these cuckoo clocks in Berne. Groups, in museums and palaces, cowed by guides, their shoulders drooping, their feet swollen. Friends and lovers in shrieking quarrels on that dreamed-of visit to a romantic city, Amsterdam, Venice, Bangkok. Weary queues in railway stations, pushing their luggage ahead inch by inch. Couples grey and silent with melancholia in any foreign hotel dining room. Young parents, laden with small children toys nappies bottles, scouring the streets for a bed and breakfast refuge. They were all pleasure-bent but seek and ye shall find does not necessarily apply to travel. Once safe again at home they could forget how awful some, much or most of it had been, bring out their souvenirs, their photos, their edited memories, and plan another holiday.

No sight is better calculated to turn anyone off travel than the departure lounge of a big airport. It's like the inscription on the Statue of Liberty, "Give me . . . your huddled masses" and let them wait. If attendance at airports was compelled by law we would protest in marches, demonstrations, picket the White House and Parliament, take the case to the World Court, write to *The Times,* raise the roof. Of our own will we sit there, knee to knee, with our hand luggage and duty-free plastic bags around us, deafened by announcements, wan and palely loitering for anywhere from one to ten hours. We look beaten, exhausted, sick of the whole thing. Then the flight is called, we make the interminable trek to the departure gate, we clamber and crush into a bus or if lucky walk straight on to the aircraft. Inside the plane, our faces change, we toss jokes about, laugh, chat to strangers. Our hearts are light and gay because now it's happening, we're starting, we're travelling again.

In temporary furnished quarters at
Claviers, Spetsai, Comino,
Icogne, Naxxar, Antigua, Ta'Xbiex,
Lindos, Symi, Marsalforn.
1975–1977